Deviant Calvinism

Deviant Calvinism

Broadening Reformed Theology

Oliver D. Crisp

Fortress Press
Minneapolis

DEVIANT CALVINISM

Broadening Reformed Theology

Scripture quotations are from the New Revised Standard Version Bible, copyright © 1989 by the Division of Christian Education of the National Council of the Churches of Christ in the USA. Used by permission. All rights reserved.

Cover design: Laurie Ingram

Cover image © Oliver D. Crisp.

Library of Congress Cataloging-in-Publication Data

Print ISBN: 978-1-4514-8613-1

eBook ISBN: 978-1-4514-8759-6

The paper used in this publication meets the minimum requirements of American National Standard for Information Sciences — Permanence of Paper for Printed Library Materials, ANSI Z329.48-1984.

Manufactured in the U.S.A.

This book was produced using PressBooks.com, and PDF rendering was done by PrinceXML.

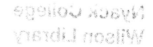

To Gavin D'Costa,
scholar and gentleman

Contents

Acknowledgments

I have been thinking about the scope of salvation in the context of Augustinian and Reformed theology for more than a decade. This volume is a product of this period of theological rumination. It has definitely been a process, and the manuscript has gone through several iterations. "Murder your darlings," says the novelist and critic Arthur Quiller-Couch about the difficult process of redaction. In my experience, implementing this instruction can be the cause of not inconsiderable literary anguish. Nevertheless, it is sound advice when it comes to the writing of books.

The finished product owes much to the gentle prodding of Robin Parry and his alter ego, Gregory MacDonald, especially chapters 6–8. The project is also indebted to Paul Helm, who may not be enamored of some of the conclusions reached but who was a fine dining companion, along with Robin, at the Air Balloon pub in Gloucestershire, England, where we talked and ate our way through a number of Friday afternoons in 2009–11. He has also read through and commented on a number of the chapters, to my great benefit. Interaction with Alan Torrance over lunch and at the theology seminar in St. Andrews way back in 2002 led directly to the writing of an earlier version of chapter 6. Gustation and theology seem to be agreeable companions. My friend and erstwhile colleague Gavin

D'Costa led a reading group with me at the University of Bristol when I taught there. We drank tea, ate biscuits, and talked through a number of papers by graduate students and faculty. Part of the first chapter was the product of our friendly but critical ecumenical interactions, and it was originally published alongside a piece by Gavin on being a Roman Catholic theologian. I have learned much from him about doing and embodying theology. I hope that he may be entertained by the thought of having a book of Reformed theology dedicated to him. Douglas Sweeney and Benjamin Myers also offered comments on an earlier draft of part of chapter 1. Doug may be happier with the characterization of Arminian evangelical thought offered in this version of the chapter than in its previous iteration. It is difficult to predict what Ben might say, but it is bound to be eminently quotable. Kevin Timpe gave me valuable feedback on the third chapter, as did Faith Pawl, much of which I have taken into account. Kevin may be disappointed to discover I stubbornly refused to substitute Alan Scott for Hal Jordan as the Green Lantern, however.

Claire Crisp listened to various readings and to my thinking out loud on numerous occasions. Her forbearance is remarkable. I am also grateful to my children and to the laughter and tears we have shared in the last few years in moving away from the familiarity of the Old World to the novelty of the New World. What rare and precious gems you are! Last, but not least, I thank Michael Gibson of Fortress Press, for his enthusiasm and efficiency in shepherding this volume through the press, and Dan Salyers for his work on the index.

Versions of several chapters have appeared previously. They have all been revised for this volume and appear here with permission. An article titled "On Being a Reformed Theologian" (folded into chapter 1) was published in *Theology* 115, no. 1 (2012): 14–25. An earlier iteration of "Experience and Doctrine" (the bulk of the rest of chapter

1) was published in *The Oxford Handbook of Evangelical Theology,* ed. Gerald A. McDermott (Oxford: Oxford University Press, 2010), 68–80. An earlier version of "Augustinian Universalism" (chapter 4) appeared in the *International Journal for Philosophy of Religion* 53 (2003): 127–45. "Universalism and Particularism" (chapter 5), the sequel to "Augustinian Universalism," originally appeared in the *Scottish Journal of Theology* 63, no. 1 (2010): 1–23. An earlier version of chapter 6 was published as "'I Teach It and I Also Do Not Teach It': The Universalism of Karl Barth (1888–1968)," in *"All Shall Be Well": Explorations in Universal Salvation and Christian Theology,* ed. Gregory MacDonald (Eugene, OR: Wipf & Stock, 2010), 305–24.

Introduction

Calvinism is rooted in a form of religion which was peculiarly its own, and from this specific religious consciousness there was developed first a peculiar theology, then a special church-order, and then a given form for political and social life, for the interpretation of the moral world-order, for the relation between nature and grace, between Christianity and the world, between church and state, and finally for art and science; and amid all these life-utterances it remained always the self-same Calvinism, in so far as simultaneously and spontaneously all these developments sprang from its deepest life-principle.

—Abraham Kuyper, *Lectures on Calvinism*

The dictum *ecclesia reformata, semper reformanda* is often taken to be a summary statement about the Reformed churches. They are "reformed" in doctrine and practice, according to the word of God. They are also "always reforming," that is, always in the process of further refining their doctrine and practice in light of reflection on the word of God. It is vital that Reformed theology holds on to both these things. Reformation of life and doctrine is not something that, once achieved, can be set aside as if the church this side of the grave can be confident that it has arrived at doctrinal and liturgical perfection. The Reformed churches have always regarded reformation as an ongoing process, a matter of continuing the work begun in the sixteenth century in the communities of the present.

We look back, informed by a tradition of rich theological reflection. But we also look forward, reforming our life under the word of God in preparation for the life to come. However, sometimes it appears that the popular perception of Reformed theology is rather more like a great shire horse stuck in the mud than a majestic Andalusian, charging ahead with its rider. Often, Reformed theology is epitomized as a project that has reified the thought of one individual, John Calvin. All subsequent theology must nod in the direction of the great Frenchman and take its cue from his work. There is much to be said for the theology of Calvin, and a great deal that the student of divinity can learn from him. However, Reformed theology was never identified with the project of one person and was never supposed to be a straitjacket binding its practitioners. As a growing consensus of historical theologians at work on this area have argued elsewhere, the Reformed tradition comprises a variegated and diverse body of theological views even on matters once thought to be definitive of those churches bearing its name, including the doctrines of double predestination and limited atonement,—to name but two of the most obvious candidates.[1]

If contemporary Reformed theologians often hold on to their heritage as thinkers in a tradition that has been reformed in doctrine and practice according to the word of God (that is, the *ecclesia reformata* aspect of our dictum), too often there is reticence to hold this together with the notion that the Reformed churches must continue to be reformed in light of the word of God. This is not a platitude; it bespeaks something substantive about method in Reformed theology, as the best practitioners of this tradition

---

1. To give two recent examples, see Richard A. Muller, *Calvin and the Reformed Tradition: On the Work of Christ and the Order of Salvation* (Grand Rapids, MI: Baker Academic, 2012), and, as an example of this sort of revisionist historiography, the essays collected together in Maartin Wisse, Marcel Sarot, and Willemien Otten, eds., *Scholasticism Reformed: Essays in Honour of Willem van Asselt*, Studies in Theology and Religion 14 (Leiden, Neth.: Brill, 2010).

demonstrate. One need only consult the differences between, say, Zwingli and Calvin, or Edwards and Hodge, or even Schleiermacher and Barth, to see this is the case. Reformed theology is always being reformed in each new generation. The churches of the Reformation continue to face new challenges and difficulties as the Christian churches encounter one another in dispute as well as ecumenical friendship and dialogue, and as other religious traditions challenge sometimes long cherished views about matters vital to the Christian faith in general and the churches of the Reformation in particular, such as the scope and nature of salvation, or the uniqueness of divine revelation in Christ.

The present work takes forward a constructive theological project in Reformed theology. That is, it seeks to show by example that the Reformed tradition is alive and well and has important resources by means of which contemporary systematic theology can be fructified. In some of my previous work, I have been drawn to the margins of theological orthodoxy or to the doctrinally eccentric, because I think that those occupying such liminal places are intrinsically interesting subjects for theological exploration. Their work also throws light upon the shape and character of more mainstream theology. Theology at the margins forces us to ask uncomfortable questions about what we think are settled issues, provided we are willing to listen to its messengers.

This book is not about theology from the margins, though it will appear to be that to many readers unfamiliar with the history of Reformed theology. This is because Reformed theology as it is usually reported today is not the whole story. We might say that for many people with only a superficial understanding of the Reformed tradition, a part of that whole has come to stand in for the whole itself. This is not so much synecdoche (a trope where the part stands in for the whole, as in the phrase "head of state") as it is a fallacy of composition (conflating a part with the whole). It would be like conflating the contemporary Tea Party of American politics with the historic Republican Party, or (to take a British example) like conflating the politics of New Labour with the historic socialist movement that coalesced into the Labour Party early in the twentieth century. In both these cases, the parts enumerated really are important features of contemporary American and British political life; both represent influential strands of a larger political party and ideology. But neither is identical with the larger whole of which it is a part, and anyone confusing the part with the whole would be thought partisan or misinformed.

Nevertheless, this is just what has happened with much (though not all) contemporary reporting of Reformed theology. Key themes have been written into the popular versions of accounts of this tradition, and—importantly for our purposes—other things have been written out of the narrative. By my restoring something of the broader doctrinal context of Reformed theology, it is hoped that readers may come to see that this particular strand of Christianity is much more variegated and diverse in its theological commitments than is often reported in popular versions of it. These differences are not trivial. Nor are the matters in question of secondary importance. In several cases, a right understanding of the doctrinal diversity tolerated within the confessional bounds of Reformed theology shows that the Reformed have permitted different and conflicting views on a particular matter that is far from being doctrinally marginal.

For instance, Reformed theology is often thought to entail or at least imply a doctrine of determinism. God ordains all that comes to pass, so God ordains all that I will do, every action I perform; in which case, I am not free to do other than what God has ordained. There have been some high-profile Reformed theologians who have taken this line, and today the view that is often reiterated on this score owes much to the work of Jonathan Edwards. His *Freedom of the Will* is perhaps the most sophisticated and unrelenting philosophical account of the relationship between divine determinism and human freedom ever penned by a Reformed theologian.[2] But his view is not identical to the Reformed view per se. Nor is it the case (contrary to popular belief) that the Reformed confessions require belief in some version of divine determinism. In Chapter 3, I deal with this in detail, arguing that the Reformed confessions neither require nor deny divine determinism. In fact, a species of theological libertarianism is consistent with Reformed theology, given certain qualifications (though I do not *endorse* such libertarianism here).

Another important example of this sort of mistaken view of Reformed theology can be found in popular accounts of the scope of atonement. Often, central tenets of Reformed theology are summed up in the acrostic tulip.[3] However, the *L* here, which stands for "limited atonement," is not the only view permissible within Reformed confessionalism. There is a strand of Reformed thinking, which goes all the way back to the early Reformers of the sixteenth century, that denies the doctrine of limited or, more accurately, *definite* or *particular* atonement. In its place, these Reformed thinkers posited a universal atonement. They thought that Christ died for all humans in accordance with the overwhelming testimony of the New Testament. The elect are given faith to believe in Christ and are saved. Those that are passed over by the Holy Spirit are left in their sins and perish as a consequence. Until fairly recently, this alternative to the definite-atonement view was regarded as the preserve of a

---

2. Jonathan Edwards, *Freedom of the Will*, ed. Paul Ramsey, vol. 1 of *The Works of Jonathan Edwards*, ed. Perry Miller (New Haven, CT: Yale University Press, 1957).

3. T = Total depravity; U = Unconditional election; L = Limited atonement; I = Irresistible grace; P = Perseverance of the saints.

vociferous minority in early-modern Reformed theology that has persisted in periodic pockets of discontent ever since. It is usually called Amyraldianism, after Moïse Amyraut, the seventeenth-century French theologian with whom this doctrine has come to be associated. However, there were many who espoused this view besides and before Amyraut, and Amyraut himself learned it from his Scottish teacher John Cameron.[4]

The scope of atonement is one of the major themes of this book. It turns up first in the chapter on eternal justification, which has to do with whether the elect are justified in eternity or from eternity, and whether coming to faith represents merely an epistemic change in the elect individual (that is, a coming to see what she already is in Christ from eternity) or whether it is more than that—a real change in time, which is foreordained by God. Chapter 3, on libertarian Calvinism, also has to do with the scope of salvation, although it is dealt with there only in passing. The claim that divine ordination does not require determinism all the way down is important when considering matters pertaining to human freedom, including human freedom with respect to salvation. But it also informs the chapters that make up the second half of this volume.

There are four chapters that bear the word *universalism* in their titles (chapters 4–7). These plot important trajectories in Reformed understandings of the scope of atonement and election. The first of these, chapter 4, sets out a version of necessary universalism commensurate with theological determinism rather than libertarianism. Necessary universalism is the doctrine according to

---

4. It is not a little ironic that a greater historical understanding of this point has arisen at a time in which there are the beginnings of a renewed interest in articulating and defending the doctrine of particular atonement among certain Reformed and evangelical theologians. For historical work on this, see the literature cited in chapter 7. A significant recent attempt to restate particular atonement can be found in David Gibson and Jonathan Gibson, eds., *From Heaven He Came and Sought Her: Definite Atonement in Historical, Biblical, Theological, and Pastoral Perspective* (Wheaton, IL: Crossway, 2013).

which necessarily all of humanity is saved through the work of Christ by divine ordinance. The Princeton stalwart Benjamin Warfield famously remarked that Calvinism is the one Protestant tradition of Christian theology whose assumptions can be pressed in the direction of universalism.[5] As this chapter shows, the fact that the Augustinian tradition in a broad sense, and the Reformed tradition as a species of Augustinianism in a more narrow sense, can be pressed in this direction raises an important issue that goes to the heart of Reformed theology on the scope of salvation. It is this: Why does God not save everyone if there is no impediment to God's doing so (assuming God determines all the salvation of those God saves)? Given that the Reformed (and Augustinians more generally) claim that election depends on the work of Christ that has an infinite value, and upon God's intention in atonement which in turn is just God's good pleasure and will, the question is, why does God not save more than God does? Why not save all fallen humans?

This problem posed by Augustinian universalism (for such we shall call it) is addressed in chapter 5, on universalism and particularism. Here a case is made to rebut the objection that if there is no impediment to God's providing salvation for all in Christ, then God *ought* to provide salvation for all in Christ. One of the central planks of this rebuttal is the claim, common in much Reformed theology, that any theater of divine action is one in which God must display all God's attributes, including mercy and justice.

Given that universalism is a doctrine much discussed in contemporary systematic and philosophical theology, and that Barth's doctrine of election has left such a deep mark upon contemporary discussion of the scope of salvation in Reformed theology, a chapter on the Barthian account of election seems appropriate. As is well

---

5. See Benjamin Warfield, *The Plan of Salvation*, rev. ed. (Grand Rapids, MI: Eerdmans, 1975), chap. 5.

known, Barth's doctrine has been the cause of not a little controversy in the secondary literature, and the contemporary discussion of his doctrine of election continues to be the subject of comment and often-heated debate in scholarly journals and popular blogs.[6] The argument presented here has been through several iterations. It now seems to me that one strand of Barth's thinking is not universalistic, though it is hopeful about the scope of salvation.[7] However, I argue in this chapter that there are other things he says that are more incautious and do press up against the doctrine of universalism. On balance, it may be that there is more than one doctrine of election in Barth's mature thought and that this tension in his thinking can be traced to his unwillingness to commit himself unequivocally to one or another of these views. At least some Barth scholars have recently argued that this tension arises because Barth himself saw a tension in Scripture between universalistic and particularistic passages and believed it inappropriate to attempt to reconcile what appear to be the paradoxical claims in Holy Writ.[8] Be that as it may, Barth's

6. Much of the recent flurry of papers on Barth's doctrine of election was stimulated by Bruce L. McCormack's essay "Grace and Being: The Role of God's Gracious Election in Karl Barth's Theological Ontology." It was originally published in *The Cambridge Companion to Karl Barth,* ed. John B. Webster (Cambridge: Cambridge University Press, 2000), and has been republished, with some emendations and changes, in McCormack, *Orthodox and Modern: Studies in the Theology of Karl Barth* (Grand Rapids, MI: Baker Academic, 2008). A recent collection of some of the journal papers on post-McCormack readings of Barth can be found in Michael T. Dempsey, ed., *Trinity and Election in Contemporary Theology* (Grand Rapids, MI: Eerdmans, 2011). The literature on this topic continues to grow apace.

7. Conversations with David Congdon and George Hunsinger have made me revise my earlier views on this topic.

8. See, e.g., George Hunsinger, "Hellfire and Damnation: Four Ancient Views," in *Disruptive Grace: Studies in the Theology of Karl Barth* (Grand Rapids, MI: Eerdmans, 2000), 226–49; and Bruce L. McCormack, "'So That He May Be Merciful to All': Karl Barth and The Problem of Universalism," in *Karl Barth and American Evangelicalism,* ed. Bruce L. McCormack and Clifford B. Anderson (Grand Rapids, MI: Eerdmans, 2011), 227–49. I should add that I have some sympathy with this view. It is a common theme in much historic Reformed theology when it is faced with apparent paradoxes in Scripture. Another example pertinent to this volume is that of the hypothetical universalism of seventeenth-century authors like Bishop John Davenant. One reason Davenant gives in his *Dissertation on the Death of Christ* (in *An Exposition of the Epistle of St Paul to the Colossians,* trans. Josiah Allport, 2 vols. (London: Hamilton, Adams, 1832) for

doctrine is an important resource for contemporary theology. One of the most important implications of his doctrine for Reformed theology is in his call for a more christologically conditioned doctrine of election. Not that other Reformed accounts are nonchristological; nevertheless, Barth's doctrine places the person and work of Christ at the heart of the doctrine of election in a way that marks a step change from much historic Reformed discussion of the topic. In this way of thinking, not only is Christ's work the means by which some of fallen humanity is saved, but Christ is also, in one important respect, the ground of election, a matter to which I have attended elsewhere.[9]

The last two chapters of the book represent an attempt to articulate a positive case for hypothetical universalism, the doctrine I earlier said has often mistakenly been conflated with the name of Amyraut. Just as there have been defenders of hypothetical universalism in the Reformed tradition from its inception, so there have been different versions of the doctrine. Amyraldianism is one; but there is an earlier and distinct version that was developed by a group of Anglican divines in the early seventeenth century, under the tutelage of Archbishop Ussher of Armagh. Perhaps the most distinguished defender of this Anglican version of hypothetical universalism is John Davenant, the lord bishop of Salisbury, leader of the British delegation to the Synod of Dort, and the onetime Lady Margaret Professor at Cambridge. In chapter 7, I offer a version of hypothetical universalism that uses Davenant's Anglican account in his *Dissertation on the Death of Christ,* an unjustly neglected piece of Reformed theology. It is usually eclipsed by John Owen's *The Death of Death,*

holding to universal atonement and the election of a particular number of fallen humanity is that both doctrines are clearly taught in Scripture. In fact, there is a striking parallel between Davenant's reasoning and that of McCormack, despite the different conclusions reached.

9. See Oliver D. Crisp, *God Incarnate: Explorations in Christology* (London: T & T Clark, 2009), chap. 2. Another interesting recent proposal that draws on Barth and the Puritan John Owen in this regard is Suzanne McDonald, *Re-Imaging Election: Divine Election as Representing God to Others and Others to God* (Grand Rapids, MI: Eerdmans, 2010).

which offers arguably the most sophisticated defense of a definite-atonement doctrine.[10] There are shortcomings with hypothetical universalism, the most important historic examples of which are dealt with in this chapter. Yet it is an important Reformed doctrine of the scope of atonement that should be taken much more seriously than it is at present. Reformed theologians have largely "forgotten" this rather different account of the scope of election and atonement.[11]

One of the most famous objections to hypothetical universalism has to do with its doctrine of universal atonement, shared in common with the Arminians, Roman Catholics, and many of the fathers of the Church. The claim is made that if Christ's work atones for the sin of all humanity, then those who are damned are punished twice for their sin: once in the person of Christ, and a second time in their own person, in hell. This seems monumentally unjust. But God is not unjust, so universal atonement must be false. Such reasoning is often given by those defending definite atonement, and Owen's articulation of this objection is celebrated. However, I argue, in keeping with the nineteenth-century American Presbyterian Robert Dabney, as well as hypothetical universalists like Davenant, that this objection fails. There is no good reason to think that those who are damned are punished twice for their sin if universal atonement is true. The damned are not punished at all in the first instance; it is Christ who acts as their surety and who takes upon himself the penal consequences of their sin. And Christ's work is not said

---

10. Recent defenders of "Amyraldianism" include the British pastor-scholar Alan Clifford, who is scathing about the influence of Owen's doctrine of definite atonement. See, for example, his *Atonement and Justification: English Evangelical Theology, 1640–1790; An Evaluation* (Oxford: Oxford University Press, 1990).

11. An example: Richard J. Mouw, in a short treatment of the definite-atonement doctrine, when faced with the fact that there are biblical texts that seem to imply a universal atonement as well as texts that imply a particular redemption, says this: "I simply live with both sets of texts, refusing to resolve the tension between what looks like conflicting themes." *Calvinism in the Las Vegas Airport* (Grand Rapids, MI: Zondervan, 2004), 42. But this is just what motivates hypothetical universalism!

to be effectual for the salvation of all humanity; it is only said to be sufficient to that end conditional upon faith, in keeping with the ancient catholic dictum that Christ's ransom is sufficient for all humanity but efficacious only for some (namely, the elect).

There is much work to be done not only in excavating forgotten doctrines of the Reformed tradition (thereby providing a more complete account of the shape of Reformed theology) but also in giving a positive statement of Reformed dogmatics for today. This volume is offered as a small contribution to that end. It is to be hoped that this is not merely a matter of interest for *Reformed* theologians, however. Many of these issues affect Christian theologians of whatever stripe who call themselves lovers of catholicity. For this reason, the whole of this book is prefaced with chapter 1, a treatment of tradition, faith, and doctrine. This sets the scene for what follows, as a chapter that is more methodologically focused. It provides an argument for thinking about the relationship between tradition, faith, experience, and doctrine that tries to show how these things belong together in a properly evangelical and catholic Reformed theology, that is, a theology of the heart. How doctrine is formed is an important issue, and this is one answer to that question, or, more accurately, the beginnings of one answer to that question. Given that there is a fundamental connection between what Reformed divines think about the scope of salvation and the sources of authority to which they appeal, this chapter seems pertinent. Perhaps others may take up this task and press it forward in a way that makes good on the claim, made by historic Reformed communions, to be engaged in the ongoing task of reforming theology.

1

Tradition, Faith, and Doctrine

Whosoever, through his private judgment, willingly and purposely, doth openly break the Traditions and Ceremonies of the Church, which be not repugnant to the Word of God, and be ordained and approved by common authority, ought to be rebuked openly, (that others may fear to do the like,) as he that offendeth against the common order of the Church, and hurteth the authority of the Magistrate, and woundeth the consciences of the weak brethren.

— Article 34 of Thirty-Nine Articles of Religion

It may seem strange to begin a book like this one that is primarily concerned about broadening Reformed theological accounts of the scope of salvation with a chapter on tradition, faith, and doctrine. Isn't this a little far afield? Yet it seems to me that the two things are related. What is said about the scope of salvation is surely connected in more than a passing way to the sources of authority and testimony to which theologians give heed. A Reformed view of these things sheds light on how formal judgments about Scripture, tradition, and doctrine play out in the material concerns about particular issues in tackling the scope of salvation (as well as other doctrines, of course). Consequently, some remarks about how a thinker in the Reformed tradition might approach these matters seem called for. Because it appears to me that Reformed views on this matter overlap with and have been developed in dialogue (and conflict) with several other constituencies and their concerns, we will need to navigate a course that includes discussion of a wider range of such "interest groups" than other, similar accounts might provide. I trust that this will be regarded as a strength rather than a liability of the chapter.

Along with many historic members of my own theological tradition (though fewer contemporary representatives), I think of myself as a Reformed Catholic. That is, my own views on matters theological are part of the tradition of western catholic Christianity that divided from the Roman branch at the Reformation. As the patristic scholar D. H. Williams has recently put it, "There is no question that the early Reformers believed they were seeking to restore the faith of the early church. The basic thrust of their mission was not to point to themselves as the begetters of a new 'protestantism' but to the establishment of a proper Catholicism."[1] The fact that branches of the Christian Church remain at odds with one another over doctrine and practice—even if their differences are expressed in more collegial ways these days—is regrettable. Like Williams, I think the Reformation was a time of great rediscovery and religious reform. But I also think it was a time of theological violence (committed in different ways by each of the parties to the conflict) that was misguided and harmful. If the Western church had taken upon itself the task of reform earlier and with more seriousness, then perhaps the Reformation would have been an intra-ecclesial debate, not the cause of disruption. But counterfactual history is not the focus of this chapter, or this book; I register this point merely to indicate my own sensibilities with respect to the relationship between the Roman and Reformed branches of Christianity. Similar things could be said about different branches of Protestantism as well. We

---

1. D. H. Williams, *Evangelicals and Tradition: The Formative Influences of the Early Church* (Grand Rapids: Baker Academic, 2005), 85.

are siblings, not enemies, related to one parent, namely, Western catholic Christendom. It is a fundamental mistake to conceive of the relationship between Roman and Reformed Christianity otherwise—as if we were two distinct religious entities or, even worse, two distinct religious traditions. We are two branches of one rich and complex religious tradition.[2]

Scripture and Tradition

To complicate matters further, Reformed Christianity is a branch of the Christian tradition that has a number of different shoots. These include churches of both presbyterian and episcopal polities. Anglicanism, despite what you may have read or experienced (pace John Henry Newman), is a historically Reformed church. Its formularies are the product of the Reformation as much as the documents and liturgies of other churches in this tradition. In fact, for some time after the Reformation, the Anglican Church was viewed by the Reformed on the continent of Europe as a sister church, not as something apart, as some contemporary Anglicans would have

---

2. It might be asked whether this characterization of the relationship between Reformed and Roman Catholicism is really to the point. For instance, article 22 of the Thirty-Nine Articles of Religion of the Church of England, a Reformed confessional document to which we shall return presently, says that the "Romish" doctrine of "Purgatory, Pardons, Worshipping and Adoration, as well of Images as Relics, and also Invocation of Saints," is "a fond thing, vainly invented, and grounded upon no warranty of Scripture, but rather repugnant to the Word of God." Similarly, article 19 of the same document says that "the Church of Jerusalem, Alexandria, and Antioch, have erred, so also the Church of Rome hath erred, not only in their living and manner of Ceremonies, but also in matters of faith." This raises two serious concerns: Can a given ecclesial body be a church if it defends errors in doctrine and practice? And if (some) Reformed communions have these statements as a confessional basis, can they be described as *siblings* of Roman Catholicism? As to the former question, much depends on the nature of the error concerned. I suppose creedally orthodox Roman Catholics are not in error about matters touching central dogmatic affirmations about the faith. That said, they may still be in doctrinal error or may practice their faith in a mistaken fashion, e.g., through some of their Mariological doctrines. As to the latter query, I suppose siblings can have periods in which their relationship is strained and difficult. The children of one set of parents may well be closely related in a biological sense even if they have not been able to get along with each other personally and are deeply divided over matters both think important. Something like that seems to be true of the separated branches of global Christianity.

us believe.[3] It is often said that Anglicanism is rooted in Scripture, tradition, and reason. But if this is taken to mean that tradition and reason stand alongside Scripture as equal partners in the theological enterprise, then this is a mistaken report of the theological roots of Anglicanism. Consider article 6 of the Thirty-Nine Articles:

> Holy Scripture containeth all things necessary to salvation: so that whatsoever is not read therein, nor may be proved thereby, is not to be required of any man, that it should be believed as an article of the Faith, or be thought requisite or necessary to salvation. In the name of the Holy Scripture we do understand those canonical Books of the Old and New Testament, of whose authority was never any doubt in the Church.

Compare this with article 34, part of which is the epigraph to this chapter:

> It is not necessary that Traditions and Ceremonies be in all places one, or utterly like; for at all times they have been divers, and may be changed according to the diversity of countries, times, and men's manners, so that nothing be ordained against God's Word. Whosoever, through his private judgment, willingly and purposely, doth openly break the Traditions and Ceremonies of the Church, which be not repugnant to the Word of God, and be ordained and approved by common authority, ought to be rebuked openly, (that others may fear to do the like), as he that offendeth against the common order of the Church, and hurteth the authority of the Magistrate, and woundeth the consciences of the weak brethren.

---

3. This point is brought out rather nicely in Jonathan D. Moore's study *English Hypothetical Universalism: John Preston and The Softening of Reformed Theology* (Grand Rapids: Eerdmans, 2007). For two very helpful introductions to Anglican thought by someone sympathetic to this line of reasoning, see Mark Chapman, *Anglican Theology* (London: T&T Clark, 2012), esp. chap. 1; and Mark Chapman, *Anglicanism: A Very Short Introduction* (Oxford: Oxford University Press, 2006).

And this:

> Every particular or national Church hath authority to ordain, change, and abolish, Ceremonies or Rites of the Church ordained only by man's authority, so that all things be done to edifying.

The message is pretty clear: Scripture is the *norma normans non normata*—that is, the norming norm that is not normed by anything else. Tradition, here understood to be a collection of divers human practices of an ecclesial nature, may differ according to locality, custom, and time, provided they are in accordance with the word of God. But tradition is implicitly subordinate to Scripture in this regard. One might compare article 21 on this matter, "Of the Authority of General [Church] Councils":

> General Councils may not be gathered together without the commandment and will of Princes. And when they be gathered together, (forasmuch as they be an assembly of men, whereof all be not governed with the Spirit and Word of God,) they may err, and sometimes have erred, even in things pertaining unto God. Wherefore things ordained by them as necessary to salvation have neither strength nor authority, unless it may be declared that they be taken out of holy Scripture.

This is an important amplification of the previous point. The article makes explicit the fact that ecclesiastical councils can be in error, the implication being that such error occurs when these bodies go beyond their scriptural warrant to propound doctrines that, ex hypothesi, cannot be binding upon the consciences of Christians.

It might be helpful to compare the sort of authority envisaged for councils in the Thirty-Nine Articles with the authority of case law in societies such as those in Great Britain and the United States. In such legal systems, law can be made by precedent, and the law is binding upon all citizens of the societies concerned. But the law is not necessarily inerrant: new laws can be enacted that repeal previous legislation, replacing them with regulations that are more just, or more appropriate to the times in which we live. This is not to denigrate the character or normative nature of the law as such; it is to understand that particular aspects of the body of legislature at any given time may be mistaken or need amending.

Let us take an example. We would not think a law that prevented citizens from normally being able to bear arms where once they were able to carry arms an unjust law, provided the new law was enacted according to due legal process, which made provision for the repeal of the previous law under certain circumstances. The fact that such process can be exceedingly complex is not to the point here. Our concern is with the normative nature of such legislation. Just as certain laws can be overturned that once were binding upon a people, so also conciliar statements may be in error, provided it can be shown that they do not correspond to the word of God. And just as there is nothing remiss in acknowledging that law can be mistaken and need repealing while at the same time acquiescing to the normative status of such law while it is in force, and of the law per se (as a system of legislation), so also there is nothing remiss in claiming that conciliar statements can be mistaken and need redressing by subsequent ecclesial bodies, which may have a better or more complete theological perspective. We might very well think a given law unjust, but this does not necessarily mean we think the law as a body of legislation, governing the way a given society is governed, is unjust. Just so, we may think a given ecclesiastical council mistaken in something it affirms. This does not necessarily call into question all conciliar authority. The point is that conciliar authority, though normative under certain conditions, is nevertheless limited in its purview by the word of God, under which it stands and by means of which it can be corrected. It has a normative status, but one the warrant for which is derived from a higher norm to which all conciliar canons are subordinate, namely, Holy Scripture. One of the important claims made by theologians of the Magisterial Reformation was that ecclesiastical authority is not without error when it comes to matters of doctrine. In this respect, ecclesiastical councils differ from Scripture.

This point is amplified and expanded upon by the fathers of that great English assembly that produced the Westminster Confession. It is one of the singular ironies of ecclesiastical history that the confessional basis of the Church of Scotland and many other presbyterian bodies is the document drawn up by a group of largely English divines, called together, at least initially, in order to revise the Thirty-Nine Articles.[4] This may be the English church's greatest gift to presbyterianism. In the first chapter of the Westminster Confession, entitled "Of the Holy Scripture," we read that

> [t]he authority of the Holy Scripture, for which it ought to be believed, and obeyed, depends not upon the testimony of any man, or Church; but wholly upon God (who is truth itself) the author thereof: and therefore it is to be received, because it is the Word of God. (1.4)

And this:

> The whole counsel of God concerning all things necessary for His own glory, man's salvation, faith and life, is either expressly set down in Scripture, or by good and necessary consequence may be deduced from Scripture: unto which nothing at any time is to be added, whether by new revelations of the Spirit, or traditions of men. (1.6)[5]

---

4. For a recent account of this see Robert Letham, *The Westminster Assembly: Reading Its Theology in Historical Context* (Phillipsburg, NJ: Presbyterian and Reformed, 2009).

5. However, note that later in this same article (1.6), the authors write that "there are some circumstances concerning the worship of God, and government of the Church, common to human actions and societies, which are to be ordered by the light of nature, and Christian prudence, according to the general rules of the Word, which are always to be observed." This is rather different from the tone of the Thirty-Nine Articles.

Although the Westminster divines allowed that not every part of Scripture is as clear as one might like (1.7), they speak with one voice about how Scripture is the norming norm of all theological judgments, in this manner:

> The infallible rule of interpretation of Scripture is the Scripture itself: and therefore, when there is a question about the true and full sense of any Scripture (which is not manifold, but one), it must be searched and known by other places that speak more clearly. (1.9)

> The supreme judge by which all controversies of religion are to be determined, and all decrees of councils, opinions of ancient writers, doctrines of men, and private spirits, are to be examined, and in whose sentence we are to rest, can be no other but the Holy Spirit speaking in the Scripture. (1.10)

Tradition certainly plays an important role in both the Thirty-Nine Articles and the Westminster Confession, but it is an ancillary one. It is a norm not alongside Scripture but subordinate to it.[6] This represents an important difference of theological judgment between confessional Protestants and their Roman brethren. We might put it like this: for the Reformation churches, Scripture is recognized by the church as being divinely inspired via the susurrations of the Holy Spirit. It is the Spirit that moved the fathers of the ecumenical councils of the church to pronounce particular books canonical. They themselves were not competent to make this judgment apart from the work of the Holy Spirit.

It is a bit like recognizing the queen as she goes on a walkabout among a crowd of people. Our recognition of her does not confer on her a regal status. Rather, we acknowledge her regal status as we recognize that this person is our sovereign. Just so, the fathers of

---

6. Compare later in the Westminster Confession, which (at this juncture) echoes the language of the Thirty-Nine Articles: "All synods or councils, since the apostles' times, whether general or particular, may err; and many have erred. Therefore they are not to be made the rule of faith, or practice; but to be used as a help in both" (31.4).

Nicaea, Chalcedon, and the rest recognized the qualities of certain documents as bearing the marks of apostolicity and divine revelation, and canonized them. This was an ecclesial act in one respect, but it was an act undertaken by a body subordinate to the work of the Holy Spirit, who authorized these texts. The fathers of the ecumenical councils did not make Scripture; they understood certain books as being authorized by God. It is the difference between *deciding* one afternoon that a particular letter one has discovered in the attic was written by one's infamous ancestor the Bristol pirate Edward Teach (a.k.a. Blackbeard), and *recognizing* by certain telltale signs that the letter one has found in the attic was the work of the infamous Teach. In the former case, some act of imprimatur has gone on whereby I make a judgment about the artifact in question that confers upon it a certain status. In the latter case, the judgment concerned is more a question of seeing qualities latent within the letter as being the sort of qualities to be found in the extant work of Teach. I say that the fathers of the ecumenical councils were engaged in an activity much more like this latter case of discovery than like the former one. And I think this sort of view is not an atypical one in the Reformed tradition.

But when the matter is put like this, it may seem that there is less separating the Reformed Catholic from the Roman Catholic position (which is all to the good, as far as I am concerned). At the very least, it is important to note that representatives of these different communions greatly value the role of tradition in the life of the church and that there is a place of eminence, though not preeminence, given to tradition in the doctrinal formularies of two of the shoots of the Reformed tradition, namely, Anglicanism and Presbyterianism.

The Role of Faith

But if the churches of the Reformation have retained an important though subordinate place for tradition in the formation of Christian doctrine, then what of the role of faith? Here, consideration of the contribution of evangelical theology, including Reformed evangelical theology, is pertinent.[7]

Evangelical theology has traditionally had a somewhat ambivalent relationship to the notion of "experience," understood here as some event lived through of which one is consciously aware. Our focus shall be upon the role *religious* experience plays in the formation, sustenance, and development of Christian doctrine. But, given the foregoing, we will also consider the relationship between religious experience as a putative source of encounter with the divine, and other sources of testimony appealed to in order to ground theological authority, such as Scripture and tradition. We will see that in Reformed and evangelical thought there are different, sometimes conflicting, accounts of the relation that experience bears to doctrine or to norms of theological authority.

But faith itself is an act that implies religious experience. So, in addition to the question of the relation between faith and religious experience of the sort just mentioned, there is a logically prior question about how faith itself is to be understood qua experience in evangelical theology. The concept of faith admits of numerous different interpretations.[8] But for most evangelicals, faith is an act that involves two components. The first is propositional content, that is, believing that such and such is the case. This we shall call the "doxastic" component of faith. The second part is trust—what we might call the "fiducial" component to faith. Some people think faith

---

7. Reformed theology is not synonymous with evangelical theology, as shall become clear in what follows.

8. See William Lad Sessions, *The Concept of Faith* (Ithaca, NY: Cornell University Press, 1994).

is essentially nonpropositional or numinous and cannot be expressed in language. I shall have nothing to say about such notions of faith in what follows—not because they are unimportant but because they do not seem to be typical of mainstream Reformed and evangelical theology.

It seems clear that faith is something that is normally acquired. For some, faith acquisition comes about through a process of discovery, reflection, careful weighing of evidence, and so on. For others, it seems to be a sudden intrusion into their lives, as it was for the apostle Paul. God's presence is somehow impressed upon that person in such an immediate way that he or she cannot deny it; it is overwhelming. Whether faith is acquired through reflection or through dramatic change, it looks like one important feature of such faith is doxastic, in that one comes to hold certain beliefs in virtue of having faith. It also seems fairly clear that such faith in God also includes a fiducial component. From this, it should be clear that reflection on the very concept of faith and the role it plays in evangelical theologies must also include consideration of how faith relates to experience, because to have faith is to undergo some sort of experience.[9]

Though the subject of disagreement between competing parties of evangelicals, the *concept* of faith in evangelical theology has historically had fairly well-defined boundaries, which is attributable in large measure to the legacy of the Reformation. The Reformers bequeathed to their theological progeny an understanding of the nature of faith and its central and defining place in Protestant thought, which evangelicals have traditionally taken very seriously. But the issue of what faith consists in—what it is, exactly—should be distinguished from the matter of what function it has in theology, what role it plays. I suggest that these two issues, the conceptual

---

9. Note that here and in what follows, "experience" is not equivalent to "feelings."

and the functional aspects of faith, correspond to two levels of disagreement among evangelical theologians on the role of faith. It is tempting to think that this question of the role of faith in the life of the believer has been what has most often divided evangelicals. But in fact, such differences are the outcome of deeper commitments about the conceptual component of faith.

This was true even when evangelical theology was in its infancy, if the story told in the recent literature by David Bebbington and those who have followed his lead is correct.[10] Assume, for the sake of argument, that Bebbington is right and evangelicalism as a movement began in the 1730s with the revivalism of John and Charles Wesley, George Whitefield, and Jonathan Edwards, at the onset of what has become known as the Great Awakening. If this is true, then it would appear that at the beginning of evangelicalism there was a difference of opinion on the nature of faith, on its role in theology, and on how it is related to religious experience, a divergence that continues to the present.[11]

---

10. See David Bebbington, *Evangelicalism in Modern Britain: A History from the 1730s to the 1980s* (London: Routledge, 1989). Bebbington argues that there are four distinctive features of theologies that are evangelical: biblicism (a high view of Scripture in all matters touching Christian faith and practice), cruciocentrism (the centrality of the atonement), conversionism (that fallen human beings need to hear and respond to the gospel), and activism (the imperative to evangelize). This characterization of evangelicalism has become known as the Bebbington Quadrilateral.

11. Garry Williams has recently argued that the elements of the Bebbington Quadrilateral were already present in Reformation and Puritan theology. If that is right, then evangelicalism was aboriginally Augustinian in its understanding of faith and experience, and only subsequently fissured along "Calvinistic" and "Arminian" lines. This would mean there was originally much more convergence on the concept of faith and on how to understand religious experience in light of faith among evangelicals than Bebbington's thesis would allow for. But even if Williams is right (and I think there is much to be said for his argument), it is still the case that there are those in the evangelical constituency who align themselves with an evangelical Arminianism, as well as those who stand within Augustinianism broadly construed. That is all I am presuming here. See Garry J. Williams, "Enlightenment Epistemology and Evangelical Doctrines of Assurance," in *The Advent of Evangelicalism: Exploring Historical Continuities*, ed. Michael A. G. Haykin and Kenneth J. Stewart (Nashville, TN: B & H, 2008), 345–74.

To see this, let us turn to consider some of the main points of convergence and divergence over the matter of faith that existed between traditional evangelical Wesleyan Arminianism and evangelical Reformed theology of the sort embraced by stalwarts of evangelical history such as George Whitefield and Jonathan Edwards.[12] We begin with the conceptual level, concerning the nature of faith. Wesleyan evangelicals have traditionally agreed with their Reformed counterparts that it is faith alone that justifies a person before God; that faith is a gift of God; that faith brings about moral and spiritual reorientation; and that (as a consequence of this) faith itself must be experiential. In other words, faith is inherently *affective*. It cannot be a merely notional or intellectual assent to a given statement or proposition, though it normally includes such assent.[13]

Following Jonathan Edwards, we might think of the *affection* as that faculty of the soul which inclines or disinclines a person to do a thing under consideration, and includes the will, the mind, and the heart in such inclination. In this view, religious affections do not admit of a bifurcation between "heart" and "mind." They are more like "reasons of the heart." This means they are not reducible to emotion, passion, or intellectual preference but involve the interplay of mind, will, and heart, as Edwards suggests.[14] That this affective

12. I choose these two strains of evangelical theology because they have clear historical precedent in the literature and entail distinct theological positions. But one could just as easily speak, in denomination-specific terms, of evangelical Baptists, some of whom have historically been Reformed (such as Andrew Fuller, Charles Spurgeon, and John Piper) and some of whom have been more Arminian in their theology (such as the late Stanley Grenz and Roger Olsen). Or one could speak of evangelical Anglicans who are Arminian or Reformed, or free Evangelicals, Disciples of Christ, charismatics, Pentecostals, and so on. The relevant issues here can be transposed, without much change, to these particular denominational contexts.

13. Does this mean one must have a consciously "affective" experience in order for a given experience to count as genuinely "religious"? Not necessarily. One can profit from reading Scripture without being conscious of simultaneously enjoying a particular "experience" of God beyond the reading. The Holy Spirit may be at work in the believer without that believer's being conscious of it, and so on. But from an evangelical perspective, the affective component to faith is vital.

understanding of faith crosses the Arminian–Calvinist divide in historic evangelical theology can be illustrated from the experience of both John Wesley and Edwards, both of whom give paradigmatic accounts of "affective" faith acquisition. Wesley's famous report of his "conversion" runs thus:

> In the evening, I went very unwillingly to a society in Aldersgate Street, where one was reading Luther's Preface to the Epistle to the Romans. About a quarter before nine, while he was describing the change which God works in the heart through faith in Christ, I felt my heart strangely warmed. I felt I did trust in Christ, Christ alone for salvation; and an assurance was given me that he had taken away *my* sins, even *mine* and saved me from the law of sin and death.[15]

Edwards' account has striking similarities:

> The first that I remember that ever I found anything of that sort of inward, sweet delight in God and divine things, that I have lived much in since, was on reading those words, I Tim. 1:17. "Now unto the King eternal, immortal, invisible, the only wise God, be honour and glory for ever and ever, Amen." As I read the words, there came into my soul, and was as it were diffused through it, a sense of the glory of the Divine Being; a new sense, quite different from any thing I ever experienced before. Never any words of scripture seemed to me as these words did. I thought with myself, how excellent a Being that was; and how happy I should be, if I might enjoy that God, and be wrapped up to God in heaven, and be as it were swallowed up in him.[16]

---

14. Jonathan Edwards, *Religious Affections,* ed. John E. Smith, vol. 2 of *The Works of Jonathan Edwards,* ed. Perry Miller (New Haven, CT: Yale University Press, 1959), 96–97. Edwards admits that "it must be confessed, that language here is somewhat imperfect" in defining religious affections (97).

15. From *John Wesley,* ed. Albert Outler, Library of Protestant Thought (New York: Oxford University Press, 1964), 66.

16. From Jonathan Edwards, "Personal Narrative," in *A Jonathan Edwards Reader,* ed. John E. Smith, Harry S. Stout, and Kenneth P. Minkema (New Haven, CT: Yale University Press, 1995), 283–84. The fact that the precise date and morphology of the conversions of Wesley and Edwards have been disputed need not detain us here.

But there are also important areas of conceptual disagreement between the two evangelical parties on the question of faith acquisition. The Wesleyans could not agree with the Reformed about the *manner* in which salvation is said to be only by divine grace through faith. Broadly speaking, Arminian theology as a genus, of which evangelical Wesleyans are a species, is often accused of being committed to a doctrine of synergism according to which there is both a human and a divine contribution to be made to the process by which faith is acquired.[17] We might say that for the synergist, humans have the freedom to embrace or reject prevenient divine grace by, or with, faith. By contrast, most Reformed theologians (though perhaps not all) are said to affirm monergism.[18] This, very roughly, is the doctrine according to which no human contribution can be made to the process by which faith is acquired. That is, for the monergist, humans are *utterly incapable* of responding to God's suasions with faith. The work of salvation is entirely a work of grace; the human decision in regeneration follows in the wake of a prior (and absolutely singular) divine act.[19] Such a distinction does serve

17. There are important doctrinal differences between the Arminianism espoused by Jacob Arminius and his immediate disciples, such as Episcopius, and later Wesleyan Arminianism. Arminian theology is a rich and variegated genus, just as Reformed theology (its theological parent) is. Both Arminianism and Reformed Christianity belong to what, to borrow another zoological term, we might call the family of evangelical theology. Recent work in historical theology has helped clarify some of the differences between species of Arminian theology. See, e.g., Richard Muller, *God, Creation, and Providence in the Theology of Jacob Arminius* (Grand Rapids, MI: Baker, 1991). Cf. Roger Olson, *Arminian Theology: Myths and Realities* (Downers Grove, IL: Intervarsity, 2006).

18. Reformed theologians are typically theological determinists, but some have advocated theological libertarianism, like the Arminians. This is a matter to which we shall return in chapter 3. An excellent discussion of Calvinistic libertarianism can be found in William Cunningham's essay "Calvinism and the Doctrine of Philosophical Necessity" (1862), in *The Reformers and the Theology of the Reformation* (Edinburgh: Banner of Truth, 1989), 471–599.

19. The reason for such human incapacity is moot. Many Reformed theologians argue that the noetic effects of sin are such that human beings are incapable of turning to God without divine grace. But the Amyraldians and, later, followers of Jonathan Edwards in New England argued that there is no natural impediment to fallen human beings trusting in God by faith, but there is a moral inability to do so. See, e.g. Jonathan Edwards, *Freedom of the Will,* ed. Paul Ramsey,

a purpose, but it is not clear to me that it is a useful distinction when applied to different branches of evangelical theology. For it is not clear to me that Arminian theologians are synergists. Careful Arminian theologians deny that fallen human beings may turn to God without the interposition of divine grace, just as Reformed theologians do. Although there is a real disagreement about how much the will of a fallen individual awakened or invigorated by the secret working of the Holy Spirit may be said to be active in the process of salvation, this is not the same thing as claiming that the will of a fallen individual contributes in any substantive way to salvation. It is not even clear what it would mean for "the will" to contribute to salvation, other than as a euphemism for the agent contributing to her or his salvation. And no evangelical theologian, Arminian or Reformed, would countenance that.[20]

This leads us to note, more briefly, the second level of disagreement between Wesleyan and Reformed evangelicals on the matter of the role faith plays in their respective theologies. We have seen that evangelicals have tended to converge on the centrality of faith for the Christian life and on the importance of the idea that one is saved only through faith, despite wranglings over what salvation *sola fide* entails. But they have disagreed among themselves about the practical consequences of this commitment in the *ordo salutis* and the life of faith. Here the different theological characters of the two evangelical traditions come into play more obviously. Consider, for example, how faith is deployed in, say, the doctrine of regeneration or perseverance. Arminian evangelicals have traditionally thought that in both regeneration and perseverance, the human subject

vol. 1 of *The Works of Jonathan Edwards,* ed. Perry Miller (New Haven, CT: Yale University Press, 1957), 156–62, 362–63.
20. For one interesting recent account of salvation that is consistent with Arminian theology and is not synergistic, see Kevin Timpe, *Free Will in Philosophical Theology* (London: Bloomsbury Academic, 2014), chap. 4.

contributes to the process involved, which the Reformed have denied. This is one important reason for the different accounts of the order of salvation and of perseverance that one finds in these two traditions.

However, it is also true to say that in the past century (and for a variety of reasons), the conceptual boundaries thought to circumscribe what is doctrinally permissible in discussion of the nature of faith in the evangelical constituency have broadened out. This means that there is now a greater range of options on the nature of faith *and* its function in evangelical thought than was true at the close of the nineteenth century. For instance, there are evangelical biblical scholars for whom Pauline faith is as much a matter of belonging to the covenant community as it is a question of having some alien righteousness imputed to the believer by God (see the work of scholars like N. T. Wright and those taking a "New Perspective" on Paul).

Thus far, we have seen that the relationship between faith and experience is an intimate one. For evangelical theologians, faith depends on experience; it is affective. It is practically impossible to have faith without such experience, even if, as a matter of fact, for some people faith in God begins at the same moment that experience of God occurs.[21] But a lively, affective faith is not enough. One can have the sort of evangelical understanding of faith just outlined and yet live a wicked life (see Rom. 6:1). Such antinomianism is a real problem for evangelicals who take seriously the experiential dimension to faith, as expounded by evangelical leaders of the past like Wesley and Edwards.[22] In the recent literature, Richard

---

21. Experience of God need not generate faith. James 2:19 tells us, "You believe that God is one; you do well. Even the demons believe—and shudder." But clearly the demons believe that there is a God without trusting in God. They have known God, have had experience of God, but have no faith in God. The same is true of many human beings—which is why it is possible to commit the unforgivable sin by rejecting the susurrations of the Holy Spirit (Mark 3:29).

Swinburne has taken the view that the best way to avoid antinomianism is to adopt a pragmatic model of faith. Whereas a number of theologians in the Western tradition, such as Thomas Aquinas or Martin Luther, have emphasized both the doxastic and fiducial elements of faith, Swinburne wants to make a case for acting as if certain things were the case. The fiducial pragmatist (as we shall call him) need not believe that there is a God, but he must act as if there is a God, living a life consistent with that belief, informed by certain moral commitments and actions. Swinburne comments: "On the Pragmatist view, a man S has faith if he acts on the assumptions that there is a God who has the properties which Christians ascribe to him and has provided for me the means of salvation and the prospect of glory, and that he will do for S what he knows that S needs or wants—so long also as S has good purposes."[23] What is potentially lacking in the Lutheran account of faith, where one believes that there is a God and trusts that through Christ's work he or she will be saved, is *good purpose*. It is this that leaves the door open to antinomianism. In short, the Lutheran view (as Swinburne characterizes it) cannot exclude the scoundrel from being a person of faith. This is precisely why Swinburne thinks the pragmatic account of faith is superior to the Lutheran. The fiducial pragmatist must have a good purpose in view, which the Lutheran view cannot guarantee.

But Swinburne clearly has a rather different conception of faith than that of evangelicals attracted to the affective account of theologians like Edwards. Swinburne thinks belief is not praiseworthy because it is not voluntary: one cannot simply bring oneself to believe a particular proposition. The mind believes a given proposition on the basis of the evidence. But trust occurs where there is an evidential gap. It is what stands "in" that gap. Thus, I trust

22. We shall return to the question of antinomianism in chapter 2.
23. Richard Swinburne, *Faith and Reason* (Oxford: Oxford University Press, 1981), 116.

God despite the lack of overwhelming evidence for God's existence. However, as Paul Helm has pointed out, this means there is a paradox at the heart of Swinburne's account of pragmatic faith. For, according to Swinburne,

> [T]o the extent that the existence of God is evidentially established it is more reasonable to believe that he exists than not, but for that very reason there is less opportunity for faith in him, for trust. Merit comes only from trust, but trust can only occur when there is evidential deficiency. . . . [T]o the extent that you have good grounds for a belief about God you at the same time reduce opportunities for trusting God, for acting on an assumption while having a good purpose, and so you reduce the opportunities for faith in God, and so lessen your chances of gaining merit by exercising such faith.[24]

The upshot of this is that for the Swinburnian fiducial pragmatist, ignorance about intellectual arguments concerning God is better for one's faith. Needless to say, this is a rather peculiar conclusion for a philosophical theologian to reach.

But, assuming that the evangelical does have a conception of faith like the Lutheran, how can she exclude the possibility of antinomianism? An affective faith might still issue in a lack of good purpose. In fact, it looks like one cannot prevent antinomianism, even if it is part and parcel of faith to be experiential, as it is in the Wesleyan and Edwardsian accounts. However, something is surely awry with the person who thinks that faith is affective and yet that such faith need not issue in good purpose. Similarly, one cannot exclude the possibility that one's spouse does not reciprocate conjugal love but simulates it from purely selfish motives. But this does not in and of itself nullify conjugal love, or the trust one places in one's spouse. The misuse of a thing does not invalidate its right use.

---

24. Paul Helm, *Faith with Reason* (Oxford: Oxford University Press, 2000), 146.

Experience and Doctrine

From consideration of Scripture and tradition, as well as faith as experience, we turn to wider concerns about faith, experience, and doctrine. Recall the initial distinction made at the beginning of the preceding section of this chapter concerning the role religious experience plays in the formation, sustenance, and development of Christian doctrine, as well as in the relationship between religious experience as a putative source of encounter with the divine and other sources of testimony appealed to in order to ground theological authority. We shall consider each of these issues in turn.

Indisputably, religious experience plays an important role in the genesis of doctrine, as well as in its sustenance and development. This holds true irrespective of one's particular theological proclivities. But it is not clear that a Reformed and evangelical account of the genesis of doctrine requires that in every instance the human authors of Scripture underwent some supernatural experience of which they were conscious, as a necessary condition for the genesis of biblical doctrine. For instance, reading Luke–Acts, one gets the impression that the author did not write because he believed he had a specific experience to communicate, nor because he believed he was "under the influence" of the Holy Spirit, but because he thought it important to leave a record of the events described. The same is not true of, say, Paul or Jeremiah, for whom particular religious experience was a fundamental motivation for his writing.

This is consistent with the claim that Luke–Acts was written under the inspiration of the Holy Spirit, because divine ministrations need not be something of which we are conscious. (I am not conscious of God upholding me at every moment of my existence. Yet the doctrine of providence suggests this is just what God does.) This has the strange consequence that a specific revelatory *experience* of

God, understood as an event lived through of which the subject is conscious, is not a necessary condition for the formation of Scripture. Yet I think this must be embraced, given that some of the human authors of Scripture appear not to have been aware of the fact that their writings were divine revelation (or, perhaps, the vehicle for divine revelation).[25] But then, what role does experience play in the formation of doctrine? One way of getting clearer on this question involves distinguishing different levels of experience in relation to the formation of Scripture. At the *mundane* level, there are those experiences which are necessary for the author to be in a position to write the sort of material he does. So, the author of Luke–Acts has the experience of growing up in a literate community, being shaped by that community, becoming a physician, meeting Paul, deciding to write Luke–Acts (or being the author substantially responsible for this document), and so on. Without these particular mundane experiences, Luke–Acts would not exist as we have it. And it is surely plausible to think that God ensures that the author of Luke–Acts has these experiences in order to bring about the writing of the portion of Scripture he writes.

But then there is another level, that of *supernatural* experience, where authors live through an event of which they are conscious and which they report in terms of a divine encounter of some kind. This is also an important feature of Scripture and happens at key moments in the biblical narrative, for example, to Moses on Sinai, to Isaiah in the temple, to Ezekiel in his vision of the valley of dry bones, on

25. Experience of God is not a sufficient condition for the formation of the canon, because other conditions are also necessary, such as the process of inscripturation, which in the case of many biblical books included a period of oral transmission of the purported experience, being written down, preserved, and redacted by a given ecclesial community and being accepted by the church as of divine origin. None of these things necessarily undermines the status of Scripture as divine revelation, any more than the recording of an interview with the prime minister and its being written down and edited at some later date for publication and dissemination necessarily undermines the status of the words on the page of the published form of the interview as being those uttered by the prime minister.

the Mount of Transfiguration, and at Paul's conversion. But it is not clear that all biblical authors are consciously aware of having had such experiences—or even that every author reports having had, or having heard about, such experiences (consider, for example, the books of Ruth, Esther, and Proverbs).

So it seems that experience is very important in the formation of Scripture and that the right concatenation of mundane experience is used by God to bring about the writing of Scripture. But in some cases, this does not appear to include the notion of a consciously apprehended religious experience informing the output, in addition to such mundane experience. In such cases, I presume God works secretly by the Holy Spirit, providentially ensuring that the mundane experience that informs the writing of a particular author of Scripture enables that author, by the inspiration of the Holy Spirit, to write the word of God. But importantly, such divine workings may be hidden from the person writing, who may not be conscious of this secret divine work.[26]

Note that this understanding of divine revelation and the process of its being encoded in Scripture need not be flat-footed about how the particular canonical form of the text came about. What is important is the claim that through these different sorts of literature, in diverse ways, using the texture and voice of particular authors, in texts brought together and edited over time, we find God speaking. These are not merely the words of human beings who, through reflection upon the divine, came to hold particular views and transmitted them,

26. Compare the Puritan theologian William Ames, who writes, "Divine inspiration was present among these writers in different ways. Some things were utterly unknown to the writer in advance, as appears in the history of creation or in the foretelling of things to come. But some things were previously known to the writers. . . . Some things were known by a natural knowledge and some by a supernatural. In those things that were hidden and unknown, divine inspiration was at work." William Ames, *The Marrow of Theology*, trans. John D. Eusden (Boston: Pilgrim, 1968), 186. See also Kenneth J. Stewart, "The Evangelical Doctrine of Scripture, 1650–1850: A Re-Examination of David Bebbington's Theory," in Haykin and Stewart, *Advent of Evangelicalism*, 398–413.

or came to have particular experiences and wrote them down for posterity. These are the very words of God communicated through the feeble, fragile, fallible medium of human beings. God so fashions and shapes these humans that all the idiosyncrasies and traits a particular author has are used by the divine author to convey exactly what that divine author intends to say. For the evangelical theologian, there can be nothing implausible in thinking that God accommodates God's self in such a complex manner as to ensure, through this process of experience, writing, and transmission, that what results is what God intended to convey to God's people. As the Old Princeton theologian Benjamin Warfield memorably put it, the different biblical authors are like the colored panes in a stained-glass window. The same light shines through them all, but it is refracted in many different and beautiful ways corresponding to the color, shape, and transparency of the glass through which it passes.[27]

But more important than this, the Christian theologian has a theological reason for thinking that it is characteristic of God to accommodate God's self in such complex ways to God's creatures. This can be seen preeminently in the incarnation, the supreme instance of divine accommodation. Christology cannot be an afterthought in an evangelical account of divine revelation and its relation to faith and experience. It must be foundational. For Christ, as the word of God incarnate, is divine revelation incarnate. We know God has revealed God's self to the extent that we know Christ is God—not because revelation includes only those places in Scripture where Christ is reported as speaking but because the Second Person of the Trinity is the word of God. He is, as it were, the speech of God, who brings forth creation and who inspires the prophets and apostles by God's Spirit. So, divine revelation is, in a way, guaranteed

---

27. Benjamin B. Warfield, "Inspiration," in *International Standard Bible Encyclopedia,* ed. James Orr (Chicago: Severance, 1915), 3:1473–83.

by the role played by Christ as God incarnate, as well as by the work performed by Christ qua word of God who by the Spirit communicates to the prophets before Christ and the apostles after his ascension. The upshot of this is that, as one aspect of the *opus dei*, revelation is a triune work. Although it terminates upon the word of God in a particular manner, it also involves the Father in its instigation and the Spirit in its communication.

This also gives some indication of how an evangelical account of the relation between experience and the formation of biblical doctrine may differ from that of classical liberal theology and its modern counterparts. Liberal theologians thought that Scripture is the codification of religious experiences. Thus, for example, Friedrich Schleiermacher's famous thesis that "Christian doctrines are accounts of the Christian religious affections set forth in speech."[28] But they denied that these religious experiences constitute an immutable divine revelation. They conceived of religious experience as what generates doctrine, including the doctrine in Scripture, but they thought doctrine was inherently revisable on the basis of new experiences of God. There is, in this way, a constant process of experiencing God, checking this with Scripture and the tradition, and using such experience to correct or adjust the testimony of the Christian faith in line with the "God consciousness" or "sense of absolute dependence" the theologian perceives in and through the person and work of Christ. Hence, according to liberal theologians, experience is normative in Christian theology in a way that Scripture is not. This picture of the relation between faith and experience is beguiling, because it captures an important truth about how doctrine is often generated through religious experience. The problem with liberal theology lies not in its placing experience of God center stage

---

28. Friedrich Schleiermacher, *The Christian Faith* (1830; repr., Edinburgh: T & T Clark, 1999), §15.

but rather in its decoupling such experience from a robust concept of divine revelation along with an insistence upon a particular conception of religious experience as fundamental to the formation of doctrine. It is this move that enabled the liberal theologians to invert the traditional Reformation idea of Scripture as the final norm in matters of doctrine, replacing it with contemporary religious experience.

So much for the role of experience in the genesis of doctrine; what of the role it plays in its sustenance and development? Like many Reformed thinkers, I take it that doctrine is propositional or can be expressed in propositional form.[29] Scripture contains propositions. It also contains lots of other sorts of things, like commands, imprecations, and tropes, which are not propositions. But this is not to deny that we find doctrine in Scripture. Similarly, we find doctrine in the catholic creeds and in the confessional symbols of particular ecclesial communities (the Westminster Confession, the Augsburg Confession, the Baptist Confession of 1689, and so on). Here, there is a way in which experience plays a role in bearing witness to Scripture in the doctrine confessed by the church. As the contemporary Anglican evangelical theologian John Webster puts it, "[A] creed or confessional formula is a public and binding indication of the gospel set before us in the scriptural witness, through which the church affirms its allegiance to God, repudiates the falsehood by which the church is threatened, and assembles around the judgement and consolation of the gospel."[30]

---

29. Karl Barth offers a different account of dogmatics as a critical science that concerns itself with the proclamation of the church. He seems to think that this task is principally concerned not with propositions but with witness. Suppose that he is right. Such an account is surely consistent with thinking that doctrine can be expressed in propositional form, which is what I am supposing here. See Karl Barth, *Dogmatics in Outline*, trans. G. T. Thomson (London: SCM, 1949), chap. 1.

30. John Webster, *Confessing God: Essays in Christian Dogmatics II* (Edinburgh: T & T Clark, 2005), 73–74.

I suggest that this is a right understanding of the role of the creeds and confessions of Christendom. The ecumenical symbols of the church were authorized by councils that were moved by the Holy Spirit (whether or not they were conscious of this and "experienced" the work of the Holy Ghost) and that witnessed to Scripture in the canons forged thereby. To the extent that these canons are extrapolations of Scripture's explicit and implicit message, they are to be upheld—but only so far. Scripture is normative in a way that not even the catholic creeds are. The same goes for particular confessions that are also witnesses—in the first instance, to Scripture, but also as echoes of those ideas found in previous creedal documents that the framers of such confessions recognized as other, more ancient witnesses to the same truth.

This, or something very like it, has been the traditional understanding of most Reformed evangelicals with respect to the creeds and confessions of the church, in common with many other orthodox Christians. The extent to which a given creed or confession effectively witnesses to Scripture is, of course, an important theological consideration, but here is not the place to explore that. It is sufficient for present purposes to understand that the authority of the creeds and confessions is derivative. The experience of those framing these documents is not normative for Christian faith, as the experience of the apostles and prophets as authors of Scripture was. The Fathers who worked on the great symbols of the church were certainly guided by the same Holy Spirit that inspired the authors of Holy Writ. But the sort of guidance needed was more by way of recognizing what to say about Scripture, what to leave out, and how to express it in language that would preserve the church and communicate to the generation to which they addressed themselves, in thought-forms and ideas inevitably somewhat removed from those of the Bible. Such guidance is very different from divine revelation.

It is like the difference between writing *Jane Eyre* and writing a study guide to *Jane Eyre*. *Jane Eyre* would exist without the study guide, but the study guide would never have been conceived without *Jane Eyre*. Just so with respect to the two sorts of literature that make up Scripture and the creeds and confessions, respectively, and the different sorts of experience each required.

This is not to deny that there is doctrinal development of a sort: the more Christians have reflected on Scripture and listened to theologians from the past, the clearer certain issues have become (although this is not always the case and this does not imply a sort of Hegelian unfolding of the true nature of doctrine through history). But an evangelical account of faith and experience cannot countenance the prospect that something might be added to Scripture or stand alongside Scripture as an equivalent source of authority. In this way, evangelicals are heirs to the Reformation *sola scriptura*. Scripture has a final authority that no other source of creaturely testimony does (bar Christ). It is alone in that sense. But, of course, Scripture is never alone in another sense. It is always read and understood within the community of faith in a tradition stretching back to the apostles, under the guidance of the Holy Spirit.

Conclusion

It does not seem likely that there will be a convergence of differing evangelical conceptions of the relation between faith and experience anytime soon. Some writers worry that the doctrinal plurality currently tolerated on a number of doctrinal loci, including issues that are part of the Bebbington Quadrilateral, is a cause for grave concern about the integrity of evangelicalism and its future as a coherent theological movement. Increasingly, theologians who are evangelicals identify themselves with one or another subgroup by adding a particular preliminary to the noun *evangelical,* such as "postconservative evangelical," "progressive evangelical," "Catholic evangelical," "liberal evangelical," and so on. It may be that in due course, the doctrinal nuances that pick out these differing subgroups will lead them in such different directions that the term *evangelical* becomes more like its German equivalent, *evangelische* (roughly, "Protestant"), than the name for a coherent theological movement or homogeneous group of beliefs held by particular theological communities. This is a real concern. But I have argued that the two main evangelical genera that emerged from the Great Awakening, namely, Wesleyan Arminianism and the evangelical Reformed thought of theologians like Jonathan Edwards, share enough in common concerning the notion of faith, especially of faith as affective experience, for them to be considered part of one family of Christian theology that has its roots in the Reformation. I have also outlined one account of the role experience plays in the formation of doctrine in Scripture, which (I submit) is consistent with an evangelical way of thinking.[31] Finally, I have given some indication of how this differs from the way in which subsequent generations have reflected on Scripture, which has been codified in the bodies of doctrine comprising the creeds and confessions, which is where we began this chapter. There is more to be said about how evangelicals view their own private religious experiences with respect to faith, and about the relationship between faith and what is often called Christian practice. But enough has been said here to indicate how discussion of such matters might begin.

---

31. It would be anachronistic to claim that the church fathers who recognized the canon of Scripture were evangelicals in the Bebbington sense of that term. The account set forth here may be thought of as a Reformed perspective on the relationship between religious experience and the formation of doctrine consistent with evangelicalism—a sort of Reformed evangelical gloss on how the Fathers came to canonize the creeds.

2

Eternal Justification

God did, from all eternity, decree to justify all the elect, and Christ did, in the fullness of time, die for their sins, and rise again for their justification: nevertheless, they are not justified, until the Holy Spirit does, in due time, actually apply Christ unto them.
—Westminster Confession of Faith, 11.4.4

When are the elect declared or pronounced righteous? It might be thought to be at the eternal "moment" in the order of divine decrees when God ordains that they will be justified through the work of Christ. However, this is not the only theologically viable possibility. Perhaps it is at the time at which Christ's work is complete; or the moment when the believer appropriates Christ's benefits, being united with him by the power of the Holy Spirit; or the public declaration of the righteousness of the individual on the last day when she or he stands before the divine judge. Each of these answers has had its defenders in the Christian tradition, and much depends on which of these responses (if any) one gives to the question. For this question connects the doctrine of election to justification and faith.

A number of Reformed theologians have defended a version of the doctrine of eternal justification, according to which God justifies the elect either *from* eternity or *in* eternity. The difference between these two prepositions is important in this context, as we shall see. The friends of eternal justification comprise some of the luminaries of the Reformed faith. These include Karl Barth, Abraham Kuyper, Herman Hoeksema, John Gill, and William Twisse, as well as a number of divines whose work is less widely known today. Among this latter group are writers like Tobias Crisp and John Brine. There are still others whose work is sympathetic to aspects of eternal justification even if it is not clear that they actually endorse the doctrine. Examples include Thomas Goodwin and Herman Witsius. However, the doctrine is not without opponents. Critics within the Reformed tradition include Herman Bavinck, G. C. Berkouwer, and Louis Berkhof, to name but three of the more recent (and vocal) Dutch opponents.[1]

The historic association of eternal justification with Reformed theology might indicate that it is the preserve of a minority in the Christian tradition, of little value to those unencumbered by an idée fixe regarding the doctrine of election. However, it seems to me that the doctrine helps clarify a cluster of important issues pertaining to the relationship of faith, justification, and election, matters that are of much wider significance in ecumenical theology today. Katherine Sonderegger, in a recent essay on the relationship between justification and election in the 1999 Roman Catholic–Lutheran Joint Declaration on the Doctrine of Justification, makes this point well. She observes that the declaration is silent regarding the connection between these two fundamental themes,

---

1. The so-called Three Forms of Unity in the Reformed tradition, that is, the Belgic Confession, the Heidelberg Catechism, and the Canons of Dort, are ambiguous on the matter of the "moment" of justification. The Belgic Confession grounds justification in the righteousness of Christ in article 23. The canons of the Synod of Dort do not address the matter directly. Neither does the Heidelberg Catechism. This silence on the matter of eternal justification is also observed by the Thirty-Nine Articles (see articles 11 and 17.) This is not terribly surprising, because the doctrine became a matter of dispute in the seventeenth century, which postdates these confessions but not the Westminster Confession, which was composed in 1646.

although election stands behind much that it does say regarding the form of the doctrine of justification and the specific matters of historic dispute between these two communions. However, as Sonderegger goes on to point out, it is impossible to avoid discussion of election in a complete account of justification. Similarly, it is impossible to avoid discussion of justification in a full-orbed doctrine of election. As she puts it, "Predestination forms the necessary context to justification, as shadow to light; without it, justification itself loses definition, rigor, and force."[2] Although Sonderegger's concerns are more about the way election and reprobation shape justification, the same is true of the relationship between the eternal decree to justify the elect and its actualization in time in the justification of believers, which is the focus of the present chapter. To these recent remarks by Sonderegger we may add the oft-reported comment of Karl Barth that election "is the sum of the Gospel" and that "it is the Gospel *in nuce* . . . the very essence of all good news."[3] If that is right, then what we think about the connection between election, justification, and faith touches the very center of the Christian life. For these reasons, discussion of eternal justification may offer one Reformed contribution to the ongoing debate about these matters among the different and disparate communions of the Christian church.

Distinguishing Justification *in* and *from* Eternity

As has already been intimated, there are at least two ways to construe the doctrine of eternal justification. Both versions of the doctrine agree upon the claim that, in one dogmatically important sense, the elect are declared righteous in eternity by divine decree. Hence, both

---

2. Katherine Sonderegger, "Called to Salvation in Christ: Justification and Predestination," in *What Is Justification About? Reformed Contributions to an Ecumenical Theme,* ed. Michael Weinrich and John P. Burgess(Grand Rapids, MI: Eerdmans, 2009), 124–25.
3. Karl Barth, *Church Dogmatics,* ed. Geoffrey W. Bromiley and Thomas F. Torrance, vol. 2, pt. 2 (1942; repr., Edinburgh: T & T Clark, 1957), 13–14.

versions of the doctrine maintain that in one carefully circumscribed respect there is good reason to think that the elect are eternally justified. Call this the question concerning the moment of "formal justification." The two versions of the doctrine diverge upon the matter of whether or to what extent there is another sense in which this act of eternal justification is incomplete until the Holy Spirit applies the benefits of this eternal act to the individual in time. Call this the question concerning the moment of "material justification." To put it another way, the distinction between these two versions of eternal justification turns on whether justification is a divine act that is, so to speak, completed in eternity, or whether it is ordained in eternity but is, as it were, realized in time. To make this difference clear, we will need to spend some time outlining the two versions of the eternal-justification doctrine. The first we shall call justification *in* eternity. It is distinct from a closely related neighbor that we will designate justification *from* eternity.

For those who hold to the justification-in-eternity view, the act of justification is complete at the moment God ordains the justification of the elect in eternity. We might say that, in this view, the moment of formal justification *is* the moment of justification. Faith in Christ is an unveiling to the elect individual of the eternal purposes of God according to which she has been justified in eternity. She does not change from being a child of wrath to being a child of grace through coming to faith. Rather, she is eternally a child of grace and comes to understand that she is included in God's eternal saving purposes in Christ at the moment when the Holy Spirit reveals this to her by means of the gift of faith given in regeneration. In this way, the justification-in-eternity view coordinates the unfolding of God's purposes in history to God's eternal decree to save and justify God's elect in and through the work of Christ.

Compare this to the justification-from-eternity view. In this way of thinking, as with the justification-in-eternity doctrine, God ordains the salvation of a certain number of individuals eternally. God also ordains that these individuals be justified on the basis of the work of Christ, an act that is also eternal but consequent upon the decree to elect some number of individuals. However, unlike the proponent of the doctrine of justification in eternity, the defender of justification from eternity thinks that the act of eternal justification is, in one sense, incomplete at the moment God ordains the justification of the elect in eternity. Although God has decreed that certain persons will be elect and justified in and through the work of Christ, this must be actualized in time through the secret work of the Holy Spirit in the hearts of the elect. As the Westminster Confession puts it, the Spirit must "apply Christ unto them" that are elect in due time, so that there appear to be two phases or aspects to the eternal decision of God to justify the elect. The first aspect is the eternal decree (the eternal "moment" of formal justification); the second aspect is the bringing about of God's eternal purpose in the justification of the elect at a particular moment in time (the temporal moment of material justification).

With this distinction between the two sorts of eternal justification doctrine made tolerably clear, we may proceed to an exposition of each of the two variations before considering some of the main objections to eternal justification.

Concerning Justification *in* Eternity

Let us begin with the doctrine of justification in eternity. Consider the following parable:

> A boy who is a member of the royal family and the heir to the throne of some faraway land is living anonymously in a remote hamlet, under the straitened circumstances that are the lot of a village peasant. The

old king dies and succession falls to the lad, who is proclaimed the new ruler of the kingdom. A royal delegation is sent to locate him, and, after much searching, they find him and bring him to the palace, where he is enthroned as monarch amid much rejoicing.

For the purposes of comparison with the doctrine of justification in eternity, there are several important things to note in this story. The first is that the child is heir to the throne even before he is aware of the fact. His royal status and claim do not depend on his *knowing* that he is a member of the royal family. The second thing to see is that his coming to know that he is a member of the royal family and the heir to the throne makes a significant change to the life of the child *once he is made aware of this fact*. From a poor, meager existence in a remote hovel, he comes to acquire the lifestyle and trappings of a prince.

The doctrine of justification in eternity makes three very similar claims. It presumes that justification is an eternal divine act according to which God ordains before the foundation of the world those who will be elect, and justifies them. Election and justification are conceptually distinct. They are not the same doctrine, and the justification-in-eternity view does not necessarily collapse the one into the other. However, they are very closely related in the order of the divine decrees, though justification is consequent upon election. As the eighteenth-century Baptist divine John Gill puts it,

> Justification may well be considered as a branch of election; it is no other, as one expresses it, than setting apart the elect alone to be partakers of Christ's righteousness; and a setting apart Christ's righteousness for the elect only; it is mentioned along with election, as of the same date with it; "Wherein," that is, in the grace of God, particularly the electing grace of God, spoken of before, "he hath made us accepted in the beloved" (Eph. 1.6). What is this acceptance in Christ, but justification in him? And this is expressed as a past act, in the same language as other eternal things be in the context, he "hath" blessed us, and he "hath" chosen us, and "having" predestinated us, so he hath made us accepted; and, indeed, as Christ was always the beloved of God, and

well pleasing to him; so all given to him, and in him, were beloved of God, well pleasing to him, and accepted with him, or justified in him from eternity.[4]

That is, in the sequence of eternal decrees, God ordains the election of some number of fallen humanity through Christ, whereupon God justifies this number by means of the work of Christ. Given that these distinctions in the divine decrees pertain to one eternal divine act of ordination, and given that if God is atemporal, there is no temporal lag between the ordering of one decree and the ordering of another (though there may be a conceptual distinction between them, and a difference in place in the order of decrees), these things do not occur at different moments in time, one after the other.

This brings us to a second point. Those who are eternally the objects of divine grace come to know that they are elect and justified at a particular time, at which they are given faith by the secret working of the Holy Spirit in order to understand that they are united to Christ. However, there is a sense in which those who are elected by God are eternally justified. The status of these individuals as those saved by the work of Christ and justified in the sight of God is contingent upon divine ordination. Nevertheless, the eternal free act of God whereby God decrees their salvation on the basis of the work of Christ as mediator makes their salvation inevitable (Eph. 1:4–11). To borrow a distinction from Scholasticism, we might say their status as elect is hypothetically necessary, or necessary consequent upon the divine decree to elect them in Christ.

Like the young prince living in ignorance of his royal status before being discovered, the individual member of the elect already belongs to the company of the redeemed prior to coming to faith. Similarly, according to the doctrine of justification in eternity, the person who

---

4. John Gill, *A Body of Doctrinal Divinity* (London: 1769), bk. 2, chap. 5, sec. 2b2.

is eternally elect in Christ is also eternally justified. Possession of faith makes no material difference to one's elect status, because it is an effect, not a cause, of justification. The act of justification must logically precede the act of faith, whether in time or in eternity, for a person must be just in the sight of God before she can be given the gift of faith in God. Similarly, someone who has been suspended on suspicion of embezzling company funds must be cleared of all charges and declared innocent before his place is returned to him.

In this way of thinking, faith is the means by which the elect individual comes to understand she is already a member of the elect, and already justified by God in Christ. The change it effects is epistemic, not ontological. It is a change of perception or of knowledge, not a change in legal or moral standing, or even in being. To put it in the concrete terms of the New Testament, the elect are not changed from being enemies of God to being children of God. This cannot be the case, for God has eternally elected them in Christ. Nor can they be changed from being outside the bounds of those divinely justified to being among those justified, because their justification has been eternally secured by divine decree. Instead, like the prince in our story, the person who is eternally elected in Christ comes to see she is elect at the moment she is granted faith in Christ. But this election is not secured or brought about at that moment. Rather, she comes to see what was eternally true about her because of the purposes of God according to God's good pleasure and will.

However, the epistemic change this secures in the life of the one elect is not necessarily trivial or superficial; it may involve a significant change in circumstance. In the case of the crown prince, this change involves going from living as a pauper in a mean rural hamlet to enjoying the trappings of royalty. Something similar may obtain in the case of the elect individual who comes to understand she is justified in eternity. From living without God and without eternal hope, the believer comes to see herself as included in the purposes of God in salvation and as numbered among those who are saved through the merit of Christ. This change, though really a change in how one understands one's status before God rather than a change in status as such, is nevertheless momentous. Concerning this change, the Dutch Reformed theologian Herman Hoeksema says,

> In his eternal counsel God has ordained Christ as Mediator and head of all the elect. And therefore it must be true that God knew the elect in Christ as justified from all eternity. The elect do not become righteous before God in time by faith, but they are righteous in the tribunal of God from before the foundation of the earth. God beholds them in eternity not as sinners but as perfectly righteous, as redeemed, as justified in Christ.[5]

That said, justification in eternity does not necessarily negate the application of this eternal divine act in time. We have already noted that justification must be received by faith, which is the instrument by means of which the believer is united to Christ and becomes a partaker in his benefits as a visible member of the church. But between the eternal "moment" of justification and the bestowal of faith in time, there is the finished work of Christ in his death and resurrection, which is the means by which justification obtains. We might put it like this: God eternally ordains the particular number of God's people, who are elected in Christ as the mediator of salvation. The mechanism by means of which this eternal act of election is actualized obtains in and through the work of Christ in time, and supremely in his death and resurrection. In this way, the work of Christ constitutes the means by which election is secured. This, in turn, is applied to the individual by faith, which is a divine gift bestowed via the secret work of the Holy Spirit. However, faith is

---

5. Herman Hoeksema, *Reformed Dogmatics* (1966; repr., Grand Rapids, MI: Reformed Free Publishing Assoc., 1973), 502.

not itself justifying; it is purely instrumental. We might say that it is the conduit by means of which we come to see that we are united to Christ and are able to become partakers of his benefits through the sacramental life of the church. Finally, to these three "moments" of justification may be added the final justification on the last day, when those who are members of Christ's elect will be declared to be the bride of Christ.[6]

Abraham Kuyper makes this apparent in his discussion of eternal justification. He is clear in his own mind that "Scripture reveals these two positive, but apparently contradictory truths, with equally positive emphasis: . . . that, *on the one hand,* He has justified us in His own judgment seat *from eternity;* and . . . that, *on the other,* only in conversion are we justified *by faith.*"[7] Yet, as we have seen, these two things can be reconciled, given a view of faith as the instrument by means of which the individual apprehends her status as justified. Kuyper seems to concur. He remarks, "It should therefore openly be confessed, and without any abbreviation, that justification does not occur when we become conscious of it, but that, on the contrary, our justification was decided from eternity in the holy judgment-seat of our God." He goes on: "There is undoubtedly a moment in our life when for the first time justification is *published* to our consciousness; but let us be careful to distinguish justification itself from its publication." Justification "does not spring *from* our consciousness, but it is mirrored *in* it, and hence must have being

6. Hoeksema makes similar remarks in ibid., 503. But these are distinctions one can find elsewhere in Reformed theology, e.g., in the homiletics of the nineteenth-century Scottish Reformed minister John Colquhoun (1748–1827). See his *Sermons, Chiefly on Doctrinal Subjects* (Edinburgh: J & D Collie, 1836), especially sermons 10–11. He speaks of the manner of justification under four heads: *intentionally,* in the divine decree and purpose; *virtually,* in the resurrection of Christ from the dead; *actually,* when faith is applied to the elect; and *publicly,* on the last day, when the elect will be absolved before all humanity by God (152–56).

7. Abraham Kuyper, *The Work of the Holy Spirit,* trans. Henri de Vries (1900; repr., Grand Rapids, MI: Eerdmans, 1946), 2:371.

and stature in itself."[8] We may now summarize the doctrine of justification in eternity:

1. God eternally decrees the number of the elect.
2. God eternally decrees that Christ is the mediator of salvation.
3. Christ is the ground of election (given that God the Son, the divine person who voluntarily assumes human nature, is a member of the divine Trinity) and the means by which election is brought about as the Elect One and mediator of our election.
4. God knows all those who are elect.
5. God knows that all the elect will be saved through the work of Christ as mediator.
6. God knows that all the elect will be justified through the work of Christ by God's divine grace alone, according to God's divine will and purpose (Eph. 1:5).
7. It is eternally true that the elect are justified by Christ's meritorious work alone (not by their own merit).
8. The secret work of the Holy Spirit applies the benefits of Christ's work to each individual member of the elect.
9. This application obtains by means of the gift of faith, bestowed on the elect individual by the Holy Spirit, uniting that individual to Christ.
10. The application of faith to the elect individual does not justify that individual; justification is an eternal act of divine grace.
11. The application of faith to the elect individual enables that person to see that she is included within the ambit of divine election and that she is justified.
12. The application of faith to the elect individual brings about an epistemic change to the person concerned.

8. Ibid., 2:370.

13. The application of faith does not bring about a moral or legal change in the elect individual.

Justification *from* Eternity

Our exposition of justification from eternity can be briefer, because there is much that the two versions of eternal justification have in common. Numbers 1–9 in the summary of justification in eternity given in the preceding section applies to both versions of the doctrine. They begin to diverge at number 10. Whereas justification in eternity makes faith merely instrumental, justification from eternity requires the application of faith in order to complete the act of justification begun in eternity. It is an integral part of the whole divine act of justification.

To extrapolate: according to justification from eternity, the change that the power of the Holy Spirit brings about in the believer through justification is more than a matter of perceptual or epistemic change; it must include a moral and legal (and perhaps, even, an ontological) change as well. Although God has ordained that certain individuals be justified eternally, there must be an application of this action to the believer in time. The application requires the work of Christ, so that his righteousness may be applied to the elect individual, thereby justifying her in the sight of God. However, and importantly, in the justification-from-eternity view, this action of God in history (in the work of Christ and in the life of the believer at the moment of justification) involves something more than a perceptual gestalt, or its soteriological analogue; it involves the moral renewal of the individual at the very moment in which the Holy Spirit applies the benefits of Christ to the member of the elect. Justification is ordained in eternity, but it is brought about in time. We might put it like this: in the justification-from-eternity view, the elect individual is outside the bounds of salvation until such time as the Holy Spirit applies

Christ's benefits to her in the moment of justification. Nevertheless, this act of the Spirit in history is one aspect of the eternal act of God whereby God has ordained that she be justified via the work of Christ at a particular moment in time. In this way, the eternal act of God in justifying the elect is completed in time, at that moment at which the Holy Spirit unites the elect individual to Christ.

We can see this as follows. Presuming numbers 1–9 from the previous summary of the justification-in-eternity view, we can add the following theses that represent the distinctive claims of the justification-from-eternity position:

10. * The application of faith to the elect individual completes the eternal act of justification; justification is an eternal act of divine grace that obtains in time at the very moment in which the Holy Spirit applies the benefits of Christ to the individual.
11. The application of faith to the elect individual enables that person to understand that she is included within the ambit of divine election and that she is justified.
12. The application of faith to the elect individual brings about an epistemic change to the person concerned.
13. The application of faith also brings about a moral and legal change in the elect individual.

The distinctive aspect of justification from eternity is rather like the difference between the issuing of a royal pardon and the time at which it is served by the sovereign's legate upon the individual in prison. At the time the sovereign seals the pardon, the person is liberated *in principle*. However, there is a temporal lag between the sealing of the decree and its execution, at which point the individual who has been pardoned is *in fact* released from bondage. Although there is not a temporal lag between God's decree to justify the elect and the execution of this decree (for the traditional doctrine of eternal justification presumes that God is atemporal, so that time does not apply to the divine life), there is a conceptual distinction between the eternal decree and its execution in time. God's eternal act is without time, but it obtains at a particular moment in time, just as I may stand outside a river but place my foot into its running waters at a particular place and time. And, of course, there is a temporal distinction from the point of view of the human subject of election: whereas there is a time at which she is elect in principle (by divine decree), she is elect in fact only once she has had the benefits of Christ's atonement applied to her by the secret working of the Holy Spirit.

Objections

This completes our exposition of these two perorations on the doctrine of eternal justification. We may now turn to some objections to this reasoning, tackling what seem to be the most pressing concerns that the defender of eternal justification must face.

The Integrity of the Doctrine

First, this characterization of the two versions of eternal justification raises a concern about their integrity. Are these two distinct variations of one doctrine, or does the one collapse into the other? It looks like there is a significant difference between the two concerning the place of faith. We have seen that, according to the justification-in-eternity doctrine, faith is merely an unveiling of what is already true of the elect individual. Her justification is a completed eternal act. The application of that act to the believer in time is a matter of helping the believer to understand her actual status before God. In this way, the story of the long-lost prince is apt. He is of the royal blood and heir to the throne, though he does not know it.

Similarly, the individual member of the elect is already justified in eternity, though he is not aware of that fact until it is revealed by the secret work of the Spirit.

Not so with justification from eternity, for in this view, the eternal act begun in the divine decree has to be completed in time in the bestowal of faith by the Spirit. So it looks like much depends on whether justification is a complete, eternal act of God independent of any temporal event (such as coming to faith), or whether it is an eternal divine act that must be completed, so to speak, by means of bringing the elect individual to faith. If this is right, then these do represent two distinct doctrines, or two distinct versions of one particular doctrine, the doctrine of eternal justification.[9]

Antinomianism

A more significant concern is that eternal justification implies antinomianism. In seventeenth-century English Puritanism, there was a heated and vituperative debate about eternal justification in which opponents argued that the doctrine encouraged, even licensed, immorality.[10] The apostle Paul at the beginning of Romans 6 famously asks, "Shall we carry on sinning that grace may abound?," to which he replies, "By no means!" It has often been thought that he was addressing some form of antinomianism at this juncture of his epistle. This is the view that those who are made partakers of divine grace through the work of Christ are released from the obligation to observe the moral law. If we are united to Christ, according to the

---

9. A useful comparison of Calvin and Barth on this matter can be found in George Hunsinger, "A Tale of Two Simultaneities: Justification and Sanctification in Calvin and Barth," in *Conversing with Barth,* ed. John C. McDowell and Mike Higton (Aldershot, UK: Ashgate, 2004), 68–89. I am grateful to Michael Gibson for this reference.

10. A very helpful account of this debate is given in Hans Boersma, *A Hot Pepper Corn: Richard Baxter's Doctrine of Justification in Its Seventeenth-Century Context of Controversy* (1993; repr., Vancouver, BC: Regent College Publishing, 2004).

antinomian, then the guilt for all our sins is included in the work of Christ, in which case we may live free from the constraint of moral law in the knowledge that the guilt and punishment for our sins have been dealt with by the incarnation and atonement. The sin of yesterday, today, and tomorrow is included in this idea, so I may, as it were, carry on sinning without penalty. In fact (for Paul's audience, at least), it seems that an increasing amount of sin was thought to correlate to increasing amounts of grace bestowed upon the sinning believer by means of Christ's finished work. That is, the more the believer sins, the more she is aware of God's grace at work in her for salvation; so it is better to continue to sin, and to sin on a grand scale, in order that one may enjoy more divine grace as a consequence.

Needless to say, this notion appears to be an invitation to licentiousness that is contrary to the heart of the Christian faith. It trades on a half-truth about the scope of divine grace relative to the application of the benefits of the work of Christ to the believer united to him. In the context of seventeenth-century Puritanism, eternal justification was thought to have this consequence. For if, reasoned its opponents, God justifies the ungodly from eternity so that faith is merely the instrument by means of which the believer comes to see that she was always and eternally elect and justified in God's purposes, then the believer may "carry on sinning that grace may abound." The moral law is, for all practical purposes, abrogated for the believer, and (so it would appear) there is no moral impediment to living the life of a sybarite. In fact, as Gerrit Berkouwer puts it, the seventeenth-century antinomians were thought to hold that "all sin and guilt, all taint and impurity were swept away and were now not merely disallowed, but impossible. Sin as guilt before God could no longer exist in the believer."[11]

---

11. G. C. Berkouwer, *Faith and Justification*, trans. Lewis B. Smedes (Grand Rapids, MI: Eerdmans, 1954), 149.

However, it is not clear why this is a particular problem for defenders of eternal justification any more than it is for those who defend the view that God justifies the sinner in time at the moment at which he is declared righteous in God's sight by the ascription of Christ's alien righteousness to him. To see this, we will need to take a little time to compare the eternal-justification views with the claim that justification obtains in history, which I suppose is the main alternative position in historic Reformed theology.

Suppose we think of God's decree to justify the elect as rather like a promise to save someone made before the act of saving that person. If I promise to save a drowning man and then jump into the water and save him, it would appear that in making the promise, I place myself under an obligation to save him. We do this sort of thing all the time. For instance, I promise to pick up my children from school and, having placed myself under the obligation to do so, make every effort to be at the school gate on time. Note that in such circumstances, the promise and its fulfillment are two distinct things. The fulfillment is the moment at which what is promised is made actual, before which there was only the expectation that what was promised would occur at some future moment.

Maybe this is rather like what happens with the decree to justify the elect and its execution in history. God's decree to justify the elect is something like a promise by means of which God places God's self under an obligation to bring about the justification of the elect in time. The proponent of this view weights the importance of the divine decree relative to its execution in time rather differently than does the defender of one of our two versions of eternal justification. The reason is that, in this view, the divine decree does not bring about justification; it merely promises or anticipates it. The fulfillment of this promise obtains in time so that (from a human perspective, at least) there is a time before its fulfillment at which the object of divine election is still a culpable sinner, and a time from its fulfillment onward at which the object of divine election is justified and no longer culpable for sin. For this reason, we may think that what we might call the "justification-in-history view" does not fall afoul of antinomianism in the way that versions of eternal justification do.

But why think that? What is it about the justification-in-history view that makes it less susceptible to this objection, if indeed it is less susceptible to it? Presumably, the thought is that, in the justification-in-history view, the elect individual is not justified *until such time as God acts in history*, imputing Christ's righteousness to her. Prior to this act, she is outside the bounds of salvation. Once justified, she is within the bounds of salvation. There is much more than an epistemic change that occurs here, for the person justified in this way undergoes a change in her legal and moral status from being without grace to being within the ambit of grace, at a definite moment in time. It is like the change that obtains when someone who is not a citizen of a country becomes a citizen: there is a time at which the person is not a citizen, and there is a time after which she is a citizen. Such change does not obtain in the two versions of the eternal-justification doctrine outlined earlier, though for different reasons.

In the case of justification from eternity, which is closer to the justification-in-history view than the justification-in-eternity position is, the application of justification to the individual in time might also involve more than an epistemic change. Although God has ordained the justification of the individual from eternity, that decision must find its fulfillment in time in the secret work of the Spirit in the life of the elect individual. This does involve an epistemic change, namely, coming to see that one is the object of divine saving grace. However, this is preceded by the ascription of the alien righteousness of Christ to the individual in question. As we have already noted, according to the justification-from-eternity view, God's action has two aspects: the eternal decree to justify the elect, and the effectual bringing about of that decree in the life of the member of the elect in time. Nevertheless, this is fundamentally an eternal act. The actualizing of it in time in the life of the believer is, we might say, the completion in time of what is "begun" in the eternal decree. However, since God's atemporal act has numerous temporal effects, this is just to say that God's decree to justify the believer in eternity includes or encompasses the bringing about of that act in time.

On the face of it, this sounds very like the justification-in-history view. The difference between the two views can be expressed in a distinction between two sorts of speech-act. The first is a declaration that immediately changes a particular state of affairs upon being uttered. The second is a promise that includes as part of its fulfillment the effect it has upon the person to whom it is directed. The promise and the fulfillment are distinct things that do not necessarily happen simultaneously in this latter case, as they do in the former.

The justification-from-eternity view is rather like the first sort of speech-act. Take the common example of wedding vows, in this case, the speech-act performed by uttering the words "I do" in the context of a wedding by the bride and groom to one another at the relevant part in the service. This string of words, when uttered in this context, constitutes an action by means of which the two people bind themselves to each other in matrimony. Technically, this is a declarative illocutionary act, that is, an act that brings about a change in a state of affairs as words are uttered. Yet we can distinguish the words (of the vow) and the action it brings about as two aspects of one whole—that is what a speech act is, after all. God's decree to justify the elect, according to the justification-from-eternity view, is analogous to a speech act. God decrees what God will do and, in *the very act of doing so*, brings it about in time. There is no temporal lag between the divine declaration and its obtaining in time, because God is not in time. God's action is an eternal one that obtains in time, in the numerous temporal effects that are the justification of the elect. Not so for justification in history. Although God's eternal decree is atemporal in this view as well, so that there is no temporal gap between decree and justification, the justification-in-history view admits of two distinct aspects of justification: there is the atemporal decree, and there is the fulfillment of that decree in history. This is more like our second sort of speech-act, that is, a perlocutionary speech-act. This speech-act includes within the action its effect upon the person or persons to whom it is directed. In this case, the idea is that God promises to justify the elect in eternity and brings about this effect in the temporal change that occurs in the person in question at the moment when she is justified in time.

As with the justification-from-eternity and justification-in-history views, according to the justification-in-eternity view, the divine decree to justify the elect is an eternal act that obtains in time. So, once again there are, as it were, two aspects to the one divine act: the declaration in eternity, and its execution in time. The difference is that, in the justification-in-eternity view, what is communicated to the believer in time is the fact that she is already justified, whereas what is communicated in justification from eternity is the very act of justification. To return to our earlier example of the prince plucked from obscurity, it is the difference between informing the boy that he is a prince when he thought he was a pauper (justification in eternity), and informing the pauper that by royal decree he has been declared a prince in an action that takes immediate effect (justification from eternity). Lest it be thought that this latter view is indistinguishable from the justification-in-history view, we can differentiate it from the two species of eternal-justification doctrine as follows. In this view, justification is a declaration to one who really is a pauper that he is a prince from that moment onward. Prior to the moment at which the declaration was proclaimed, he really was a pauper.

This brings us back to our worry about antinomianism. There clearly is an important difference between the two versions of eternal justification and the justification-in-history view in the matter of precisely what change occurs in time in the life of the believer. However, this difference in and of itself does not imply anything about antinomianism. Why? Because whether one is an antinomian is a matter that is independent of any consideration about when justification takes place. We can see this if we apply antinomianism to our three "moments" of justification in our three versions of the justification story just outlined.

Suppose one holds to the justification-in-history view. This does not imply that the individual, once justified, is absolved from following the moral law, or that she may "carry on sinning that grace may abound." She was outside the bounds of divine grace before her justification and is within those bounds once justified. Yet, having been justified, she is still bound by the demands of the moral law; but her capacity to fulfill those demands is still partial and incomplete, given her state of sin. However, because she is justified, she is no longer culpable for her moral shortcomings, having had the alien righteousness of Christ imputed to her. The consequence of this is clear and does not imply antinomianism.

Suppose one adopts the justification-in-eternity view. This does not imply antinomianism either. To see this, let us return yet again to the example of the prince plucked from obscurity. He comes to understand that he is the heir to the throne, of royal blood, where previously he thought of himself as a commoner. Does this epistemic change render him immune from moral censure thereafter? That is, on coming to understand that he is a prince, is the boy absolved from acting in a way consistent with the law of the land and with the moral law? Not obviously. Indeed, if the prince were to begin to act without moral constraint upon coming to understand himself as a member of the royal line, he would be thought guilty of misbehaving, even of failing in his duty to the realm. A tyrannical or amoral king is a terrible thing, and no one (not even the most ardent royalist) would think that the king is without moral constraint or that, in virtue of understanding himself to be a prince, he is absolved from acting in a way consistent with the moral law and law of the land. Still less would it be thought that, in virtue of coming to understand himself as a prince, the boy has a license to act in whatever manner he so desires. That would be a travesty of monarchy.

The same applies, mutatis mutandis, to the question of antinomianism as applied to justification in eternity. If the individual justified in eternity comes to understand this justification at a certain point in history via the susurrations of the Holy Spirit, this does not automatically grant the individual in question moral carte blanche. Nor does it give the individual warrant to "carry on sinning that grace may abound." Indeed, one might think that in coming to understand oneself as a member of God's elect, justified in eternity, one has a *greater* moral responsibility than previously, not a lesser one. The person who is ignorant of moral obligations that accompany his status because he is ignorant of that status is not released from that moral obligation upon coming to understand that he has the status in question. Rather, in coming to understand that he has a particular status, he comes to see that having this status includes acting in a manner consistent with that status. In the case of the pauper who discovers himself to be a prince, this means acting in a manner consistent with benevolent monarchy. In the case of the member of the elect, justified in eternity, this means acting in a manner consistent with the discovery that he or she has been justified in eternity and included in the scope of divine salvation as a child of God.

Given that justification in eternity is the stronger of our two versions of eternal justification, the worries about antinomianism with respect to the justification-from-eternity view should be easier to meet. This is just what we find upon examination. Recall that, according to justification from eternity, the one eternal divine act of justification includes the moment at which the elect individual is justified in time. She is eternally elect, and eternally justified, but this act must be "completed" or "actualized" in time. Does this give the justified individual reason to think she may act in a manner inconsistent with the moral law? No, it does not, any more than it does in the justification-in-eternity view. In fact, in a manner like the justification-in-eternity view, one might think that upon coming to understand one's justified status in the sight of God at a particular moment in time, one also comes to see that one has a responsibility to act in accordance with that status, that is, as a child of God. On the face of it, and as with the justification-in-eternity view, if anything, this gives the believer a reason to think she has a greater responsibility to act in accordance with her status as one who is justified, once she comes to understand that status.

However, perhaps there is another way to construe the antinomian worry. Maybe the concern is that if a person is eternally justified, then how he behaves—even whether he has faith—is, in a sense, immaterial to his status in the eyes of God. The same cannot be said of the justification-in-history view, so this objection goes, because in that view, the individual is not always justified but comes to be justified only at a particular moment in time. However, once again, this seems to be wide of the mark. The boy prince was always a prince, but his coming to understand that fact does nothing to alter his status with respect to his obligation to act according to the moral law.

Perhaps the objection can be refined yet further. What if the worry is that the sinner acts immorally before conversion and is morally reoriented after conversion according to the justification-in-history view, whereas she is immoral but justified from the get-go according to eternal justification. There is no moral reorientation in the latter case, and that is what motivates the concern over antinomianism. If there is no moral change that occurs or needs to occur in the *ordo salutis*, then it appears that one may sin with impunity. But why think that? None of the views we have canvassed suggest that, prior to salvation, an individual is not under the constraint of the moral law or may act immorally without censure. That does not change upon coming to see that one is elect. Even if there is more motivation to act morally upon coming to see that one is justified and elect, this does not mean that there is no motivation to act morally before this realization. Still less is there reason to think that, before coming to see that one is justified, one may act lawlessly. The prince was still bound to act according to the law of the land when he thought himself a pauper. On realizing his status as a prince, he has even more reason to act morally, not less reason. Similar considerations apply to the elect individual, according to our two versions of eternal justification, mutatis mutandis.

Thus, I conclude that justification from eternity does not imply antinomianism, nor (more surprisingly, no doubt) does justification in eternity, although some theologians in the past have thought the latter version of the doctrine pernicious in this respect. However, in order for the doctrine to be pernicious, one would need to add to justification in eternity a thesis about the moral responsibility of those who understand themselves to be included within the scope of salvation. I suppose that no responsible Christian theologian would accede to such a thesis, and I do not see why justification in eternity, taken as a view about the relationship between election and justification in the eternal purposes of God, should be thought to imply an antinomian thesis about moral responsibility. Hence, this objection fails against both versions of the eternal-justification doctrine.

Unwarranted Theological Speculation

A related objection to the worry about antinomianism is that eternal justification is an exercise in unwarranted theological speculation. In his treatment of the topic, the twentieth-century Dutch Reformed divine Gerrit Berkouwer is particularly exercised about this in relation to the seventeenth-century version of the doctrine (though not its modern counterparts, such as in the work of Kuyper). He writes, "This concept of eternal justification reveals how a speculative logic can invade a scriptural proclamation of salvation and torture it beyond recognition."[12] The logic of the doctrine finally "estranges itself from scriptural reality." What is more, "it robs divine revelation of its unique and saving significance and devaluates the historical characters of the activity of God."[13] In this view, he says, eternity swallows up the significance of time with the worry that this doctrine cannot do justice to the historical shape of Christian dogma like the incarnation and redemption of Christ: "The reality of justification in time must never be by-passed via a speculative strain of thought concerning eternity."[14]

This objection has undoubted rhetorical power. However, upon examination, its content is a little thin. Unwarranted theological speculation is clearly a bad thing. However, the question is whether

12. Ibid., 150.
13. Ibid.
14. Ibid., 151. Berkouwer ends his tirade against the Puritan version of the doctrine by saying, "Antinomianism is a sorry chapter in the Church's history, but it can serve well as a sharp warning to every member of the Church that the way of Christian truth is not the thin thread of speculation, but the concrete revelation of God in Word and Act" (151).

eternal justification is a doctrine that is unwarranted in the manner Berkouwer claims. Later in the same chapter, he rails against theological speculation, saying that "[t]heology is not an excursion into the stratosphere that lies beyond the borders of faith's speech in time; it may not travel beyond the borders of faith's perspective. Beyond the word of Scripture we dare not go, in speech or in theological reflection; for it is in this word that God's love in Jesus Christ is revealed. There is nothing beyond that." What is more, "[s]peculation which seeks after 'depth' in place of or beside this 'practical' word must be directed back to the simple witness of revelation."[15]

There are two issues here. The first concerns unwarranted theological speculation, and whether eternal justification falls into this trap. The second is the relationship between time and eternity in the purposes of God, and whether, in Berkouwer's evocative phrase, eternity has swallowed up the significance of time. As to the first, it would seem that there is data in Scripture relevant to the issue raised by the doctrine of eternal justification. The opening passage of Eph. 1:3-14 certainly deals with divine ordination and its relation to justification, if one allows that the concepts may inform the discussion even if particular terminology does not. Similarly, Rom. 8:28-30 deals with election, calling, and justification in its famous *ordo salutis*; and there are other relevant passages besides these two.

Perhaps Berkouwer's concern is not that there is no biblical material relevant to the matters the doctrine raises, but that the doctrine presses these biblical passages beyond what they actually disclose. It would be rather like being told by a friend that he has been given a financial gift sufficient to buy a house, and then pressing

15. Ibid., 160.

him to divulge how much he has to spend. There is an answer to that question, but it may be impolite or inappropriate to ask. Similarly, there is an answer to whether God eternally justified some number of fallen humanity, but prying into the particulars of divine ordination may be inappropriate. This is a venerable principle of theological modesty, and one that has a historic association with Reformed theology. It is, after all, something John Calvin invokes on a number of different occasions in his *Institutes*.

However, it seems to me that the defender of eternal justification may rightly claim that where the biblical material implies some doctrine that is not explicitly taught therein, we are warranted in drawing the inference just as we do with other central dogmas of the faith, such as the Trinity and the incarnation. No orthodox Christian would say that inferring God is triune from the biblical material is inappropriate. Why think that a similar hermeneutical strategy is unwarranted when applied to another doctrine implied by Scripture, such as the conjunction of election and justification? This is not to say that there are no theological issues that are idle, unwarranted, or speculative in the pejorative sense. For instance, whether Adam and Eve had navels may be idle or speculative, because Holy Writ is silent on the topic and does not imply a particular view on the matter. The issue of eternal justification is not speculative in this way. It is not clear to me that it is speculative in any way that is theologically inappropriate or damaging, and without further argument it is difficult to see why one might think it is inappropriate or damaging.

What of time and eternity in the purposes of God? Does eternal justification imply that eternity "swallows up the significance of time"? It does place a lot of emphasis on protology rather than eschatology. That, in many ways, is characteristic of much Reformed theology—with some notable exceptions, like Jürgen Moltmann.

However, if God is atemporal, as much classical theology has presumed, then it makes sense to think that God's eternal act of creation and redemption, the *exitus* and *reditus* of the divine life, is not something that happens at a particular moment in time, though it may obtain at a particular moment in time. It is something bound up with what God has ordained "before" the foundation of the world, according to God's good pleasure and will. It is a small (though significant) step from here to the claim that God's eternal purposes comprehend the election and justification of individuals, however one understands the relationship of these two things. Moreover, as we have seen, in at least one version of eternal justification, the justification-from-eternity view, the moment in time at which a person is justified is intimately bound up with God's decree to elect and justify that person. So, it appears that Berkouwer's objections can be met, given a consistent interpretation of the relevant biblical passages and the applications of some careful distinctions about God's relationship to time that are the common property of classical Christianity.

Coda

I have argued that there is more to be said for eternal justification than is often thought. There may be important theological reasons, including reasons that have application to ecumenical theology, for considering the merits of this doctrine. Having set out the two versions of the doctrine, it seems to me that the weaker of the two, namely, the justification-from-eternity view, is easier to defend than the justification-in-eternity view, because it makes the act of justification in history something that is included within the eternal divine act of justification. There are serious objections to these two perorations of the doctrine over against what I have called the justification-in-history view. Yet it seems to me that these objections are not as overpowering as has sometimes been thought, and that there may be resources with which to meet these objections. How one might apply these insights to the current ecumenical discussions about the place and shape of justification relative to the doctrine of election is an interesting and potentially fruitful avenue of research that may help bring something of the "definition, rigor, and force" to the doctrine that Katherine Sonderegger (with whom we started this chapter) believes current ecumenical discussion lacks.

3

Libertarian Calvinism

1st, there is nothing in the Calvinistic system of theology, or in the Westminster Confession of Faith, which *precludes* men from holding the doctrine of philosophical necessity. 2d, There is nothing in the Calvinistic system of theology, or in the Westminster Confession, which *requires* men to hold the doctrine of philosophical necessity.

— William Cunningham, "The Doctrine of Philosophical Necessity"

In his well-known book *The Reformed Doctrine of Predestination,* Lorainne Boettner affirms that "[e]lection is a sovereign free act of God, through which He determines who shall be made heirs of heaven."[1] Later, in distinguishing the Reformed view from fatalism, he remarks, "There is, in reality, only one point of agreement between the two, which is, that both assume the absolute certainty of all future events."[2] The certainty of a particular human action, says Boettner, is consistent with its being an act for which the person concerned is both free and responsible: "Nor does it follow from the absolute certainty of a person's acts that he could not have acted otherwise. He could have acted otherwise if he had chosen to have done so. Oftentimes a man has power and opportunity to do that

---

1. Lorainne Boettner, *The Reformed Doctrine of Predestination* (Philadelphia: Presbyterian and Reformed, 1932), 111.
2. Ibid., 151.

which it is absolutely certain he will not do, and to refrain from doing that which it is absolutely certain he will do."[3] What is more, "God controls our actions so that they are certain although we act freely. His decree does not produce the event, but only renders its occurrence certain; and the same decree which determines the certainty of the action at the same time determines the freedom of the agent in the act."[4]

Boettner is typical of those who regard the Reformed view on human freedom as synonymous with a version of theological compatibilism. In this way of thinking, God ordains (that is, efficaciously brings about or determines) all that comes to pass, and human freedom must be understood as consistent with this divine ordination. (Biblical passages that appear to support this position include Prov. 16:33, Eph. 1:3-11, and Rom. 8:28-30.) However, if this is thought to be the only view of human freedom consistent with Reformed theology, then it is a mistaken view of the matter—as we shall see.

To begin with, consider these words from chapter 3 of the Westminster Confession, entitled "Of God's Eternal Decree":

I. God from all eternity, did, by the most wise and holy counsel of His own will, freely, and unchangeably ordain whatsoever comes to pass; yet so, as thereby neither is God the author of sin, nor is violence offered to the will of the creatures; nor is the liberty or contingency of second causes taken away, but rather established.

II. Although God knows whatsoever may or can come to pass upon all supposed conditions; yet has He not decreed anything because He foresaw it as future, or as that which would come to pass upon such conditions.

Then there this, from chapter 9, "Of Free Will":

3. Ibid., 156.
4. Ibid., 157.

I. God has endued the will of man with that natural liberty, that is neither forced, nor, by any absolute necessity of nature, determined good, or evil.

II. Man, in his state of innocency, had freedom, and power to will and to do that which was good and well pleasing to God; but yet, mutably, so that he might fall from it.

We may note the following things about these passages. Chapter 3 of the Confession states that God ordains all things yet without offering violence to the will of the creature or removing secondary causation. God knows all "supposed conditions" but does not decree things, because God foresees them as future (to God) or as things that would come to pass upon such future conditions. It also says, in chapter 9, that the human will has a "natural liberty" that is not determined to good or evil by any "absolute necessity." Third, the Confession makes it clear that the first human pair had free will consistent with alternate possibilities. They had the power to will and to do what was pleasing to God, and the power to fall from that state.

Now consider the rest of chapter 9 of the Confession:

III. Man, by his fall into a state of sin, has wholly lost all ability of will to any spiritual good accompanying salvation: so as, a natural man, being altogether averse from that good, and dead in sin, is not able, by his own strength, to convert himself, or to prepare himself thereunto.

IV. When God converts a sinner, and translates him into the state of grace, He frees him from his natural bondage under sin; and, by His grace alone, enables him freely to will and to do that which is spiritually good; yet so, as that by reason of his remaining corruption, he does not perfectly, or only, will that which is good, but does also will that which is evil.

V. The will of man is made perfectly and immutably free to do good alone in the state of glory only.

Postfall, humans are unable to "will . . . any spiritual good accompanying salvation" and can do nothing to convert themselves. God has to act in order to regenerate the sinner. As the Confession makes clear elsewhere, no fallen human can contribute to his regeneration or to the preparation of himself for salvation. This is what the Confession takes "being dead in your sins" to mean.

The Westminster Confession is only one of the great Reformed symbols. Yet is it one of the most influential, because it has been the historic standard for so many Presbyterians. It is also one of the few historic confessions of the sixteenth- and seventeenth-century Reformed churches that deal with the question of human free will in detail. Given that the Reformed churches are confessional bodies (unlike, say, Pentecostals or many Baptists), the place given to such statements is also doctrinally significant. The Westminster Confession has a greater authority in the Reformed communions for which it is a subordinate doctrinal standard than, say, the work of a particular theologian, for the work of no single theologian is theologically binding in Reformed theology in the way that the confessions are. After all, no single-authored theological work is a doctrinal standard in such churches. Consequently, what the Confession teaches about human free will is of greater dogmatic significance than the work of any single theologian, even the works of divines who stand at the head of this tradition, like John Calvin, John Knox, or Huldrych Zwingli.

It would be significant, therefore, if it transpired that what the Westminster Confession says about this matter of human freedom does not commit its defender to some form of stoic fatalism (as it would have been understood in the sixteenth- and seventeenth-century debates when the historic Reformed confessions were compiled) or hard determinism (as we understand it today).[5] It seems to me that in what the Confession does say, there is the conceptual space, so to speak, to prescind from determinism touching all human choices and to affirm some limited version of libertarianism. It is to these twin concerns that I want to direct attention in what follows.

The Theological Debate about Human Free Will

Let us begin by rehearsing some commonplaces in the theological debate about human free will. A common misconception of Reformed views on human free will is that Reformed theology (including the theology of the Westminster Confession) implies or even entails hard determinism. Call this the "folk version" of Reformed theology on human free will, or the "folk view" for short. It has been around long enough to find its way into a number of great works of literature, such as James Hogg's *Confessions of a Justified Sinner* and Robert Burns's *Holy Willie's Prayer*.

The reasoning usually invoked by advocates of the folk view goes something like this: According to the Reformed, God eternally ordains whatsoever comes to pass. Now, if God ordains whatsoever comes to pass, then I am not free at any moment to choose to act contrary to what God ordains I do at that moment. But free will requires the ability to do otherwise at the moment of choice, in which case the Reformed view must deny that I have free will.

Much more would need to be said in order to iron out some of the ambiguities in this popular version of the complaint against Reformed theology raised by the folk view if we were to spend our time analyzing it in detail. Nevertheless, the intuition driving

---

5. I realize that fatalism is not equivalent to hard determinism. However, in historic Reformed theology, determinism is a latecomer. The sixteenth- and seventeenth-century divines who were responsible for the major Reformation confessions did have stoic fatalism in view when thinking about predestination, for this was something that Renaissance humanism had brought back into the discussion. However, determinism came into the debate much later, in the nineteenth century. In important respects, the worries raised by stoic fatalism are close enough to worries about hard determinism that these two have often been conflated in the literature.

the objection should be clear. It is that freedom, in the full-blooded sense of the term relevant to questions of free will, requires alternate possibilities. If a particular choice is really free, in this sense, then it must be one that was not determined in advance, whether by God or by any other cause. It must be up to me how the choice goes, and it must be the case that at the moment of choice I was able to do something other than what I actually chose to do. If the Reformed deny this, then they deny human freedom in the sense relevant to the free-will debate.

It is not clear to me that the Reformed do in fact deny this, or even that they must deny it (because their view has this implication whether they are aware of that or not). Nor is it clear to me, from what we have seen thus far, that the Westminster Confession, one of the representative statements of Reformed theology, requires this. Now, it is one thing to show that the Reformed position on human free will does not entail or even imply hard determinism. It is quite another to show that Reformed thinking on this matter is consistent with some version of libertarianism. Let us begin by showing that the Reformed are not necessarily committed to hard determinism. This rebuts the objection to Reformed theology encapsulated in the folk view. We may then turn to the rather more ambitious project of articulating a species of libertarian Calvinism.

To derive hard determinism from the sort of Reformed confessional statements one finds in places like the Westminster Confession, the objector would need to provide evidence that the Reformed view (if we may call it this) implies or entails hard determinism. I do not deny that there is much Reformed theology that appears to be consistent with theological compatibilism of the sort Boettner articulates (that is, with the compossibility of divine determinism and human free will). A number of noted Reformed theologians have advocated such views, such as Jonathan Edwards and, I think, Francis Turretin. However, hard determinism is a species of *incompatibilism*, because the hard determinist claims that determinism is incompatible with human free will. This is clearly inconsistent with theological compatibilism: if one is a theological determinist, one must choose whether or not one thinks this is consistent with human free will, and must opt for compatibilist or incompatibilist versions of determinism accordingly.

Suppose the Reformed view implied hard determinism. Then there would be a significant problem to overcome with respect to ascription of moral responsibility to human actions. There is a sophisticated philosophical literature on this topic, with several recent authors adopting something like what I am calling hard determinism, or views that have the same upshot with respect to human moral responsibility. However, I take it that such a position would normally be regarded as theologically untenable, even unorthodox. The presumption in almost all Christian theology, including Reformed theology, is that human beings do have free will (whatever that means), and that they are morally responsible for those actions that are free. That is, there is a presumption among such theologians (I think, among almost all traditional, orthodox Christian theologians) that human beings must be free in some sense in order for their actions to be morally responsible. Moral responsibility is not decoupled from freedom in this theological literature. Indeed, to decouple these two things would be regarded as a step away from orthodox Christian belief.

Be that as it may, for present purposes we need only the much more modest claim that the Reformed view expressed in the Westminster Confession requires that humans have free will in some sense. This seems evident from the gobbets cited at the beginning of the chapter. So it would seem that the stated view of (at least some of) the Reformed as found in the Confession is contrary to hard determinism, given that hard determinism is a species of incompatibilism. Still, it may be that the Reformed view is internally disordered, such that it implies hard determinism in some places even if in other places some notion of free will is affirmed. Here, I have in mind something like the following. If Jones holds to doctrine x and x implies y, then Jones's view commits him to y even if he is not cognizant of this. Examples are not hard to come by. Here is a simple one: Suppose Jones says that he endorses the political views of Karl Marx but denies that he is a communist. It may be that he is unaware of the fact that commitment to Marx's political views implies communism (assuming Marx's views do imply communism). Suppose that is right. The fact that Jones does not know that his commitment to Marx's political views implies commitment to communism as a political philosophy does not mean he is not committed to communism. If he is committed to Marx's political vision, then (arguably) he is committed to communism whether or not he is aware of this and affirms it. Clearly, this also holds if he endorses Marx's political philosophy and thinks this does not commit him to communism. That is, if Jones accedes to Marx's political views and denies he is a communist, though commitment to Marx's views imply communism, then it looks like Jones has disordered, even contradictory, political beliefs. He is unaware that one of those beliefs has implications that undercuts the other belief.

Perhaps something like this is true of the Reformed position expressed in the Westminster Confession or in one of the other great confessions of this tradition. I do not deny that this is possible. However, it seems to me that this is very unlikely, and I know of no one who has attempted to argue this. There is nothing I can find in the Westminster Confession that implies hard determinism. This is also true of the other great Reformed symbols of the sixteenth and seventeenth centuries. If it does transpire that the great Reformed symbols are internally disordered in this fashion, then there would be a significant doxastic problem with Reformed theology. Charity (and a nod to Thomas Reid) would seem to require that we presume that these historic confessions that have served so many Christians for so long and have been scrutinized by a great number of thinkers, friendly or otherwise, are most likely not disordered in this obvious way and are innocent of this charge until proved otherwise.

Similar but much more plausible is the claim that the Reformed view as expressed in its confessions appears in some places to affirm views that are compatibilist, whereas in other places some version of libertarianism appears to be in view. This is a much more plausible objection, because it is clear from what we have already noted that the Westminster Confession does state that God ordains whatsoever comes to pass and that humans have free will. One recent example of this sort of objection can be found in the work of the Christian philosopher Jerry Walls.[6] He focuses his attention on another section of the Confession, chapter 10, which deals with effectual calling. There, we find the following:

> I. All those whom God hath predestinated unto life, and those only, He is pleased, in His appointed time, effectually to call, by His Word and Spirit, out of that state of sin and death, in which they are by nature to grace and salvation, by Jesus Christ; enlightening their minds spiritually and savingly to understand the things of God, taking away their heart of stone, and giving unto them an heart of flesh; renewing their wills, and, by His almighty power, determining them to that which is good, and effectually drawing them to Jesus Christ: *yet so, as they come most freely, being made willing by His grace.* (emphasis added)

The second section of chapter 10 goes on to say that the elect human upon whom God secretly works in this way is "altogether passive" in

6. Jerry L. Walls, *Hell: The Logic of Damnation* (Notre Dame, IN: University of Notre Dame Press, 1993). See also his more recent article "Why No Classical Theist, Let Alone Orthodox Christian, Should Ever be a Compatibilist," *Philosophia Christi* 13, no. 1 (2011): 75–104.

this divine action of regeneration until, being quickened by the work of the Holy Spirit, "he is thereby enabled to answer this call, and to embrace the grace offered and conveyed in it."

Walls detects a subtle sleight of hand going on in this part of the Confession. For there is a difference between saying that

(i) because a person is determined to do an action by God making him willing to do that thing, the person is able to do that thing

and that

(ii) a person is enabled to do that thing by God, but it is up to the person whether he does the action in question.

According to Walls, both of these claims are present in different sections of the Westminster Confession, and this is a problem. For, on the face of it, the second sort of claim is consistent with libertarianism (in other words, and very roughly, with the claim that humans have free will and that possession of free will is inconsistent with determinism). Yet the first claim is consistent not with libertarianism but with compatibilism. Walls comments:

The fact that Calvinism has these two conflicting streams of thought is, I think, quite significant. It may explain how Calvinists can, with an air of plausibility, deny the unwelcome implications which follow from their premises. By trading on both conceptions of freedom [that is, a libertarian conception and a compatibilist one], it seems possible to hold both that God determines all things in the strictest sense, and that human beings are truly responsible for their sin. . . . If the preceding argument is correct, such a position is ultimately due to confusion.[7]

The upshot of this is that, first, the Reformed view does not imply or entail hard determinism, and second, the Reformed view (at least, as expressed in the Confession) does have a prima facie problem with

7. Walls, *Hell*, 68.

which view of human free will it affirms alongside the claim about the divine ordination of all things whatsoever.

Metaphysical Underdetermination of the Confessions

A solution to whether the Reformed view is consistent with libertarianism may also provide an answer to the conundrum Walls poses for Calvinism. For it may be that the Reformed view is consistent with the notion that at least some human actions are libertarian in nature as well as the claim that certain human actions are determined by God, contrary to what Walls supposes.

However, before addressing this matter, it is important to get clear what I meant earlier when I stated that libertarian Calvinism may be consistent with the Confession though it is not required by the Confession. It seems to me that it is often the case in matters theological that particular views espoused in official ecclesiastical documents are what we might call metaphysically underdetermined. By this I mean that many official ecclesiastical documents (and here I am thinking of confessions, catechisms, and the canons of church councils in particular) are often deliberately framed so that they commit the church and its adherents to a conceptual minimum regarding dogma and doctrine, and regarding the metaphysical implications that a particular doctrinal formula has. Often, I think, this is a deliberate ploy of those framing such documentation. Rather than providing what we might call a maximal account of a particular doctrine or dogma, theologians and clergy working on such documents often (perhaps usually) attempt to provide a minimal account of a particular doctrine or dogma so as to meet the particular need the confession or canonical document is a response to, while minimizing the theological and metaphysical hostages to fortune. A classic example of this is found in the "definition" of the Council of Chalcedon regarding the person of Christ. As has often been pointed out, the canons of that council actually give us a sort of conceptually minimal core, so that what the Fathers regarded as orthodox doctrine may be upheld but without the definition of key terms like *person* and *nature*.[8]

My claim is that the Reformed view might be like this. It might be sufficiently open-textured that it is consistent with more than one account of the compossibility of the divine ordination of all things with human freedom. This is not quite as outlandish as it first sounds. In the development of early Reformed thought, there was a doctrinal plurality on a number of matters that was tolerated while Reformed theology was still in its pliant phase, before some key matters were hammered out on the anvil of ecclesiastical controversy. For instance, Jacob Arminius lived and died as a Reformed pastor and professor at Leiden, though he espoused a version of Molinism and may even have been responsible for the introduction of Molinism into Protestant thought. Although the Synod of Dort repudiated a number of his views in its canons, this was subsequent to his death. During his lifetime, his views were merely controversial; they were not unorthodox. What is more, his views are more measured and careful than the Remonstrant party that took up his cause at the synod.

Arminius is not the only example of someone whose views were at odds with the common perception of Reformed theology. The theologians at the French Academy of Saumur are another example, as are their theological cousins the Anglican divines John Preston, Bishop John Davenant, and Archbishop Usher of Armagh. All three of this triumvirate espoused a version of hypothetical universalism, like the Saumur divines (a matter to which we shall return in chapters

---

8. I tackle this issue at greater length in "Desiderata for Models of the Hypostatic Union," in *Christology Ancient and Modern: Explorations in Constructive Dogmatics,* ed. Oliver D. Crisp and Fred Sanders (Grand Rapids, MI: Zondervan Academic, 2012), chap. 1.

7 and 8). Recall that this is the view according to which God ordains the salvation of all humanity by means of the sufficient work of Christ, dependent on saving faith, which is provided to the elect alone. This is significant for our purposes, because Bishop John Davenant headed up the British delegation to Dort at the behest of King James I and affirmed the canons the synod produced, canons usually thought to imply a doctrine of particular redemption—that Christ died only for the sins of the elect, not for the sins of the whole world. However, Davenant's position denied this, and he was not alone in this matter as a delegate at the synod. This is puzzling. However, it may be that he was happy to affirm the synodical canons because he thought them sufficiently conceptually porous, so to speak, that he could do so without giving up what he considered to be theologically nonnegotiable, an interpretation that has recently received some support from historical investigation into the matter.[9] My suggestion is that something like this may be true of the Confession and its claims about human freedom relative to libertarianism. That is, it may be that there is metaphysical room, as it were, for the libertarian to affirm the Confession—even a libertarian Calvinism.

The Case for Libertarian Calvinism

We come now to the case for libertarian Calvinism. It has several parts. To begin with, there is the question of the free will of our first parents. In early-modern Reformed theology (the context of the Westminster Confession), this question was conceived in terms of a historic Adam and Eve.[10] The issue was this: Was the primal sin of

---

9. See Jonathan D. Moore, *English Hypothetical Universalism: John Preston and the Softening of Reformed Theology* (Grand Rapids, MI: Eerdmans, 2007), and chapter 7 for more on this matter.
10. This question can be recast in terms of the libertarian freedom of some original hominid community for those worried about the historicity of some aboriginal human pair.

Adam and Eve freely entered into? Were they free to sin and free to refrain from sinning at the moment of choice? To this question, the libertarian Calvinist, in keeping with the symbols of Reformed theology like the Westminster Confession, can offer an affirmative response. They were free to act in this way.[11]

Second, there is an issue about what effect the fall has upon human free will. As is well known, the Reformed churches have a rather severe view about the extent and depth of the moral damage wrought by original sin. Suppose they are right about this. Then we might ask, are fallen human beings capable of freely choosing to be reconciled to God? Can fallen humans choose salvation or reject it? Do they have such options at some putative moment of choice? Here, the answer is negative. Fallen human beings have no freedom to choose to be reconciled to God. Possession of original sin places certain choices relevant to salvation beyond reach.[12]

Third, and following on the heels of the previous point, does this mean that fallen human beings cannot make free choices in matters other than those touching human salvation? That is, are fallen human beings free in making choices for which they are morally responsible in areas of their lives other than those that have to do directly with their own eternal destiny? In answer to this question, the libertarian

11. In addition to the words of chapter 9 of the Confession cited earlier, chapter 4, on creation, says that Adam and Eve in their state of original righteousness had "the law of God written in their hearts, and power to fulfil it." Yet they were "under a possibility of transgressing, being left to the liberty of their own will, which was subject unto change."

12. "I. All those whom God hath predestinated unto life, and those only, He is pleased, in His appointed time, effectually to call, by His Word and Spirit, out of that state of sin and death, in which they are by nature to grace and salvation, by Jesus Christ; enlightening their minds spiritually and savingly to understand the things of God . . . *renewing their wills*, and, *by His almighty power, determining them to that which is good,* and effectually drawing them to Jesus Christ: *yet so, as they come most freely, being made willing by His grace.* "II. This effectual call is of God's free and special grace alone, not from anything at all foreseen in man, who is *altogether passive* therein, until, being quickened and renewed by the Holy Spirit, he is thereby enabled to answer this call, and to embrace the grace offered and conveyed in it" (Westminster Confession, chap. 10; emphases added).

Calvinist can give an affirmative response. Even in a fallen state, human beings have the freedom to do otherwise in many—perhaps most—choices other than choices that pertain to their salvation. So, Jones cannot choose to be reconciled to God. That can be only a divine work, dependent on the election of God, and Jones can do nothing to place himself in a position where his being saved is more likely by virtue of his having performed such-and-such actions. He cannot contribute to his being saved, he cannot choose to be saved. Nor can he choose to choose to be saved. Choosing a thing is usually called a first order choice in the contemporary literature, whereas choosing to choose a thing is a second-order choice (because one is deliberating about a given choice). So Jones cannot have first- or second-order free choices that might contribute to his being saved. This the Reformed are adamant about. However, Jones may make all sorts of free choices about things outside the sphere of salvation that have momentous consequences for him. For instance, he may freely choose to vote Democratic, he may freely choose his mate, he may freely make a decision that leads him to become physically and psychologically addicted to a substance, and so on. In short, according to libertarian Calvinism, fallen human beings have significant free will in all sorts of mundane choices, some of which are important and influential (such as choosing to become a presidential candidate, or choosing to become a research scientist working on vaccines to prevent a pandemic). However, fallen human beings are incapable of making free choices about salvation.

This is perfectly consistent with the Reformed confessions and with the Westminster Confession, the representative symbol with which we are concerned. Recall that although God eternally "ordains whatsoever comes to pass," God does so in such a way that no "violence [is] offered to the will of the creatures; nor is the liberty or contingency of second causes taken away, but rather established"

(Westminster Confession, 3.1). What is more, "God has endued the will of man with that natural liberty, that is neither forced, nor, by any absolute necessity of nature, determined good, or evil" (9.1). It is true that "[m]an, by his fall into a state of sin, has wholly lost all ability of will to any spiritual good accompanying salvation: so as, a natural man, being altogether averse from that good, and dead in sin, is not able, by his own strength, to convert himself, or to prepare himself thereunto" (9.3). However, this is entirely consistent with the claim that fallen humans have libertarian free will in many choices other than those beyond their reach because of sin, such as willing "good accompanying salvation."

An analogy may help make this clear. Consider Hal Jordan. He is a normal human being who is able to make all sorts of free choices in his life that require the ability to do otherwise, consistent with libertarianism. However, he is unable to make choices that would require him to have the superpower of actualizing his thoughts immediately in concrete ways. As John Locke famously quipped, we cannot really choose to fly, because we are incapable of flying; in which case arguing that being unable to freely choose to fly is evidence that I lack the free will to fly is idle. Jordan is like this. He may want to fly, but he cannot; he has no superpowers. That is, until one day, when they are bestowed upon him by a dying alien who gives him a ring powered by a green lantern that acts as a catalyst by means of which he is able to transform his desire to fly into action. It gives him the superpower of being able to actualize his thoughts (with certain important limitations and qualifications that need not trouble us here). Because he has the ring, he now can fly, where before he could only dream of flying.

Now, Hal Jordan (a.k.a. the Green Lantern) is like a fallen human being on the libertarian Calvinist account of human free will in this important respect: like the Green Lantern, fallen human beings are incapable of freely choosing to perform certain actions absent intervention from an external agency. In the case of the Green Lantern, this agency is an alien with a power ring. In the case of the fallen human being, this agency is divine. In both cases, there is a class of actions that the agent cannot perform without the interposition of an external agent who brings this class of actions within reach: for the Green Lantern, this class includes actions that actualize thoughts about flying; for the fallen human being, this class includes choosing salvation.

Note that this libertarian Calvinism does not deny that God ordains whatsoever comes to pass. It denies that God *determines* or *causes* whatsoever comes to pass. In this way of thinking, there appear to be (at least) two sorts of human action. There are those actions which are determined by God, the supreme example of which is human salvation, which is a work instigated and effected by the secret work of the Holy Spirit upon the individual, bringing about a human action (penitence and the spiritual renewal of the fallen human person so that he or she may turn to God for reconciliation). Then there are those actions which are not determined by God but are foreseen and permitted by God. According to libertarian Calvinism, this is a much larger class of actions than is usually admitted in what we might call compatibilist Calvinism. For according to the libertarian Calvinist view, many—perhaps most—mundane human actions are ones for which the human in question is able to do otherwise at the moment of choice and is morally responsible.

Objections to Libertarian Calvinism

Let us turn to some objections to the libertarian Calvinism just outlined.

Libertarian Calvinism Is Conceptually Confused

The most obvious objection to this libertarian Calvinism is that it is conceptually confused. Consider the following line of reasoning:

a. God ordains whatsoever comes to pass;
b. some human actions are free actions (that is, actions that are the exercise of free will) for which the humans concerned are morally responsible; and
c. free will requires the ability to do otherwise.

One might think that the problem with libertarian Calvinism lies in affirming one or more of these three statements. But that cannot be right, because, without further elaboration, it does not appear that these claims are obviously inconsistent—and many historic Arminian theologians have been willing to affirm all three, given certain qualifications regarding what is meant by things like divine ordination. The problem is not with the scope of divine ordination as such but with how we construe "divine ordination." If God's ordination of whatsoever comes to pass is thought to be equivalent to "God *causes* whatsoever comes to pass," then divine determinism follows. However, it might be that divine ordination includes both the determination of certain actions and the bringing about of states of affairs in which other actions are foreknown and permitted but not determined. This, I suppose, is what the libertarian Calvinist wants to affirm. God does cause (or otherwise effectually brings about) certain things, such as the salvation of a certain number of fallen human beings through union with Christ. The fallen humans in question are incapable of performing this action for themselves apart from divine intervention, because this class of action is placed beyond their reach by original sin. So, God has to ensure their salvation by determining that outcome.

It looks like libertarian Calvinism is a sort of mixed or complex view about human freedom and moral responsibility. Divine ordination includes elements of determinism (with respect to choices leading to the salvation of an individual) and indeterminism (with respect to many other mundane choices). The elements that are determined are what Protestant Scholastic theologians would have called hypothetically necessary. That is, they depend upon God's design to bring about the salvation of a particular individual. The indeterminist elements depend on God's bringing about certain states of affairs where the actions of fallen human beings are foreknown but not determined, as many theological libertarians maintain is the case with all human actions that are free and morally responsible ones. This does not appear incoherent, though it does mean divine ordination is a complex of two different sorts of thing.

The idea that there may be actions that are placed beyond our reach until such time as they are made within reach by some external agency is one that we are familiar with in other circumstances. Here is a peroration on an example often used in the free-will literature:

Suppose Smith has become physically and psychologically addicted to alcohol. He began his adult life free from such encumbrance, but through a series of bad choices, choices which were free in the sense that he could have done otherwise at the moment of choosing, he began the slow descent into alcoholism. At a certain point, Smith became an addict. He can no longer function effectively without alcohol. This does not mean that Smith is incapable of making *any* free decisions once addicted. Nor does it mean that he no longer has free will. There are many decisions Smith makes in everyday life, including important decisions, that are still such that he could have done otherwise at the moment of choice, and he is morally responsible for the choices he makes. Nevertheless, he is an addict, and it may be that there are certain actions that are no longer available to him because of his state of addiction. Although at one time he was able to make those choices, once he crossed the threshold of addiction, these actions were beyond him. He may think wistfully about performing the sorts of actions that are unavailable to him as an addict, but he knows he cannot will them in his current condition. For example, he cannot will not to be dependent on alcohol immediately and henceforth. He can will to take steps toward becoming less dependent on alcohol with a view to eventually becoming free from his dependency, but this involves a series of graduated steps over time. Now, suppose that, as a matter of fact, Smith will never freely begin the road to recovery. He just cannot bring himself to make those decisions that would lead to less dependency; he is "weak-willed" in this respect. He is enthralled to his addiction and will remain so until and unless some other agent steps in to change this state of affairs.

Happily for Smith, a benevolent scientist has developed a chemical switch that can rid him of his dependency, as they say, "cold turkey" (that is, without his imbibing any more alcohol until free from physical dependence), with a 100 percent success rate. The scientist does not wait for Smith's consent, for (recall) Smith will never freely choose to begin the road to recovery; he is weak-willed. Instead, the scientist injects Smith with a serum that delivers this wondrous chemical switch while he sleeps. He awakes without any symptoms of physical dependence and is able to begin the long process of ridding himself of his psychological addiction.

This story, a peroration on many such stories in the free-will literature, tracks the sort of view the libertarian Calvinist has of human bondage to sin, free will, and salvation fairly well. From an original state of libertarian freedom, humans fell into sin by making bad choices that constitute the primal sin. Thereafter, no fallen human could be rid of the thrall to sin without divine intervention (rather like the benevolent scientist). However, this is not to say that fallen humans are incapable of making any libertarian free choices while in a state of sin, only that they are incapable of making choices leading to an immediate and complete end of the addiction to sin. Even when addicted to sin (or alcohol), the persons in question are able to make at least some choices that require the ability to do otherwise and for which they are morally responsible. This seems true even in the case of addiction that raises issues of diminished responsibility (for example, the alcoholic who kills a pedestrian while driving drunk). In such cases, we do not say that the alcoholic is blameless; rather, we say responsibility is *diminished* (if it is diminished at all). Perhaps the same can be said of some sins committed while in a state of sin, or sins for which one has to be in a state of sin to feel the temptation, such as fornication.

Libertarian Calvinism as a Species of Arminianism?

A second sort of objection to libertarian Calvinism is that it is no different from its theological cousin Arminianism. Recall that, for present purposes, Arminianism is a sort of deviant or rogue Calvinism, one that is incompatibilist. According to the Arminian, free will requires the ability to do otherwise at the moment of choice, and this is inconsistent with divine determinism. The fact is that both Arminianism and libertarian Calvinism are incompatibilist in this respect. Like Arminianism, libertarian Calvinism denies that divine determinism is commensurate with human free will. The difference between the two positions lies in the fact that the libertarian Calvinist affirms that some human actions are determined by God. Naturally, these are actions that are not free and for which the fallen human beings in question are not responsible.[13] The Arminian presumes that God elects on the basis of foreknowledge.[14] The libertarian

13. Or, rather, these actions are not free in the sense that they are freely undertaken by the fallen human beings in question without divine instigation. Recall that the Confession admits that God frees the fallen creature "from his natural bondage under sin; and, *by His grace alone, enables him freely to will and to do that which is spiritually good*" (9.4; emphasis added.) Perhaps God heals our fallen capacities so that willing what is spiritually good is within reach. God then ensures that the redeemed human chooses this good and desires it. This is more than a reordering of human desire, however; it must be a change that is effectual. Regenerate humans are not merely enabled to make the right choice and be reconciled with God; they are effectually renewed by God so that they desire God.

14. In outlining his position on predestination in his *Declaration of Sentiments,* Arminius writes, "God decreed to save and to damn certain particular persons. This decree has its foundations in divine foreknowledge, through which God has known from all eternity those individuals who through the established means of his prevenient grace would come to faith and believe,

Calvinist denies this, claiming that God elects according to God's "good pleasure and will" (Eph. 1:5) without taking into consideration any creaturely action. It is because God does this that God must ensure that those God elects are redeemed, by effectually bringing about their regeneration.

Libertarian Calvinism as a Species of Calvinism?

A further objection has to do with whether this libertarian Calvinism counts as a species of Calvinism at all. After all, the folk view of Calvinism has a considerable grip on the popular imagination. Even if one does not think Calvinism is equivalent to hard determinism, it is commonly thought to be determinism of a soft variety—specifically, theological compatibilism (that is, the view according to which human freedom is compatible with divine determinism). We have seen that libertarian Calvinism affirms a limited determinism regarding choices pertaining to human salvation. However, it denies that determinism is compatible with human free will. So, it is a species of incompatibilism that allows for a circumscribed divine determinism, on the one hand, and libertarian free will, on the other. Does this "mixed view" mean it is something other than Calvinism, some sort of tertium quid that is neither one thing nor the other, neither Calvinism nor Arminianism? It seems to me that in order to derive that conclusion, one would have to be able to show that libertarian Calvinism was not consistent with the Reformed symbols. For, as was argued earlier, Reformed theology is confessional in nature, and the great confessions have historically served as a doctrinal framework for what counts as permissible Reformed

and through his subsequent sustaining grace would persevere in the faith. Likewise, in divine foreknowledge, God knew those who would not believe and persevere." *Arminius and His Declaration of Sentiments: An Annotated Translation with Introduction and Theological Commentary,* ed. and trans. W. Stephen Gunter (Waco, TX: Baylor University Press, 2012), 135.

theology. Upon examination, it looks like libertarian Calvinism makes good sense of what the Westminster Confession says about the relationship between the divine ordination of all things whatsoever and human free will. It may be that the Confession is also consistent with some version of compatibilism; well and good. Our task in this section of the chapter was to show that libertarian Calvinism is not inconsistent with the Confession, that it is a permissible interpretation of the relevant confessional statements on the subject, not that it is the only permissible interpretation of the relevant confessional statements or even that it is the best or most plausible interpretation of the relevant confessional statements.

The Walls Objection Revisited

The fourth objection we shall consider brings us back to the work of Jerry Walls, raised earlier. Recall that Walls thinks the Confession is internally disordered, because it affirms things in certain places that imply libertarianism and affirms things in other places that imply compatibilism. He specifically cites the Confession on effectual calling, which he thinks affirms both that

> (i) because a person is determined to do an action by God making him willing to do that thing, the person is able to do that thing

and that

> (ii) a person is enabled to do that thing by God, but it is up to the person whether he does the action in question.

Walls has in mind chapter 10 of theConfession, where it says this:

> I. All those whom God hath predestinated unto life, and those only, He is pleased, in His appointed time, effectually to call, by His Word and Spirit, out of that state of sin and death, in which they are by nature to grace and salvation, by Jesus Christ; enlightening their minds spiritually

and savingly to understand the things of God, taking away their heart of stone, and giving unto them an heart of flesh; renewing their wills, and, by His almighty power, determining them to that which is good, and effectually drawing them to Jesus Christ: *yet so, as they come most freely, being made willing by His grace.* (emphasis added)

However, if we understand this passage in terms of libertarian Calvinism, it does not seem to be internally disordered at all. Walls claims that the Confession (and Calvinists more generally) is confused. Calvinists want to hold "both that God determines all things in the strictest sense, and that human beings are truly responsible for their sin." But we have seen that the Confession does not say that God *determines all things in the strictest sense*. It might be that Walls, in reading chapter 3 of the Confession, on God's eternal decree, has understood the second section, cited at the beginning of this chapter, as warrant for the claim that God determines all things in the strictest sense. Recall that the relevant section of the Confession says this:

> II. Although God knows whatsoever may or can come to pass upon all supposed conditions; yet has He not decreed anything because He foresaw it as future, or as that which would come to pass upon such conditions.

But this is an anti-Arminian statement, which teaches that God does not decree what God does on the basis of foreknown outcomes, though God certainly knows all future conditionals (more precisely, God knows the truth-value of propositions that are future conditionals *to us*). This does not mean God determines all things in the strictest sense, because it is not equivalent to causal determinism. How could it be, when God is not a material object and therefore cannot bring about change in the world by physical action, which is what language of material causation requires?[15] What is more, the Confession does not deny that humans have libertarian free will in mundane choices. It denies only that humans can freely choose salvation absent prevenient divine grace. That is, it denies that humans have access to free choices pertaining to salvation without being enabled to make those choices by an act of divine grace. It appears that the Walls objection is premature if libertarian Calvinism represents one viable interpretation of the Confession.

A Historical Note

Let me end with a note on the history of this discussion. Libertarian Calvinism is not a novelty. In the nineteenth century, the Southern Presbyterian divine John Girardeau advocated this sort of view, although he did not call it libertarian Calvinism.[16] Earlier in the same century, the apparently deterministic consequences of the Reformed view was discussed at length by the moderate commonsense philosopher Sir William Hamilton (who denied that determinism was consistent with the standards of Presbyterianism) and by William Cunningham, an eminent historical theologian at Edinburgh University, who argued that the Westminster Confession neither precludes nor requires a doctrine of "philosophical necessity."[17]

15. Granted, God incarnate has a physical body, but this does not imply that the Second Person of the Trinity is a physical object. Nor does it imply that the Second Person of the Trinity incarnate brings about physical action. For I suppose it is possible that God the Son acts upon God's human soul in order to bring about physical change in God's body.

16. See John L. Girardeau, *The Will in Its Theological Relations* (Columbia, SC: Duffie, 1891), esp. chap. 8, which summarizes his position.

17. As we have already noted at the beginning of this chapter, Cunningham argued as follows: "1st, There is nothing in the Calvinistic system of theology, or in the *Westminster Confession*, which precludes men from holding the doctrine of philosophical necessity. 2d, There is nothing in the Calvinistic system of theology, or in the *Westminster Confession*, which requires men to hold the doctrine of philosophical necessity." See William Cunningham, "Calvinism and the Doctrine of Philosophical Necessity," in *The Reformers and the Theology of the Reformation* (1862; repr., Edinburgh: Banner of Truth, 1989), 483. There is also an illuminating discussion of this in Richard A. Muller, "Jonathan Edwards and the Absence of Free Choice: A Parting of the Ways in the Reformed Tradition," *Jonathan Edwards Studies* 1, no. 1 (2011), http://jestudies.yale.edu/index.php/journal/article/view/63.

More recently, something similar to what I have been calling libertarian Calvinism has been the subject of heated and ongoing discussion after the recent publication by Dutch scholars Willem J. van Asselt, J. Martin Bac, and Roelf T. te Velde of their book *Reformed Thought on Freedom*.[18] In each of these cases, two things stand out, the two very things with which we have concerned ourselves in this chapter. These are whether the Reformed view implies or entails some sort of determinism all the way down, so to speak, and whether there is a place within the confessional standards of Reformed theology (as well as the thinking of key Reformed theologians) for a doctrine of free will, which includes the ability to do otherwise. In each case, the authors have argued that the Reformed view is not necessarily determinist all the way down. They have also argued that some of the earliest theologians and confessions of the Reformed tradition admit that both human choices before the fall and mundane choices after the all are free in the sense of the ability to do otherwise. Such views can hardly be said to represent the majority report on the subject in Reformed thought. Nevertheless, they do raise interesting issues that might offer an ecumenical olive branch in theological discussions on a matter long mired in unproductive, and often vituperative, disputation.

---

18. Willem J. van Asselt, J. Martin Bac, and Roelf T. de Velde, eds., *Reformed Thought on Freedom: The Concept of Free Choice in Early Modern Reformed Theology* (Grand Rapids, MI: Baker Academic, 2010). Muller's "Jonathan Edwards" is a contribution to this debate. Paul Helm has also written several articles on the topic. See Helm, "Synchronic Contingency in Reformed Scholasticism: A Note of Caution," *Nederlands Theologisch Tijdschrift* 57 (2003): 207–22; reply by A. J. Beck and Antonie Vos, "Conceptual Patterns Related to Reformed Scholasticism," *Nederlands Theologisch Tijdschrift* 57 (2003): 223–33; and a rejoinder from Helm, "Synchronic Contingency Again," *Nederlands Theologisch Tijdschrift* 57 (2003): 234–38. See also Paul Helm, "Reformed Thought on Freedom: Some Further Thoughts," *Journal of Reformed Theology* 4, no. 3 (2010): 185–207; Paul Helm, "'Structural Indifference' and Compatibilism in Reformed Orthodoxy," *Journal of Reformed Theology* 5, no. 2 (2011): 184–205; and the commentary by Roelf T. te Velde, *The Doctrine of God in Reformed Orthodoxy, Karl Barth, and the Utrecht School: A Study in Method and Content* (Leiden, Neth.: Brill, 2013), 670–76. There is also a forthcoming symposium on the matter in the *Journal of Reformed Theology*.

4

Augustinian Universalism

[I]f we take the universality of redemption in its whole range (which cannot really be conceived without the high-priestly dignity of Christ and all its consequences), then we must also take fore-ordination to blessedness quite universally; and that limits can be imposed on neither without curtailing the other.

—Friedrich Schleiermacher, *The Christian Faith*

It is often thought that Augustinianism requires a doctrine of particularism, according to which God saves some number of fallen human beings less than the total number of human beings. Indeed, it is often thought that Augustinians in general, and the Reformed as a species of Augustinian, develop their particularism in conscious opposition to universalism, which stands at the opposite end of the spectrum of views possible on the scope of salvation in Christ. However, this is a misconception. Augustinianism and universalism are compatible. Or, more specifically, the central moral and metaphysical intuitions behind Augustinianism are compatible with universalism. In this chapter, I will show how this is the case.

The central claim of this chapter is part of a larger set of theological-philosophical concerns. In recent philosophical-theological discussion of eschatology, there has been an interest in what has become known as the soteriological problem of evil. This is the contention that an all-powerful, loving God would ensure that none of humanity suffers everlasting punishment in hell. Theological libertarians who have written on this problem have claimed that God may be absolved of moral responsibility for those who are damned if they exercise their libertarian free will and reject God. But this avenue is not open to Augustinians who are also theological determinists (as opposed to libertarian Calvinists). The argument for Augustinian universalism is one way in which an Augustinian who is a determinist could respond to this problem by embracing universalism (in which case the problem dissolves, because there is no soteriological problem of evil: all human beings are saved). But this has a theological cost that most traditional Augustinians will find too high (namely, that universalism does not comport with a traditional understanding of Scripture).

Two Sorts of Universalism

A considerable literature has grown up over the last two decades that has sought to rehabilitate the doctrine of universalism. This rehabilitation has taken one of two different forms. The first, an argument for contingent universalism, claims that although it is possible that some people might end up in hell, as a matter of contingent fact no one will end up there. The second, necessary universalism, states that, given the essentially benevolent nature of God, it is inconceivable that anyone will ever end up in hell forever. In fact, given divine benevolence, God will necessarily save all people.[1]

---

1. See, in particular, John Hick, *Death and Eternal Life* (London: Collins, 1976), chap. 13, as an example of contingent universalism; and Thomas Talbott, "The Doctrine of Everlasting Punishment," *Faith and Philosophy* 7 (1990): 19–42, as an example of necessary universalism.

I will postpone comment on this debate until chapter 5. Meantime, in this chapter, I want to present a new problem of universalism. This version of universalism is a problem for theists in the Augustinian tradition in particular. This chapter will outline this version of universalism and show that it is both coherent and plausible to claim that someone could be both a traditional Augustinian (which includes, but is not restricted to, the Reformed) and a universalist. Moreover, although there may be theological grounds for rejecting Augustinian universalism, such a rejection yields a problem of evil for Augustinians.

Traditional Augustinianism

To begin with, I shall outline traditional Augustinianism. I take it that most traditional Augustinians unpersuaded by libertarian Calvinism align themselves with the doctrines of election and theological determinism of a compatibilist variety. Representative exponents of these views include theologians like Calvin and (the later) Augustine. So, for instance, Augustine claims that

> God Almighty, the supreme and supremely good creator of all beings, who assists and rewards good wills, while he abandons and condemns the bad (and yet he controls both good and bad) surely did not fail to have a plan whereby he might complete the fixed number of citizens predestined in his wisdom, even out of the condemned human race. He does not now choose them for their merits seeing that the whole mass of mankind has been condemned as it were in its infected root; he selects them by grace and shows them the extent of his generosity to those who have been set free not only in his dealings with them but also in his treatment of those who have not been freed.[2]

2. Augustine, *City of God*, trans. Henry Bettenson (Harmondsworth, UK: Penguin, 1972), 14.26, pp. 591–92. I am aware that there is a scholarly debate about whether Augustine was a compatibilist. But there is a long tradition of thinking he was and that this was his mature position. For a recent defense of the claim that Augustine was not a compatibilist, see Kevin Timpe, *Free Will in Philosophical Theology* (New York: Bloomsbury, 2014), chap. 4. That he was a compatibilist is defended in Jesse Couenhoeven, *Stricken by Sin, Cured by Christ: Agency,*

And in a similar vein, Calvin famously maintained that

> [w]e call predestination God's eternal decree, by which he compacted with himself what he willed to become of each man. For all are not created in equal condition; rather, eternal life is foreordained for some, eternal damnation for others. Therefore, as any man has been created to one or the other of these ends, we speak of him as predestined to life or to death.[3]

Let us formulate these views a little more carefully. Theists of this sort claim that theological compatibilism is true with respect to free will and that a constituent of this view is that God ordains all things that come to pass. Moreover, God predestines all those who will be in heaven and all those who will be in hell. Thus Francis Turretin:

> All things were decreed of God by an eternal and unchangeable counsel; hence they cannot but take place in the appointed time; otherwise the counsel of God would be changed, which the Scriptures declare to be impossible (Is. 46:10; Eph. 1:9).

And this:

> Thus the elect indeed have that for which they may give thanks to God (i.e., the bestowal of grace, which they have not merited), but the reprobate cannot complain because God was not bound to bless anyone, nor had he pledged himself by any promise to bestow upon the reprobate the same grace which is given to the elect; and because, if they examine themselves, they will discover in their own sin the most just foundation both of their preterition and punishment.[4]

Necessity, and Culpability in Augustinian Theology (New York: Oxford University Press, 2013), chaps. 4–7.

3. John Calvin, *Institutes of the Christian Religion,* ed. John T. McNeill, trans. Ford Lewis Battles, vol. 3 (1559; repr., Philadelphia: Westminster, 1960), 21.5, p. 926.

4. Francis Turretin, *Institutes of Elenctic Theology* ed. James T. Dennison Jr., trans. George Musgrave Giger, vol. 1 (Phillipsburg, NJ: Presbyterian and Reformed, 1992), 4.4.4, p. 320, and 4.14.23, p. 387, respectively.

It is usually understood that those who defend this sort of position are also committed to the belief that those members of humanity whose final destination is heaven (let us call them, with Calvin and others, the elect) are distinct from those members of humanity whose final destination is hell (the reprobate), as Turretin explains. Furthermore, those who will be in heaven comprise all and only the elect and are exclusive of those who will be in hell, who comprise all and only the reprobate. Moreover, theists in this tradition typically assume that there is no hope for those who are reprobate; there is no possibility that a member of the reprobate might become a member of the elect, because God has foreordained the number of those who will occupy heaven and hell.

Alongside this commitment to notions of election and reprobation, traditional Augustinians maintain that the postmortem destination of all human agents is fixed by divine decree such that the soteriological state a person is in at the point of death is the state that characterizes her postmortem existence. If she is regenerate, she is elect and will be in heaven; if unregenerate, she is (probably) reprobate and will be in hell. There may be instances of persons who are unregenerate but elect at the point of death; in that case, such persons will also be in heaven.[5] Whether this is possible or not, the issue is whether the postmortem destination of all peccable human agents is fixed at the point of death and thereafter. Almost all historic Augustinians respond that it is fixed in this way.

This effectively forecloses any discussion of postmortem conversion or of the possibility, mooted recently by Charles

---

5. It is accepted in the Augustinian tradition that there will be those among the elect who did not have the opportunity to hear the gospel and therefore may not be regenerate, for example, Abraham. What is less clear is whether this applies to "righteous" pagans who may have never heard the gospel. I leave this question open, because a clear answer to it is not necessary to the current discussion. I also leave open the question of whether there are those who die unregenerate but who may yet be among the elect because they are incapable of responding to the gospel, such as infants and the severely mentally handicapped.

Seymour, that there might be those who begin their postmortem existence in hell but see the error of their ways, repent, and are accepted into heaven.[6] It also precludes the elect from ever falling into sin postmortem after their acceptance into heaven and being expelled from heaven to hell. Furthermore, it denies any notion that the reprobate might be punished for a period postmortem in order that they are purified of their sin, so that they may enter heaven.[7] In short, the eschatological destiny of all humanity has been ordained by the decree of God, and nothing can change that decree: it is immutable.

It is also understood by traditional Augustinians that the punishment meted out in hell is infinite; there is no end to the punishment of the damned. This precludes any notion of annihilation or conditional immortality.

In what follows, I shall refer to this group of theists collectively as traditional Augustinians. I do not claim that this is anything more than a term of art for the purposes of this argument, although it seems to me that there is such a tradition including the theologians just cited.[8]

6. See Charles Seymour, "Hell, Justice, and Freedom," *International Journal for Philosophy of Religion* 43 (1998): 82. There is also a developing Protestant literature defending purgatory. See, e.g., Jerry Walls, *Purgatory: The Logic of Total Transformation* (New York: Oxford University Press, 2012).

7. Compare Hendrikus Berkhof: "[T]he darkness of rejection and God-forsakeness cannot and may not be argued away, but no more can and may it be eternalized. For God's sake we hope that it will be a form of purification." In *Christian Faith: An Introduction to the Study of the Faith,* trans. Sierd Woudstra (Grand Rapids, MI: Eerdmans, 1979), 532.

8. Paul Helm has pointed out to me in private correspondence that, as a matter of historical fact, Augustinian theists typically appealed to several factors as sources in their deliberations, including a retributive-justice argument, experience (particularly the experience of observing that some people do not appear to be saved), and, of course, Scripture. My model of Augustinian theism may, as a result, seem a little too restrictive, perhaps even artificial. I am happy to concede the point and allow that "traditional Augustinianism" in what follows should be taken to represent a central feature, though by no means the only feature, of Augustinianism per se. In any case, this does not affect the substantial point being made here.

Let us apply these elements of a traditional Augustinianism to a doctrine of hell. To begin with, I shall assume there is a domain comprising all (peccable) human agents. (I leave to one side the problem of angelic agents, if there are any such.)[9] Within this domain, there is the set of the elect, comprising all those peccable human agents who are elect by God according to God's divine decree. There is also another set within this domain, comprising all those peccable human agents who are reprobate according to the divine decree. (For the purposes of this argument, let us leave to one side questions of whether the decree[s] to elect one set and to reprobate another are *supralapsus* or *infralapsus*. Nothing in this argument hinges on one or the other position.) Now, the two sets of the elect and the reprobate are disjoint. That is, there are no members of the set elect that are also members of the set reprobate, and conversely. The number of the reprobate is predetermined by divine decree, and the number of the elect is also predetermined by God's decree, such that no member of one set will ever be a member of the other set. (For example, a member of the reprobate cannot become a Christian and be transferred to become a member of the elect.)

Moreover, in this traditional Augustinian view, God ordains those in the set of the elect to display God's mercy and grace and reprobates those in the set of the reprobate in order to display God's wrath and justice. (It might be that God ordains this for other reasons besides the display of these particular attributes as well.) According to this traditional Augustinianism, God requires that both God's mercy and

---

9. Traditional Augustinians take the view that the election and reprobation of angelic beings is a separate issue from the election and reprobation of human agents, and that reprobate angelic beings cannot be among those to whom the saving benefits of Christ are applied. See, for example, Augustine, *Enchiridion*, trans. Ernst Evans (London: SPCK, 1953), 9.26–27. There, Augustine also makes his curious claim that God elects the number of humanity God does to fill the gap left by those angels who fell with Lucifer.

grace and God's wrath and justice are displayed in God's creatures. That is, God could not bring about a state of affairs that involved the actualization of one set but not the other (a set of the elect, say, that was coextensive with the domain of peccable human agents, where the set of the reprobate was an empty set).

Typically, traditional Augustinians reply that both the actualization of the set of the elect, which displays God's mercy and grace, and the actualization of the set of the reprobate, which displays God's wrath and justice, are needed in order that the essential attributes of God be displayed in the created order. These essential attributes include divine benevolence displayed in God's grace and mercy, and divine holiness displayed in God's wrath and justice. If we then ask why it is that God should require both these sorts of attributes to be displayed in creation, there are several responses that traditional Augustinians give to justify their position. For instance, Jonathan Edwards claims that a failure to display both divine grace and mercy and divine wrath and justice would be a failure to display the fullness of the divine character and/or a central aim and end of creation, namely, to display all the divine attributes to God's own greater glory. This is the position he defends in his treatise *God's End in Creation*:

> The great and last end of God's work which is so variously expressed in Scripture, is indeed but one; and this one end is most properly and comprehensively called, "the glory of God"; by which name it is most commonly called in Scripture. . . . [T]hose things, which are spoken of in Scripture as ultimate ends of God's works, though they may seem at first view to be distinct, all are plainly to be reduced to this one thing, viz. God's internal glory or fullness extant externally, or existing in its emanation. And though God in seeking this end, seeks the creature's good; yet therein appears his supreme regard to himself.[10]

10. Jonathan Edwards, *God's End in Creation*, in *Ethical Writings*, ed. Paul Ramsey, vol. 8 of *The Works of Jonathan Edwards*, ed. Perry Miller (New Haven, CT: Yale University Press, 1989), 530.

Alternatively, it could be that it would be an affront to God's honor not to display both God's mercy and justice. Anselm has a similar argument to this in *Cur Deus homo* 1.11–15 and *Proslogion* 10. There, he argues that God's honor must be upheld, and this means God's visiting wrath upon some and justice upon others. So, for instance, in *Proslogion*, he says, "For when thou punishest the wicked, it is just, because it is consistent with their deserts; and when, on the other hand, thou sparest the wicked, it is just, not because it is compatible with their deserts, but because it is compatible with thy goodness."[11]

The point in these attempts at justifying the need for the display of both divine mercy and divine justice is to show that God has a reason for so acting, a reason that has to do with some end God envisages in creation that pertains to God's self-glorification, the vindication of divine honor, or a combination of these ends in view (or, indeed, some other end or ends not stated here that yield the same results). But what the two positions of Edwards and Anselm share is a concern with the consistency of the attributes of divine benevolence and divine justice as they are displayed in the salvation of some and the damnation of others. The assumption behind these views appears to be that God has to manifest both grace and mercy and wrath and justice in order that God is seen to be just as well as merciful. What

---

11. Anselm, *Proslogion*, in *St. Anselm: Basic Writings*, trans. S. N. Deane, 2nd ed. (La Salle, IL: Open Court, 1962), 10.63. Marilyn McCord Adams has questioned this rationale for justifying God's action in damnation (a constituent of traditional Augustinianism as I have outlined it), maintaining that Anselm's argument violates a principle of natural justice, that "no-one should be treated better than they deserve" (see Marilyn McCord Adams, "Hell and the God of Justice," *Religious Studies* 11 [1974]: 435). However, this seems implausible, for it may be that God does treat the elect better than they deserve, strictly speaking, and yet this not be unjust. Secular analogues to this problem are not hard to find. For instance, a man who owes a large amount of money to a loan shark may have his debt paid in full by someone else acting on his behalf. This may mean that he is treated better than he deserves, because he should have paid the loan shark himself, having accumulated the debt in the first place through his own deliberate fault. But may not a friend and benefactor agree to graciously step in to help the poor wretch in such circumstances? It may not be what he deserves, strictly speaking, but this does not mean that the friend acts unjustly. So Adams's principle of natural justice does not seem to pose a problem to the Augustinian theist.

we shall see is that this claim conflates two crucial issues, namely, the requirement that these essential attributes be exemplified, and the requirement that they be exemplified in a particular set of God's creatures. God's justice may be meted out, God's holiness vindicated, and God's benevolence displayed in God's gracious election without a single human agent being allotted to the set of the reprobate. However, before exploring this issue, we turn to a related problem having to do with the structure of the traditional argument.

The Problem of Arbitrariness

There is a significant problem with this brand of traditional Augustinianism, which we shall call the problem of arbitrariness.[12] It is this: given that the number of the elect is actually some number, n, which is less than the total number of human beings, there is a possible world where the number of the elect is $n + 1$. The question then is, why does God actualize this world rather than another world where there are $n + 1$ more elect than in the actual world?

In other words, God could actualize a world in which God elects one more member to the set of the elect, such that the set of the reprobate has one less member. (God could also actualize a world where God creates one more member of the elect ex nihilo, but this is a separate point. Our concern is with God electing $n + 1$ more individual[s] to the set of the elect from the domain of peccable human agents that already exist in a particular world.) The fact that God does not actualize such a world appears, prima facie, to be arbitrary. God could, of course, add many more members than this

12. Jonathan L. Kvanvig also deals with an arbitrariness problem that a strong (here read traditional) doctrine of hell could throw up, namely, that it seems arbitrary to select the strong doctrine from other, weaker alternatives without some reason for believing the stronger, over the weaker, doctrine of hell. See Kvanvig, *The Problem of Hell* (New York: Oxford University Press, 1993), 55. As will become apparent, my use of an arbitrariness problem is slightly different from Kvanvig's.

to the number of the elect. But for any number of members in the set of the elect, so long as there is at least one person in the set of the reprobate, we can ask, why is there not one more member in the set of the elect than there actually is, given that God's justice is still served if only one person is in hell? For in the logic of traditional Augustinianism, what is crucial is that divine wrath and justice are made manifest in God's creation such that God's divine attributes are clearly displayed. There is nothing in the logic of Augustinianism that stipulates the number of those benefiting from divine grace or being punished for divine justice. All that this argument for the exemplification of divine justice requires is that at least one person be in hell, so that at least one person is punished for his sin in order that divine justice be displayed and divine holiness vindicated.

And this one person need not be a human person; for it seems possible that there is a world where the set of the elect comprises all humanity and all but one angelic beings (including demons). The set of the reprobate would then comprise the one remaining demon (perhaps Abaddon or Lucifer, or some such), who would receive a just punishment for his sin in hell. In this way, divine grace and mercy would be seen to be overflowing even to those humans and demons who rejected the rule of God. For although God's justice would be made manifest in the damnation of one recalcitrant demon, the glory of the divine nature would be displayed in God's created order, as per the traditional Augustinian argument.

What this goes to show is that traditional Augustinianism suffers from a problem of arbitrariness, for it seems arbitrary that God should fix the number of the elect at the particular percentage of the total population of moral agents that God does, rather than at some higher number. Indeed, it seems that it would be objectively morally better for God to include within the elect all moral agents bar one, in hell, who would manifest God's wrath and justice. The fact that this world does not obtain, nor any world where the number of elect is higher than it is in the actual world, means that the number of elect that has been fixed by God, presuming with traditional Augustinians that this number is far short of all human agents, appears arbitrary.[13]

It must be said, by way of response to this problem, that traditional Augustinians typically appeal to the inscrutability of the divine will on the question of why the elect and the reprobate, respectively, are fixed at the numbers they are. It might be that God has a reason for limiting the number of the elect to the number God does but we do not know why God does this (Augustinians could cite passages like Deut. 29:29 in this regard). And, to borrow an idea from the probabilistic-problems-of-evil debate of some years ago, it could be that we humans simply have no condition of reasonable epistemic access (Stephen Wykstra's CORNEA principle) that might supply the grounds for some judgment about the morality of God's electing this number of elect but not a moral agent more.[14] For us to be able to make such a judgment would mean for us to have the epistemic access to all the data on God's electing decree to hand, which we simply do not have. Hence, although it may appear arbitrary that God elects this number to the set of the elect and not more, it does not follow that it is arbitrary. God may have reasons for electing the number of moral agents God does that we know nothing about.

However, in the spirit of William Rowe's response to Wykstra on the question of the CORNEA principle, we might want to claim that this particular view conflates two intuitions: The first is whether

---

13. Of course, in Augustine's doctrine of angels in *Enchiridion*, mentioned earlier, the number of the elect would not be arbitrary as such, because his point is that the number of the elect fills the gap left by the fallen angels. But then we might want to ask why this should be the case, and what it is that is so important about this particular number of elect.

14. Stephen Wykstra's CORNEA principle is found in "The Humean Obstacle to Evidential Arguments from Suffering: On Avoiding the Evils of Appearance," in *The Problem of Evil*, ed. Robert Merrihew and Marilyn McCord Adams (Oxford: Oxford University Press, 1990), 138–60.

the magnitude of suffering in hell for sin is worthy of an essentially loving God who is able to display God's justice where there is significantly less suffering. The second is that, if it is possible for God to actualize a world where this level of suffering is reduced to only a single person (and God's justice is still satisfied by this and is adequately "displayed"), then the fact that God has not actualized such a world, opting instead for a world where there is objectively morally more suffering and less happiness than there could be, seems to disconfirm either the essential benevolence of God or the existence of God.[15]

The problems with such a Rowe-type response to an Augustinian use of the CORNEA principle are that they assume God is essentially benevolent and that God's benevolence must have a universal extension to all God's creatures. But it need not be the case that an essentially benevolent being always acts in a benevolent way. God could be essentially benevolent without being benevolent to all God's creatures, and this seems to be a view that at least some Augustinians have espoused.

Naturally, this Augustinian counterclaim makes its own assumption, that essential benevolence need not be exemplified in every act of an essentially benevolent being. Is this plausible? If a particular being is essentially good, then does it not follow from this that all the acts of that being will be good? It does not. All that follows from this is that the acts of an essentially benevolent being will not be morally bad. For instance, it might be that God permits a certain evil to occur that a greater good state of affairs might be brought about that could not otherwise be brought about without the actualization of the prior evil action. Thus, an essentially good God could allow

---

15. I have borrowed these two intuitions from Rowe's debate with Wykstra. See William Rowe, "Evil and the Theistic Hypothesis: A Response to Wykstra," in Merrihew and Adams, *Problem of Evil*, 166–67.

evil for some greater good that would not be actualized without the presence of some prior evil, as in the case of the atonement. Moreover, it appears to be the case that there are some actions an essentially benevolent agent does that are morally indifferent, such as creating Smith with dark rather than red hair.

So, if it is the case that an essentially benevolent being has the property of essential benevolence but not that this being must therefore only ever act benevolently toward other moral agents, then God may be essentially benevolent but not benevolent to all human agents. For it might be (contra a Rowe-type response) that in damning a particular number of reprobate, God brings about an objectively greater good that could not be actualized without the damnation of this number. As we have already seen, traditional Augustinians might claim that such greater good is the glory of God, brought about by the display of God's justice and holiness in the punishment of sin. In this way, God's act of damnation might not be arbitrary after all.

Nevertheless, this Augustinian counterclaim still assumes that God has to damn at least one moral agent for God's justice to be vindicated and this greater good actualized; but there is no reason why this need be the case. God may vindicate God's justice and actualize the greater good of divine self-glorification without damning any human agent to hell, which leads us to consider how that might be the case in a doctrine of Augustinian universalism.

Augustinian Universalism Expounded

To begin with, we shall analyze the traditional Augustinian doctrine of election, to show that it is consistent with a version of universalism. Let us call this traditional Augustinian defense of a limited number of members in the set of the elect "the restricted elect." (By this I mean a number smaller than the domain of moral agents as per traditional Augustinianism.)

So, to the content of the restricted-elect view. It has three parts:

a. the need for an infinite retributive punishment to be meted out for the sin of those human agents who are fallen[16]
b. the need for sin to be atoned for (in Christ's death on the cross) for sinful human agents to be counted among the elect[17]
c. the need for the display of both God's grace and mercy and God's wrath and justice in the created order.

Augustinian universalism is able to satisfy these three aspects of a restricted-elect view. It seems to me that these three intuitions do not require that the set of the elect be restricted. That is, the requirements of (a)–(c) can be met by a version of Augustinianism that does not entail that the number of the elect must be restricted. If this is the case, then Augustinians can remain faithful to the core beliefs of the tradition while rejecting its appeal to the restriction of the elect. This is a rejection not of the logic of Augustinianism but only of a false belief that Augustinians have held, namely, that God elects only some but cannot elect all peccable human agents in order for God's justice and holiness to be vindicated in creation. Augustinians may, in all consistency, deny the belief in a restricted elect while retaining their belief in the requirement that (a)–(c) be satisfied.

---

16. Thomas Talbott maintains that this sort of traditional view of hell relies upon a retributive model of punishment. See Talbott, "Punishment, Forgiveness, and Divine Justice," *Religious Studies* 29 (1993): 151–68. I am sympathetic to this way of thinking and have attempted a defense of divine retribution in "Divine Retribution: A Defence," *Sophia* 42 (2003): 35–52. A comparison of these two positions is given in Dror Ehrlich, "Some Further Reflections regarding the Talbott–Crisp Debate on the Augustinian Concept of Everlasting Punishment," *Religious Studies* 47 (2011): 23–40.
17. The notion that Christ's atonement has a value equal to or greater than the value of the punishment to be meted out to one or more sinners is theologically uncontroversial in the Augustinian tradition.

Next, to an analysis of these three principles. All three seem to be crucial to the Augustinian's case for a limited, or particular, atonement and the division of all human agents into the elect and the reprobate. They also explain why a universal atonement (that is, the notion that the atonement is universally effectual for all human agents) is often thought to be alien to traditional Augustinianism, because Augustinians assume that God's decree to elect is restricted to one group of humanity only, in order that the rest of humanity, who are reprobate, display God's justice in damnation. Thus, Jonathan Edwards claims that

> [t]he glory of God is the greatest good; it is that which is the chief end of the creation; it is of greater importance than any thing else. But this is one way wherein God will glorify himself, as in the eternal destruction of ungodly men he will glorify his justice. . . . God hereby indirectly glorifies his grace on the vessels of mercy. . . . Hereby the saints will be made more sensible how great their salvation is.[18]

However, this sort of assertion is no reason for denying Augustinian universalism.[19] In fact, Augustinian universalism is perfectly compatible with the principles that make up the restricted-elect view. This requires some explanation. In order to provide such an explanation, consider the following argument, which is compatible with the restricted-elect position outlined here:

---

18. Jonathan Edwards, "The Eternity of Hell Torments," sermon 11 in *The Works of Jonathan Edwards,* ed. Edward Hickman (Edinburgh: Banner of Truth, 1988), 2:87 (original emphasis).
19. Nor, as we shall see when dealing with hypothetical universalism, in chapter 7, is it actually a good reason to think that Augustinians *must* reject a universal atonement.

1. God decrees to create and elect all human agents.
2. God decrees that the mechanism by which the sin of all human agents is atoned for is the death of Christ.
3. The sin and guilt accruing to all sinful human agents is transferred to Christ, who is punished on their account on the cross.

Thus,

4. All human agents are saved; none are lost, and none are in hell.

This is a version of necessary universalism, the view that it is necessarily the case that all human agents are saved, in this particular case because of a divine decree to that effect.[20] What is more, God decrees this outcome and, as with much traditional Augustinians, all human agents have freedom, understood in compatibilist terms. But this presents only the bare bones of Augustinian universalism. Let us flesh it out somewhat with reference to the restricted-elect position.

First, regarding (a), it should be clear from items (1)–(4) that retributive punishment is meted out for sin in the Augustinian universalism view. It is not distributed to a particular number of the human agents comprising some number less than the domain of human agents. However, the condition of (a) is still met in Augustinian universalism, because the sin of all human agents is atoned for in the death of Christ.

---

20. I qualify this with "in this particular case" because this version of necessary universalism is different from the one mentioned in the introduction to this essay. In any case, a question that arises here is, necessary in what sense? For it seems that God could have actualized a different world, if God is able to bring about worlds other than those that actually obtain (*pace* Leibniz). Perhaps this is consequentially necessary, that is, necessary in the sense that, although this world is logically dependent on the divine decree that ordains this world rather than some other world, given that God has ordained this rather than some other world, this world is necessary, the metaphysical reason being that once God has decreed this world, it is a hard fact that this world has been decreed by God.

This also meets the requirement of (b), for if the sin of all peccable human agents is atoned for in Christ, then all peccable human agents are elect and the set of the reprobate is empty. In other words, according to Augustinian universalism, the set of the elect is coextensive with the domain of peccable human agents. That is, there are no human agents who are not in the set of the elect: all are saved, none are reprobate. (Of course, this means that only the set of reprobate human agents is empty. It does not entail the additional claim that hell is empty, because it could be that there are demonic beings who are damned and whose sin is not atoned for by Christ. Such beings could still be in hell. If they were, then they would presumably be in a set comprising all fallen angelic beings in the domain of angelic agents.)[21]

Contrary to first appearances, the internal logic of this doctrine is compatible with traditional Augustinianism, for traditional Augustinians adhere to the principle that the atonement of Christ is sufficient for all sin but efficient only for the sin of the elect. This principle presumes that Christ's atonement has a merit sufficient to the purpose of saving all human agents (in fact, an infinite merit, because his death atones for one or more sins which themselves incur an infinite demerit by being committed against a being of infinite worth).[22] But typically, Augustinians claim that this atonement is

21. It may be argued that if there is at least one demon in hell, then Augustinian universalism is not a form of universalism at all. But this would be overhasty. It is true that Augustinian universalism as I have presented it is ambivalent about the soteriological status of angelic beings; but the point is issue is whether it is possible for all peccable human agents to be in the set of the elect, not whether all angelic beings could also be elect. It could be that hell is still occupied by one or more demons and that a form of universalism (with respect to human agents) obtains. Alternatively, it could be that hell is empty and all humans and angelic beings are elect. It could also be that there are no angelic beings, only elect (or reprobate) humans. Whether there are angelic beings and whether they are elect or reprobate is not an issue that falls within the remit of this chapter, given that, as I have already pointed out, traditional Augustinians tend to think that the soteriological status of angels is a separate issue from that of humans.

22. This view—that all sin incurs an infinite demerit, which requires an infinite punishment in hell—is what Kvanvig calls the "infinite-punishment thesis." See Kvanvig, *Problem of Hell*, chap. 1.

effective only for the members of the set of the elect, not for members of the set of the reprobate.

However, these typical claims are all logically contingent. God may choose to elect only some people via Christ's sufficient death, or God may choose to elect all human beings by Christ's sufficient death. Moreover, in saving all human agents, God is not violating part (a) of the restricted-elect position, because all that (a) requires is that retributive punishment be meted out for the sin of peccable human agents. But this is met in a version of (b) where the punishment for sin is transferred to Christ, who atones for it instead of the human agents who have sinned. Thus, the difference between the way (a) and (b) are understood in the traditional Augustinian's position and the way (a) and (b) are understood in Augustinian universalism depends upon the scope of the efficacy of the atonement that is envisaged. But, crucially, it does not depend upon (a) and (b) being satisfied, given that, in both views, (a) and (b) can both be met without cavil. Christ dies for all human agents in Augustinian universalism, thereby atoning for the sin of all human agents and satisfying the requirement of retribution for the sin of all human agents (not just some, as in the traditional model). Thus, Augustinian universalism satisfies (a) and (b), just as traditional Augustinianism does. It also satisfies (c), for, according to Augustinian universalism, God's grace and mercy are shown to all human agents in their election (in Christ), and God's wrath and justice are shown in the death of Christ, which atones for the sin and guilt of all fallen human agents.[23] Thus, Augustinian universalism satisfies the requirements of

---

23. I have deliberately sidestepped questions on the nature of the atonement. There are several different views that traditional Augustinians have expressed on this matter, and I do not propose to adjudicate between them here. All that the present argument requires is the notion that the sin and guilt of fallen moral agents are, in principle, transferable to Christ, who suffers their punishment in their stead. This appears to me to be compatible with at least two traditional Augustinian views of the atonement, namely, the satisfaction and penal-substitutionary models. Whether these two views are defensible or not I cannot enter into here.

traditional Augustinianism and avoids the pitfall of arbitrariness that the traditional view is susceptible to. It also presents a coherent case for necessary universalism.

A Barthian Doctrine?

One might think that this sounds remarkably like the doctrine advocated by Karl Barth, which we will consider in greater detail in chapter 6. In *Church Dogmatics,* volume 2, part 2, Barth departs from much of the Reformed tradition, denying the doctrine of double predestination (the notion that God elects some of humanity and damns the rest as reprobate) and opting instead for the view that God elects all humanity through the Elect One, Christ. Here is a representative gobbet from Barth on the matter:

> This, then, is the message with which the elect community (as the circumference of the elect man, Jesus of Nazareth) has to approach every man—the promise, that he, too, is an elect man. It is fully aware of his perverted choice. It is fully aware of his godlessness. . . . It is fully aware, too, of the eternal condemnation of the man who is isolated over against God, which is unfailingly exhibited by the godlessness of every such man. . . . It knows of the wrath and judgment and punishment of God in which the rejection of the man isolated over and against God takes its course. . . . It knows that God, by the decree He made in the beginning of all His works and ways, has taken upon Himself the rejection merited by the man isolated in relation to Him; and on the basis of this decree of His the only truly rejected man is His own Son; that God's rejection has taken its course and been fulfilled and reached its goal, with all that that involves, against this One, so that it can no longer fall on other men or be their concern. The concern of other men is still the sin and guilt of their godlessness—and it is serious and severe enough. Their concern is still the suffering of the existence which they have prepared for themselves by their godlessness (in the shadow of that which the One has suffered for them)—and it is bitter enough to have to suffer this existence. Their concern is still to be aware of the threat of their rejection. But it cannot now be their concern to suffer the execution of this threat, to suffer the eternal damnation which their godlessness

deserves. Their desire and their undertaking are pointless in so far as their only end can be to make them rejected. And this is the very goal which the godless cannot reach, because it has already been taken away by the eternally decreed offering of the Son of God to suffer in place of the godless, and cannot any longer be their goal.[24]

Barth's view seems to mean that the set of reprobate human agents is empty of all but Christ, who is the Reprobate One.[25] However, unlike Augustinian universalism, Barth maintains that there is a domain of peccable human agents within which is the set of the elect, which comprises only one member, Christ himself. Those human agents who are elect, are elect only in a derivative sense, inasmuch as they participate in the election of Christ. Hence, this election "in" Christ is not, as with the Augustinian universalist model, merely a question of all the sin of humanity being cast upon Christ, whose death atones for it. Instead, God elects human agents because of the (logically) prior election of Christ, and it is in him that humanity is counted as elect or not. So, it seems that Barth envisages a state of affairs in which those human agents who are derivatively elect are elect only by virtue of being related to the set of the nonderivatively elect, comprising Christ alone.[26]

24. Karl Barth, *Church Dogmatics*, ed. Geoffrey W. Bromiley and Thomas F. Torrance, vol. 2, pt. 2 (1942; repr., Edinburgh: T & T Clark, 1957), 318–19. Of this view, Bruce McCormack says, "Taken on the most superficial level, the revolution which Barth effected in the Reformed understanding of predestination was to replace Calvin's version of double predestination with a universal election. . . . Jesus Christ is the Subject of election and its Object, the electing God and the elected human. That is the fundamental thesis which shapes the whole of Barth's doctrine of election." From Bruce McCormack, "Grace and Being: The Role of God's Gracious Election in Karl Barth's Theological Ontology," in *The Cambridge Companion to Karl Barth*, ed. John Webster (Cambridge: Cambridge University Press, 2000), 93.

25. Barth can say things like this: "[*Christ*] stands under the wrath and judgment of God, *He* is broken and destroyed by God. It cannot be otherwise. It has to be like this. . . . He, the electing eternal God, willed Himself to be rejected and therefore perishing man." *Church Dogmatics*, vol. 4, pt. 4 (1969), 175.

26. Barth's notion that Christ is both the Elect One and the Reprobate One is rather unhelpful in this regard. I suppose he thinks that Christ can suffer in place of human beings as the Elect One, but at times he says things that seem to go beyond this. If Christ is the Reprobate One, then it is difficult to see how he can be both the one entity rejected by God forever and the one entity

This represents an important shift in emphasis from the Augustinian model, where the sin of an individual who is a member of the set of the elect is accounted to Christ, who suffers for that sin in the place of the sinner on the cross; and the Barthian model, where an individual is somehow incorporated into the election of Christ, rather like (to borrow a biblical parallel) a shoot from one grapevine that is grafted onto another vine, becoming organically united with the larger whole by being "incorporated" into its life. In a similar fashion, those in the set "elect in Christ," in Barth's model, are elect only insofar as they share a relation with the one who is *the* elect, namely, Christ.

This election is coordinate with the atonement of Christ, which sounds similarly universalistic in tone: "The rejection which all men incurred, the wrath under which all men lie, the death which all men must die, God in his love for men transfers from all eternity to him in whom he loves and elects them, and whom he elects at their head and in their place."[27] It might appear from this that Barth's doctrine is very similar to Augustinian universalism. Barth claims that all humanity is incorporated into the election of Christ, that Christ atones for all sin at the cross, and that this is an effective, not merely a potentially effective, atonement for all sin. Thus, it is in Christ that election and atonement are realized. However, there are some important structural differences between the two views, for the Barthian model does away with the traditional doctrine of election, replacing it instead with an elect person, Christ, in whom the members of the set "elect in Christ" are incorporated (like the vine graft and the vine) via the doctrine of

elected by God forever. I have discussed this in "On Barth's Denial of Universalism," *Themelios* 29 (2003): 18–29.

27. Barth, *Church Dogmatics,* vol. 2, pt. 2,123. In commenting on this passage in Barth, Colin Gunton observes that "the cross is a substitutionary bearing by God in Christ of God's rejection of human sin. Barth can speak of the one rejected, because through Jesus' rejection the rejection that the human race has merited is taken away." Colin Gunton, "Salvation," in *The Cambridge Companion to Karl Barth*, 145.

the atonement. By contrast, the model of Augustinian universalism retains the internal logic of traditional Augustinianism in the notion that there is a set comprising all those moral agents who are elect, and that all the members of the set of the elect have their sin dealt with in the atonement, thereby satisfying divine retributive justice and displaying unmerited grace and mercy.

This is not merely a question of terminological wrangling. What is at stake in the argument I have laid out is whether the internal logic of traditional Augustinianism entails a restricted election. I have argued that it does not, and that a legitimate construal of the logic of Augustinianism is compatible with a version of necessary universalism. Barth, by contrast, rejects the traditional picture, replacing it with his own doctrine of the Elect One, Christ. It is precisely because he rejects the traditional logic of Augustinianism in this matter that Barth has been viewed with suspicion by traditional Augustinians. My point, against both Barth and many traditional Augustinians in this respect, is that the traditional position is compatible with a version of universalism, and that this goes further than Barth himself would wish to go. Thus, we have a peculiar situation, where Augustinianism may legitimately be construed in a way that results in an eschatology more extensive than that espoused by Barth!

Hence, whether or not Barth's view entails universalism (a matter to which we shall return in chapter 6), his view is distinct from that of Augustinian universalism. Whereas Barth at times denies that his position regarding the scope of salvation *entails* universalism, Augustinian universalism has the double benefit of retaining a traditional view of election and reprobation while denying that the traditional view is incompatible with a version of (necessary) universalism.

A Deviant Calvinism?

But if this is not a Barthian doctrine, might it be a deviant version of Calvinism? There are two principal candidates here to which Augustinian universalism might sound similar.[28] The first is Arminianism. The followers of Jacob Arminius claimed that the scope of the atonement is universal and coupled this with a libertarian view of free will. This yields the following thesis: the atonement is potentially universal in extent but effective only for those who choose to accept Christ, whom God has foreknown will accept Christ. This means that if a particular individual chooses to freely accept Christ, then God holds the belief that this person will freely choose Christ, whereas if that person had not freely chosen to accept Christ, then God would not have held the belief regarding the salvation of that person that God did in fact hold. Instead, God would hold the belief that this person would not freely choose Christ. In this way, the libertarian freedom of the individual to choose salvation is preserved, while the sovereign mercy of God is given its widest possible remit, albeit a remit that will never be fulfilled, because, presumably, not everyone freely chooses Christ. What is important about Arminianism in the present context is that, as a matter of fact, not all people do choose Christ, God foreknows that, and therefore some people are damned to hell.

But it should be clear that this is not the same thing as Augustinian universalism. In the Augustinian model, God ordains whatever comes to pass, whereas in the Arminian model, God does not ordain human free actions. Moreover, in the Augustinian model, God can ensure that the scope of the atonement is universal or particular; in the Arminian model, God cannot ensure this. Finally, according to

---

28. For a brief overview of these two views, see Louis Berkhof, *Systematic Theology*, vol. 3 (Edinburgh: Banner of Truth, 1958), 6.B, pp. 393ff.

Augustinianism, it is not the case that some humans may freely choose not to turn to Christ (as per Arminianism); their actions are determined by divine decree, which means they must choose Christ.

The second possible form of deviant Calvinism that Augustinian universalism might be confused with is hypothetical universalism. This is the view that the atonement is sufficient for the salvation of all humanity, depending on the condition of faith. However, only the elect are given faith, so the atonement is efficacious for them alone. This is a subtle and careful position, to which we shall return in chapter 7. Nevertheless, it is clearly not the same thing as Augustinian universalism, for in Augustinian universalism, the divine decree for universal salvation is realized in the atonement. Christ really does die to save all humanity, thereby satisfying the need for divine retributive punishment for sin and bringing about the salvation of all people. In other words, according to Augustinian universalism, the atonement is both sufficient to atone for all human sin and efficacious for the atonement of all sin, because all of humanity is saved by it.

Supralapsarian Universalism?

Yet, despite the preceding discussion, it would be curious indeed if no one had ever voiced a view similar to that espoused in this chapter. And indeed, there has been (at least) one exponent of something similar in tone to Augustinian universalism in the past. William Hastie, professor of divinity at Glasgow University at the end of the nineteenth century, advocated a view similar in tone, though not in content, to Augustinian universalism. He seems to have held a version of supralapsarian universalism. In the context of a discussion about the place of absolute predestination in Reformed theology, he claimed,

> [T]he principle [of absolute predestination] can rest no longer in the old .traditional dualism and particularism, with the final termination of the whole process of the world in an eternal hell, whose tortured denizens

are for ever separated from God and heaven. The ideal of the Reformed eschatology is an endless progression in the future life under conditions modified by the result of the present development, and carrying that development forward under new conditions of divine determination.

And this:

The Reformed theology has not yet fully solved this profoundest problem of all, but it is passing in this connection through a new period of vital development. And the issue shall be a deepened belief in the endless development of all created souls till the absolute purpose of God shall be realized.[29]

Hastie goes no further than this by way of supplying the content of his views to his readers. He merely hints at the hope that Reformed theology might see that universalism is entirely consistent with the logic of absolute predestination. It seems from the foregoing that Hastie is entirely right in this matter: Augustinianism is compatible with either a restricted or a universal election.[30]

29. William Hastie, *The Theology of the Reformed Church in Its Fundamental Principles* (Edinburgh: T & T Clark, 1904), chap. 6, 281 and 282, respectively. A recent insightful study of supralapsarianism can be found in Edwin Christian van Driel, *Incarnation Anyway: Arguments for Supralapsarian Christology* (New York: Oxford University Press, 2008). As the epigraph to this chapter makes clear, Friedrich Schleiermacher also held to a doctrine of universalism. It may be that his views influenced Hastie.
30. Another apparently similar position is that of Jeremiah White (1630–1707), who was an independent minister and chaplain to Cromwell. Morwenna Ludlow, in a recent article on White and several other universalists in the closing years of the seventeenth century, says that White did not believe in reprobation. But, unlike Augustinian universalism, he took the view, common among universalists, that God will simply forgive those who sin. What is novel in White's thinking is that God does this after a probationary period of cleansing in hell. See Morwenna Ludlow, "Universal Salvation and a Soteriology of Divine Punishment," *Scottish Journal of Theology* 53 (2000): esp. 455. See also Louise Hickman's essay "Love Is All and God Is Love: Universalism in Peter Sterry (1613–1672) and Jeremiah White (1630–1707)," in *"All Will Be Well": Explorations in Universalism and Christian Theology, from Origen to Moltmann*, ed. Gregory MacDonald (Eugene, OR: Cascade, 2011), 95–115.

A New Augustinian Problem of Evil

It has often been said that traditional Augustinians believe in hell but wish that universalism could be true, even though it is not. I have tried to show that it is possible to be an Augustinian and a universalist, and that this does no violence to the notion of retributive justice lying behind the traditional Augustinian model of hell, which has been the theological stumbling block to universalism for the Augustinian. In fact, it is possible to satisfy the requirements of retributive justice and offer the prospect that all people will necessarily be saved.

However, there may be other grounds that lead the Augustinian theist to retain his or her notion of a particular atonement and limited number of elect. It might be argued that this is the plain teaching of Scripture and that, although the argument for Augustinian universalism is a possible alternative to traditional Augustinianism (perhaps even conceding that it is consistent with traditional Augustinianism in all its major points except this one respect), it simply does not reflect the teaching of the Bible. This is undeniably the view of the majority of Christian thinkers down through the ages.[31]

Nevertheless, even if this is the case and traditional Augustinianism is demonstrably the doctrine of the Bible, the argument for Augustinian universalism raises a problem of evil that traditional Augustinians must address. It is this: if God could have created the

---

31. Stephen T. Davis articulates pretty much the majority view in "Universalism, Hell, and the Fate of the Ignorant," *Modern Theology* 6, no. 2 (1990): 176–77. Thomas Talbott maintains that the consistent teaching of the New Testament is universalistic. See his "Doctrine of Everlasting Punishment," 19–20. There are several other contemporary theologians who hold to a similar position, and their number is growing. See, e.g., Gregory MacDonald, *The Evangelical Universalist*, 2nd ed.(Eugene, OR: Cascade, 2012); Brad Jersak, *Her Gates Will Never Be Shut: Hope, Hell, and the New Jerusalem* (Eugene, OR: Wipf & Stock, 2010); and Jan Bonda, *The One Purpose of God: An Answer to the Doctrine of Eternal Punishment* (Grand Rapids, MI: Eerdmans, 1998). The most sophisticated philosophical defense of universalism to date is Eric Reitan and John Kronen, *God's Final Victory: A Comparative Philosophical Case for Universalism* (New York: Bloomsbury, 2011).

sort of world outlined in Augustinian universalism, why did God not do so, given that there appears to be no reason, according to the tenets of traditional Augustinianism we have examined, why God could not create a world where all human agents were in fact elect because all their sin was dealt with in Christ. Or alternatively, to return to the arbitrariness problem for traditional Augustinians, God could actualize a world where only one moral agent was in hell and all other agents were elect. (We might call this version of Augustinianism the "limited-damnation view.") Both of these options satisfy the retribution thesis beloved of Augustinians and appear to display the glory of God in a way that is objectively better than the world that God did, in fact, create.

5

Universalism and Particularism

The great and universal end of God's creating the world was to communicate himself. God is a communicative being. This communication is really only to intelligent beings: the communication of himself to their understandings is his glory, and the communication of himself with respect to their wills, the enjoying faculty, is their happiness. God created the world for the shining forth of his excellency and for the flowing forth of his happiness. It don't make God the happier to be praised, but it is a becoming and condecent and worthy thing for infinite and supreme excellency to shine forth: 'tis not his happiness but his excellency so to do.

— Jonathan Edwards, *miscellany*

In chapter 4, I argued that, contrary to popular belief, the central tenets of traditional Augustinianism (of which the Reformed are a species) are in fact compatible with a version of universalism. Augustinians usually claim that only a particular group of humanity less than the total number of human beings (the elect) is the object of special divine grace and will be saved. The rest of humanity (the reprobate) are the object of only common grace and will not be saved. But, if Augustinianism is compatible with universalism, then this claim is false: all human beings are the objects of special divine grace and will be saved; none will be rejected. Naturally, most Augustinians will reject such reasoning on the basis of their understanding of the biblical-theological case upon which their argument stands or falls. However, this sets up an Augustinian problem of evil: if God, on the basis of Augustinian principles, could have elected all humanity to salvation and did not, then God does not appear to be benevolent. Thus, the problem posed by the soteriological problem of evil can be solved according to Augustinian principles, but at the cost of embracing a version of universalism.

But is universalism a problem for those who believe that not all of humanity is the object of special (that is, saving) divine grace? In this chapter, I shall explore two ways in which an Augustinian could rebut the argument of Augustinian universalism, in order to show that God may well have good reason for rejecting some of humanity. One of these rebuttals is unsuccessful; the other is, I think, a successful rejoinder to the Augustinian universalist thesis. In the course of the argument, I will not make any comment about the form that damnation might take, whether temporary or everlasting punishment or annihilation (or something else).[1] Instead, I shall restrict my remarks to a defense of the view that salvation is restricted to an elect that is less than the total number of humanity. Let us call this view "particularism" or "particular salvation," because the idea here is that salvation is effective only for that group of humans (less than the totality of humanity) whom God has elected to be the objects of

---

1. For example, it could be that God "reprograms" those who reject God, so that they desire God and are ultimately saved. Thomas Talbott has espoused such a view. He thinks it is a good and beneficial thing if God acts in this way toward recalcitrant sinners. I am less sanguine about this. It seems to me that if God has to reprogram sinners in order to ensure their salvation, as Talbott claims, this significantly reduces the appeal of Talbott's argument for universalism on the basis of libertarianism; for if human beings have significant moral freedom in all moral decisions apart from the one momentous decision humans can make, namely, choosing or rejecting God, then the moral utility of Talbott's libertarianism is greatly reduced. See his several contributions to the debate—"Towards a Better Understanding of Universalism," "Christ Victorious," "A Pauline Interpretation of Divine Judgement," and "Reply to My Critics"—in *Universal Salvation? The Current Debate*, ed. Robin Parry and Christopher Partridge (Grand Rapids, MI: Eerdmans, 2004), and "The Doctrine of Everlasting Punishment," *Faith and Philosophy* 7 (1990): 19–42.

God's special grace. In this way it is particular to these people. (Of course, universalism could be said to be particularist. A universalist could claim that salvation is particularly and effectively applied to all humanity. But theologians usually reserve the term *particularist* for those who maintain that salvation refers to an elect less than the totality of humanity. It is in this sense that we shall deploy the term here.)

Some Initial Distinctions

We shall begin by making clear some of the terms of the argument. Let "the elect" refer to that group of human beings who are the objects of special divine grace, who will be saved—perhaps all humanity, perhaps only some. The notion of "election" we shall use does not specify the number of people who are among the elect. And let "the reprobate" refer to those humans who are objects of only common grace and who will ultimately be rejected by God. Once again, this does not specify the number of reprobate. It is conceivable that no one is numbered among the elect apart from Christ.[2] All humanity could be the object of common divine grace but not special divine grace. However, I take it that this is not a live option in Christian theology. For present purposes, "special grace" refers to the grace conferred on a particular individual by God that ensures his or her salvation. "Common grace" refers to that grace supplied by God to all humanity, including such things as being created and sustained by God, having and enjoying the pleasures and beauty of the created order, and so on. In this way, the elect are the objects of both common and special grace, whereas the reprobate are the

---

2. This claim should be distinguished from Barth's view that Christ is the Elect One and humanity as a whole is somehow derivatively elect "in" him—a matter to which we shall return in chapter 6. My claim here is just that the set of the elect could have comprised one member only: Christ. Then no one else would be elect; everyone else would be damned.

objects of only common grace. In addition, let "universalism" refer to any one of that family of arguments which maintain that (a) God is essentially benevolent, and (b) God necessarily will bring about or ensure that all human beings are ultimately saved.[3]

In the recent philosophical literature, universalist theories have usually been distinguished as either necessary (hard) or contingent (soft), as was mentioned in passing at the beginning of chapter 4. There are some drawbacks to this distinction, however. Recall that necessary universalism is the view that it is not merely true but *necessarily* true that all humanity will ultimately be reconciled to God. Contingent universalism is the view that is it merely true as a matter of contingent fact that all humanity will ultimately be reconciled to God.[4] The problem with this putative distinction between different versions of universalism is that contingent universalism turns out not to be a true universalism, that is, one that can guarantee a universalist outcome. Jonathan Kvanvig claims that contingent universalism fails because it only modally masks the moral problem of hell. In other words, contingent universalism means that, as a matter of contingent fact, in the actual world, no one will be damned; all people will be ultimately saved. But, if universalism is merely a contingent fact, a fact that obtains in this world but that might not have obtained had things been different, then there are some possible worlds where not

---

3. Compare Trevor Hart, who cites Richard Bauckham with approval as saying, "Only the belief that ultimately all men will be saved is common to universalists. The rationale for that belief and the total theological content in which it belongs vary considerably." Cited in Hart, "Universalism: Two Distinct Types," in *Universalism and the Doctrine of Hell,* ed. Nigel M. de S. Cameron (Carlisle, UK: Paternoster, 1992), 2. It is true that there are numerous arguments for the conclusion of universal salvation, but my interest is in the logical form of these arguments, not in the variety of arguments.

4. See Jonathan L. Kvanvig, *The Problem of Hell* (New York: Oxford University Press, 1993), 74, for these characterizations of necessary and contingent universalism. Kvanvig has returned to this discussion in "Universalism and the Problem of Hell," in *Destiny and Deliberation: Essays in Philosophical Theology* (Oxford: Oxford University Press, 2011), chap. 3. There, Kvanvig rehearses his earlier distinctions and offers a rather different rebuttal of universalism, but one that does not include Augustinian universalism as we have characterized it.

everyone is saved and some people do end up in hell; in which case the moral problem of hell remains, albeit in a counterfactual form. (For if there are worlds at which some people are damned to hell, then this raises a serious concern about the justice of God, the concern that motivates Augustinian universalism in the first place.)

The problem with contingent universalism is that it does not satisfy the second conjunct of a definition of universalism (that is, item *b* in the foregoing definition). If a requirement for a given theory about eschatological salvation is that God brings it about or somehow ensures that all humanity is ultimately saved, this cannot be met by contingent universalism; for in contingent universalism, there are possible worlds where not all humanity is saved. The fact that, according to contingent universalism, all the members of the human race in the actual world are saved (it is hoped) is not sufficient to meet the requirement of this aspect of universalist theories. To show why this is the case, consider the following scenario, which uses the nomenclature introduced to these debates by Alvin Plantinga.[5]

Let us imagine a world populated by human beings with libertarian (that is, strong) free will. To borrow an Alvinism, God weakly actualizes such a world. In this world, all human beings suffer from transworld depravity. That is, they all have the property of being depraved. Their individual essences (which may be defined, roughly, as that conjunctive property which a concrete individual possesses whose conjuncts are all those properties essential to the being of that person) cannot be actualized without the property of depravity. So, in every possible world in which such a person exists, he or she exists as depraved: hence "transworld" depravity.[6] Individuals who are transworld depraved are sinners; they are in

---

5. See Alvin Plantinga, *The Nature of Necessity* (Oxford: Oxford University Press, 1974), chap. 9.
6. I am not concerned here to argue whether human beings have transworld depravity. I am concerned only to use Plantinga's ideas in order to show that contingent universalism is a nonstarter.

need of salvation. As a matter of contingent fact, not all of these individuals freely choose salvation during this earthly existence; but, happily for those who are recalcitrant in their depravity, they are all given second chances postmortem while in a hell-like environment that is sufficiently unpleasant to make them realize, at some point in their existence there, that it might be a good idea to repent, become objects of special divine grace, and ask permission to leave their unpleasant abode and enter heaven. Better still, as a matter of contingent fact, all those recalcitrant sinners in this temporary hell-like state eventually do repent and become objects of special divine grace. Thus, ultimately all humanity is saved, though not all in this present life.

This sort of counterfactual thought experiment has been popular in the recent philosophical literature on hell; but it is specious for a number of reasons, several of which are pertinent to the question of the incoherence of contingent universalism. To begin with it is not clear (to me at least), that individuals with transworld depravity will all, at some point in their existence, either in this life or in some postmortem existence, choose God. Perhaps some forms of sin are so habitual and so ingrained in an individual that no matter how many chances to repent such a person is offered, he or she will always refuse.[7]

Corollaries to this notion are not hard to find. Consider the case of those who are substance abusers, physically and psychologically addicted to alcohol or drugs. Some such people, however many chances they are given to rehabilitate, are never able to kick their drug habits. Some even die as a result. Their habit has become so ingrained that they cannot conceive of life without it; or perhaps

---

7. Kvanvig offers other lines of reasoning for rejecting contingent universalism in "Universalism and the Problem of Hell" that are worth consulting. Kevin Timpe's discussion in *Free Will in Philosophical Theology* (New York: Bloomsbury, 2014), chap. 5, also repays careful reading.

they are so enthralled to the substance they abuse that they cannot conceive of any way of living without its support; or they have become so "weak-willed" that they cannot seriously consider a life in which they are not enthralled to this drug. Whatever the reason for their continued addiction, there are addicts like this who never manage to live without their drug of choice, once addicted to it. One might think this is the case because such people have only a finite number of chances to change. If they were given an infinite amount of chances to change (or at least many more chances), they would eventually kick their habit.

However, one might think that the fact that an infinite number of chances are on offer does not mean that a particular sinner will require an infinite number of chances to make up his mind to serve God; a very large finite amount of chances might do. Perhaps this is so. Even if it is, though, it still raises the question of moral consequences. Presumably, for contingent universalists, the potential but unactualized alternative is to remain in the hell-like state forever. And presumably, some contingent universalist will think that the number of chances recalcitrant sinners need to be given in order to come to salvation is a small price to pay for the end result of universal salvation in the actual world. Such a solution to this moral-consequence problem for postmortem second-chance doctrines might be viewed as a form of satisficing consequentialism, a less-than-optimal solution that nevertheless is morally justified in view of the outcome. It is less than optimal because it raises questions about the justice of giving one opportunity after another for salvation until the desired outcome is reached. It might be thought that such a constitution of things skews divine justice, because, as a matter of contingent fact, no human being in the actual world will ever suffer the fitting desert for sinning against an infinite and perfect being.

But contingent universalists cannot say, in addition to this, that no human being who exists in the actual world could *ever* suffer the fitting desert for sinning against an infinite and perfect being, for the fact that no one actually suffers this moral consequence is merely a matter of contingent fact (if it is a contingent fact in this world). There are possible worlds, possible states of affairs, and possible situations in which the recalcitrant sinner never chooses to serve God and does suffer the consequences in hell. This seems to count against the universal aspect of contingent universalism.

However, one might think that it counts only against the modal aspect of the argument. At least in the actual world, all humanity is saved. If we are skeptical about the semantics of possible worlds, we might say that this is all that counts in the matter of who is saved. For the sake of the argument, let us concede this point to the contingent universalist. Even if we were to overlook the problem of modal masking that contingent universalism involves, there is a further, debilitating issue. This is that the contingent universalist cannot ensure the consequence of her position. It simply does not follow from a contingent matter of fact that all people will be saved; for how can this outcome be assured if it is contingent on the libertarian free choices of human beings? And if the inevitable salvation of all cannot be guaranteed, then I fail to see how contingent universalism is truly a version of *universalism*. As John Hick, himself a contingent universalist, admits,

> The customary proof of universalism runs as follows: The God whom we worship is a God of love, whose gracious purpose is to save all men. God's relation to the universe, as its creator and ruler, is such that he is able to fulfil his purposes. Therefore all men will in the end be saved. However, confronting this reasoning is an equally perspicuous disproof. This does not deny the premises that it is God's loving purpose to save all men. But it adds another premise that apparently prohibits us from drawing the universalist conclusion. This additional premise is that God

has endowed us with a genuine freedom, so that we cannot be saved without our own positive and voluntary response to him.

From which argument Hick draws the following conclusion:

> It therefore remains possible that some will fail to co-operate and will instead become so hardened in a self-enclosed blindness as never to respond to God. Accordingly, we are not entitled to make the positive affirmation that all *will* eventually be saved.[8]

This, it seems to me, counts conclusively against contingent universalism's being a version of universalism at all. It might be better to speak of it instead as "optimistic particularism" so as to avoid confusing it with necessary universalism. This, in turn, should be distinguished from a weaker but more defensible doctrine, namely, "hopeful universalism." This is the view that we hope all will be saved, though we cannot guarantee it, which sounds something like Hick's position and can be found in the work of modern theologians like Hans Urs von Balthasar. This is not a species of universalism strictly speaking but, rather, the hope that all will be saved. It is the difference between the whole class being invited to and participating in Smith's birthday party, and the hope that the whole class will participate in Smith's birthday party to which they have been invited. To my way of thinking, the only form of universalism that can guarantee the salvation of all is necessary universalism, of which Augustinian universalism is an example. It is to this sort of argument that we shall address ourselves in the remainder of this chapter.

The Argument against Particularism

Let us begin the argument proper by laying out the case against particularism. For present purposes, I shall be dealing with

---

8. John Hick, *Death and Eternal Life* (London: Collins, 1976), 242–43 (original emphasis).

particularists in the Augustinian tradition (in a manner similar to chapter 4), which includes the Reformed. Recall that the phrase "Augustinian tradition" is a term of art. Nevertheless, I think it represents the majority of classical Christian theologians who have been (a) compatibilists on the question of free will (that is, God's determining what comes to pass is compatible with human freedom and moral responsibility for their actions) and (b) particularists with respect to salvation. Such Augustinians have traditionally claimed that God restricts the number of elect to some number less than the total number of humanity. This we called the restricted-elect view. It has three parts:

- The need for an infinite retributive punishment to be meted out for the sin of those human agents who are fallen

- The need for sin to be atoned for (in Christ's death on the cross), for sinful human agents to be counted among the elect

- The need for the display of both God's grace and mercy and God's wrath and justice in the created order

A few brief comments on each of these three conditions are in order. First, Augustinians claim that divine justice as it bears upon human sin is principally retributive rather than, say, reformative. A central moral intuition here is that the punishment must fit the crime. Let us say that God is a being of infinite worth and honor. Then a single sin against an infinite being incurs an infinite demerit, which is worthy of an infinite punishment. So, the fit between crime and punishment means that all human beings are worthy of an infinite punishment by virtue of being sinners who sin. Second, Christ's work (in particular, although not exclusively, his work on the cross) is the only means by which human sin can be dealt with. The idea here is that God cannot simply forgive sin or ignore it or pretend it never happened or pass it by. God's nature as a holy and just God requires that God deal with sin by punishing sin. Third, both the divine mercy and divine justice must be displayed to all creation in order that the divine nature is vindicated and God is seen to be a good and just being, both gracious and merciful and justly judgmental of all wrongdoing.

The problem with the constitutive factors of a restricted-elect view is that they can all be met in a version of necessary universalism that is compatible with traditional Augustinianism:

1. God decrees to create and elect all humanity.
2. God decrees that the mechanism by which the sin of all human agents is atoned for is the death of Christ.
3. The sin and guilt accruing to all sinful human agents are transferred to Christ, who is punished on their account on the cross.
4. All human agents are saved; none are lost, and none are in hell.

This argument is compatible with the restricted-elect view for the following reasons. First, all sin is dealt with in an infinite punishment (or a punishment of infinite worth), namely, the punishment Christ suffers on the cross. Assuming that Christ's death has an infinite worth, or at least a worth equal to the atonement of all human agents, Christ's death can atone for the sin of all. But this means that divine justice is meted out to Christ. God's justice and mercy are displayed in the created order, and God's name is vindicated via the death of the Son, whose sacrifice displays the divine wrath against all sin, dealt with by Christ's work. Moreover, Christ's sacrifice also shows forth divine mercy to all humanity. Thus, sin is dealt with and atoned for by Christ's work, and no violence is done to the divine nature in the process.

As we saw in chapter 4, this seems to be a very serious argument against traditional Augustinian particularism. Without a response to it, Augustinians are left with three possible options. First, they admit defeat and become necessary universalists. This is, of course, possible. A number of theologians who claim to be in the Augustinian tradition have embraced universalism, although none that I know of have done so via this sort of argument. Almost all who have done so have abandoned one or more constituent of the restricted-elect view. My point is that an Augustinian can remain entirely orthodox in his or her Augustinianism and embrace universalism. In case some think that such a view is very far from classical Augustinianism, I cite Benjamin B. Warfield, who, although not defending a version of universalism as such, is nevertheless far more sanguine about the number of those saved than Calvinists are often thought to be:

> It must be borne well in mind that particularism and parsimony in salvation are not equivalent conceptions; and it is a mere caricature of Calvinistic particularism to represent it as finding its center in the proclamation that there are few that are saved. . . . So far as the principles of sovereignty and particularism are concerned, there is no reason why a Calvinist might not be a universalist in the most express meaning of that term, holding that each and every human soul shall be saved; and in point of fact some Calvinists (forgetful of the Scripture here) have been universalists in this most express meaning of the term.[9]

Alternatively, Augustinians could fall back upon a biblical argument in favor of particularism. And this is what Augustinians usually do. However, as I pointed out in chapter 4, this is not a happy option for the Augustinian, because it generates an Augustinian problem of evil: if God could have created a world where God saved all humanity yet has not done so (because the Bible says God has not), why has

9. Benjamin B. Warfield, *The Plan of Salvation*, rev. ed. (Grand Rapids, MI: Eerdmans, 1975), 97–98. Compare Paul Helm's essay "Are They Few That Be Saved?," in Cameron, *Universalism and the Doctrine of Hell*, for more on this question.

God not done so? There seems to be no good philosophical reason for God's not doing so, apart from the argument of Scripture, and a very strong moral argument for doing so.

A third option is for traditional Augustinians to abandon Augustinianism for some version of global theological libertarianism, in which case the problems raised by the restricted-elect view do not arise; because, as I take it, global libertarianism is not consistent with the notion that God ordains and brings about (that is, ensures) the salvation of anyone. (Recall that libertarian Calvinism concedes that some decisions pertaining to personal salvation are not free choices, so that there are certain things ordained by God over which we creatures have no control or say. This is different from what I am calling global theological libertarianism. One important difference is that the libertarian Calvinist can opt for a doctrine of election like the one envisaged in the restricted-elect view, with all the problems this raises regarding Augustinian universalism.)

There is a fourth option: embrace the contradiction. But I take it that this is not a live option for traditional Augustinians who wish to remain traditional Augustinians.

The Argument for Particularism

So what is the poor Augustinian particularist to do? I want to suggest two possible ways in which Augustinian particularists could rebut the argument of Augustinian universalism without giving up either their Augustinianism or their convictions about particularism, convictions that are usually taken to be rooted in Scripture. Of these two arguments the first fails, but the second succeeds in counteracting the argument of Augustinian universalism. (There may well be other arguments for this conclusion that I have not encountered or thought of. That is all to the good. My claim is merely that there are two such arguments, one of which seems to be cogent.)

John Owen on the Necessity of Faith for Salvation

The first argument in favor of Augustinian particularism has been suggested to me in reading through book 3 of John Owen's *The Death of Death in the Death of Christ*. In the course of enumerating a number of arguments against universal atonement and in favor of a particular redemption, Owen makes the following claim: "I cannot . . . be persuaded that God hath made a covenant of grace with all, especially those who never heard a word of covenant, grace, or condition of it, much less received grace for the fulfilling of the condition; without which the whole world would be altogether unprofitable and useless." The central reason behind this claim is that Owen thinks faith is a necessary condition for salvation. If salvation cannot be had without faith and if many human beings never have faith in Christ, then many human beings are not saved by Christ's work. It would be useless to say that God could effectually procure the salvation of all human beings through the work of Christ but then not ensure that they all had faith in order to make that effectual salvation effective in the life of individual human beings:

> In brief; an intention of doing good unto any one upon the performance of such a condition as the intender knows is absolutely above the strength of him of whom it is required,—especially if he knows that it can no way be done but by his concurrence, and he is resolved not to yield that assistance which is necessary to the actual accomplishment of it—is a vain and fruitless flourish.[10]

Let us call Owen's argument the "requirement-of-faith argument," or "RF argument" for short. There are several things that can be said by way of response to this line of argument, assuming the view, common among Augustinians, that saving faith is a gift of God's

---

10. John Owen, *The Death of Death in the Death of Christ*, in *The Works of John Owen*, ed. William H. Goold, vol. 10 (1850–53; repr., Edinburgh: Banner of Truth, 1967), 3.2, pp. 237 and 242, respectively.

grace, not an action that originates with human choice (see, for example, Eph. 2:8-9). Even if the gift of saving faith is committed to human beings in such a way that involves human action in concurrence with divine action, the point is that human choice alone is insufficient for saving faith. At the very least, in an Augustinian model of salvation, God and the human being in question are both necessary but only jointly sufficient conditions for saving faith. Some Roman Catholic Augustinians seem to take a view similar to this one. Other Augustinians advocate a stronger position than this. In fact, Owen's view, in common with that of many other Reformed theologians, is considerably stronger than this, denying that the human will is able to choose divine grace without the interposition of prior divine grace to enable that choice. Be that as it may, my point here is simply to show that, even if an Augustinian were to take the weaker view and allow a concurrence between human choice and divine choice (however that might come about), the human choice is not sufficient for saving faith without the divine will's acting upon it.

With this condition in place, let us assume for the sake of argument that faith in Christ is a necessary condition for salvation, as per the RF argument. Then either God gives faith to all and all are saved, or God gives faith to some and they are saved, or to none and none are saved. Owen says God does not give faith to all, because all are not saved. Many human agents are born and die without a knowledge of Christ and without faith in him. So, on the logic of his position, these individuals cannot be saved. Perhaps this is true; but how does this help rebut Augustinian universalism? Recall that Augustinian universalism says merely that God *could* save all people and that this is consistent with the tenets of Augustinian thinking. The problem Augustinian universalism raises is that God could have brought about a world both Augustinian and universalist, not that God has done so.

For the idea here is that if God *could* have done this, God *should* have done this, even if, in fact, God has not done this.

Owen's argument can be incorporated into a version of Augustinian universalism. We could say God creates an Augustinian universalist world and ensures that all human beings attain salvation by faith in Christ. Naturally, not all will do so in this life, because not all people will hear about Christ or have the chance to trust in him. But God could surely ensure that all have such a chance either immediately prior to bodily death (in a near-death experience, say) or postmortem. Presumably, God could ensure that all those who have not believed in Christ during this life do so in some postmortem existence and are acted upon by divine grace in such an irresistible way that they all (eventually) choose Christ and are saved. There is no element of contingency here, as there is with contingent universalism, because God ensures that all have a saving faith, as per Eph. 2:8-9. If a follower of Owen were to respond by saying that, whether or not God could have done this, God has not done this, so such reasoning is idle, then he or she has missed the point of the Augustinian universalist argument. The point is this: if God could have done this and there is no moral impediment to God's doing this, why has God not done so? So it seems that the addition of the faith condition of the RF argument to traditional Augustinianism does not rebut Augustinian universalism.

We might take this Owen-type argument in a different way, however. Perhaps saving faith is not a condition of salvation, because knowledge of this salvation is not a prerequisite of salvation. We might put it like this: a particular salvific event could be *ontologically* necessary for salvation but not *epistemically* necessary for salvation. Then, Christ's saving work is ontologically necessary for my salvation (his death has to be efficacious for me); but it does not follow from this that I have to know that it is efficacious for me.

Famously, Karl Rahner maintained something like this in his doctrine of anonymous Christianity:

> If, however, he [the righteous pagan] has experienced the grace of God—if, in certain circumstances, he has already accepted this grace as the ultimate, unfathomable entelechy [realization of what was previously only potential] of his existence by accepting the immeasurableness of his dying existence as opening out into infinity—then he has already been given revelation in a true sense even before he has been affected by missionary preaching from without.[11]

Let us call this second line of argument the "inclusivist-universalist Augustinian argument," or "IUA argument." (For present purposes, I am assuming that inclusivism, the doctrine with which Rahner's "anonymous Christianity" is often associated, is just the view that Christ's work is ontologically but not epistemically necessary for salvation. Hence inclusivist-universalist Augustinianism.) Perhaps Augustinian universalists could say that those who do not know and trust Christ may yet be saved via Christ's work even if they are ignorant of that work.

One might think that if I do not know that some event would be salvific for me, it cannot be salvific for me, because I would not know I was saved. But this is surely mistaken. Let us say that my wife will treat me to a special birthday meal at a local restaurant this evening. I, however, am blissfully unaware that she has arranged this. Clearly, my present ignorance of a future birthday treat has no bearing on whether my wife will actually treat me to this meal. She will take me out for a meal although I do not know this now and

---

11. Karl Rahner, "Religious Inclusivism," in *Philosophy of Religion: Selected Readings*, ed. Michael Peterson et al., 4th ed. (New York: Oxford University Press, 2010), 511. I say that Rahner endorsed something like this in his version of inclusivism because it is not clear that his anonymous-Christianity doctrine actually entails that those with no knowledge of Christ will be saved. He seems to think that there is a sort of subconscious or unconscious knowledge of Christ that means some righteous pagans will be saved, even if that knowledge is never exercised in conscious faith in Christ in this life.

will not know it until we walk into the restaurant foyer. In a similar fashion, current ignorance of some future salvation has no bearing upon whether one is among those who will be saved. Transpose this thinking onto the Christian scheme of salvation: A headhunter from Papua New Guinea never knows the great things of the gospel. He eats every missionary sent to him before the poor creatures manage to utter a word about the good news. Lacking any other means by which he might come to a knowledge of Christ, the headhunter dies ignorant of the gospel. Is he damned? According to Owen's RF argument, he is. But why should we follow Owen in this? Assume with Augustinian universalism that the headhunter, like the whole of humanity, is among the elect, saved via Christ's work. He does not know now and will not know in this life that he is one of the elect. To be sure, his salvation will be a great surprise to him. But it could be that he is saved via the salvific event of Christ's work even if he is ignorant of that work. Owen's point is that the only effective way in which a person can be in a position to benefit from the work of Christ is to be given the faith to participate in the benefits of that work. But that need not apply if God actualizes a world where the work of Christ is automatically applied to each individual person whether or not he or she is aware of it (that is, where conscious faith in Christ is not a requirement of salvation).

This IUA argument may be stretching the "Augustinian" component of Augustinian universalism somewhat. One might think that someone who takes such a view ceases to be an Augustinian, because Augustinians would agree with Owen that faith is a necessary condition of salvation. Well, perhaps something like that is right—but perhaps not. Maybe a weaker version of the IUA view can be made compatible with the biblical claims that faith is a prerequisite of salvation for human beings, adding that this is the normal or conventional but not necessarily the *only* way in which human beings are saved. Maybe some human beings, like the Old Testament saints, have no saving knowledge of Christ (no conscious faith in Christ) and yet are saved via Christ's work.[12] It seems to me that many Christian theologians would accept this. But this does not denigrate faith. Faith is still the normal means to salvation if one accepts this particular version of IUA universalism. Nor does it mean that, on the basis of such an argument as this, Christians have no reason to proselytize those who are ignorant of salvation because they will be saved whether or not they hear of the gospel. Surely it is better to know one is saved than to be in ignorance of the fact? Surely it is better to know where one is bound rather than to go blindly there? The point I am making here is that a person could be saved irrespective of whether she knew she was saved, not that there is a moral equivalence between being in a state of ignorance about one's salvation and being in a state where one is aware of it. So, although this IUA counterargument to Owen's RF view requires the Augustinian to give up the necessity of saving faith in Christ for all humanity, this need not be so great a concession, provided some argument can be mounted to show that those who never hear the gospel and die in ignorance of it might be sufficiently like the Old Testament saints or those incapable of conscious faith who are in just this sort of position with respect to salvation.

Owen is not unaware of the sorts of responses that might be made to his view (although he does not respond to exactly the sorts of arguments I have mounted here). On the question of the requirement of faith as a necessary condition for salvation, he has this to say:

---

12. Of course, there are other limit cases, too, also mentioned in chapter 4. How can severely mentally handicapped people be saved, or children who die in childbirth? If the Augustinian believes that (at least some) such persons will be among the elect, then conscious faith in Christ cannot be a requirement for salvation, contra Owen.

That unbelief, is it a sin, or is it not? If it be not, how can it be a cause of damnation? If it be, Christ died for it, or he did not. If he did not, then he died not for the sins of all men. If he did, why is this an obstacle to their salvation? Is there any new shift to be invented for this? Or must we be contented with the old, namely, because they do not believe? That is, Christ did not die for their unbelief, or rather, did not by his death remove their unbelief, because they would not believe, or because they would not themselves remove their unbelief; or he died for their unbelief conditionally, that they were not unbelievers. These do not seem to me to be sober assertions.[13]

This is a rather compressed argument, so I shall unpack it a little in order to make its structure clear:

1. Unbelief is a sin and is a cause of damnation.

Unbelief is a sin because it involves not giving due honor and regard to God. Presumably, unbelief is not the only cause of damnation. Possession of a corrupt moral nature supplied by original sin would be another cause—in fact, the very thing that gives rise to unbelief in the first place.

2. Either Christ died for the sinful unbelief of all humanity, or he did not.
3. If Christ did not die for the sinful unbelief of all humanity, then he did not die for all the sins of all humanity, and all are not saved.

The reason for this is as follows:

4. If Christ had died for the sinful unbelief of all humanity, he would have atoned for the unbelief of all humanity as one of the sins of all humanity, and all humanity would have been saved.

---

13. Owen, *Works*, 10:249.

But, says Owen, the evidence of Scripture and experience shows that not all are saved. Alternatively, there is this possibility:

5. If Christ did die for the sinful unbelief of all humanity, then all humanity would be saved, because he would have atoned for all the sin of humanity, unbelief included.
6. But then unbelief would not be an obstacle to salvation, and (presumably) all would be saved.

Owen thinks that this counts against the doctrine of universal atonement, though we can adapt his reasoning to Augustinian universalism. All are not saved, so Christ cannot have died to save them from their sinful unbelief; otherwise they would be saved from it. But is that right? In Augustinian universalism, Christ does atone for unbelief, because he atones for all sin. How is it, then, that some go to the grave without a knowledge of Christ and are saved? Perhaps because, like the patriarchs, they go to some postmortem existence where Christ is revealed to them in a saving fashion. Or perhaps conscious faith is not a requirement for salvation, and the work of Christ can be applied to all human beings irrespective of whether they have conscious faith in Christ. So, it seems, Owen's reasoning, when adapted to present purposes, does not offer a convincing argument against Augustinian universalism.

A New Argument for Particularism

In the last section of this chapter, I want to offer a new argument in defense of an Augustinian account of particularism that may fare better than the argument adapted from Owen.

The question of whether God must create the best possible world is a hoary old chestnut in the philosophy of religion. Philosophers have been divided over the question of whether the notion of a best possible world even makes sense and, if it does, whether God has to create the best anyway. I side with Richard Swinburne on this question. He maintains that there can be no best possible world, because, for any optimal world we care to imagine, it can always be made better by the addition of one more person or one more planet, such that the overall objective moral worth of that particular world is greater than the previous world, and so on ad infinitum.[14] Swinburne is not alone in his denial of a best-possible-world thesis. Thomas Aquinas famously denied that there was a single optimal sort of world that God had to create. There is, Thomas argued, an infinite number of possible worlds all compatible with divine benevolence, and God could have chosen to bring about any one of them:

> God, in willing his own goodness, wills things other than himself to be insofar as they participate in his goodness. But, since the divine goodness is infinite, it can be participated in in infinite ways, and in ways other than it is participated in by the creatures that now exist. If, then, as a result of willing his own goodness, God necessarily willed the things that participated in it, it would follow that he would will the existence of an infinity of creatures participating in his goodness in an infinity of ways. This is patently false, because, if he willed them, they would be, since his will is the principle of being for things, as will be shown later on. Therefore God does not necessarily will even the things that now exist.[15]

This sort of reasoning seems plausible to me. Let us assume, for the sake of argument, that it is plausible. And let us assume, with classical Christian theology, that God is essentially benevolent, that is, essentially morally and metaphysically good. Then, according to Thomas, there is no single best possible world God could and should

---

14. See Richard Swinburne, *The Existence of God,* rev. ed. (Oxford: Oxford University Press, 1991), 113ff.

15. Thomas Aquinas, *Summa contra gentiles,* 1.81.4. Katherin Rogers's discussion of this issue is helpful. See Rogers, *Perfect Being Theology* (Edinburgh: Edinburgh University Press, 1998), 103–4.

have created. In fact, there are an infinite number of worlds God could have created consistent with God's benevolence.

Let us add to this a further notion: that this world, and worlds very similar to this one, are among the set of worlds that God could have created, because they are worlds consistent with divine benevolence. This seems plausible. For consider the following sort of reasoning: Salvation is a matter of divine grace, not divine obligation. That is, God is not obliged to save anyone who is a sinner, although he may do so if he so wishes. I take it that a gracious action is an act of supererogation.[16] That is, it is an act that one did not have to perform but that one chose to perform. By contrast, acts of obligation are acts one should perform. So, love of God might be an obligation. I am obliged, on the basis of the Ten Commandments, say, to love and honor God. If I fail in this, I am culpable for my lapse, because I am morally obligated to love God. I am not morally obligated to give a large chunk of my savings to Oxfam (*pace* Peter Singer), but perhaps I do so. If I do, then I perform something that might be supererogatory. Now, if salvation is a work of supererogation, then God could create a world where no one is saved, and this would be a world consistent with God's divine benevolence. In such a world, all human beings would be damned because of their sinfulness; and God would be acting according to God's just nature if God were to damn all humanity. Not only would God be acting according to divine justice but God would also not be acting in a way inconsistent with God's divine benevolence. For if salvation is an act of supererogation, then God cannot be obliged to save anyone. In such a world, God saves no one, and this is consistent with God's benevolence. However, this world does have

16. Robert Adams says that grace means "a disposition to love which is not dependent on the merit of the person loved," in "Must God Create the Best?," in *The Virtue of Faith* (New York: Oxford University Press, 1987), 56. His definition seems weaker than an act of supererogation but not necessarily inconsistent with it.

a significant disadvantage for the Augustinian universalist. It is this: In such a world, divine benevolence and divine grace are not both displayed, because divine grace is not offered to any of the human agents God has made in this world. Yet, as we have already seen, it is an important constituent of traditional Augustinianism that both divine justice and divine mercy are displayed in the creation in order that God's name is vindicated. Thus, although such a world would be consistent with the divine nature, strictly speaking, it would not be consistent with the way in which God behaves according to traditional Augustinianism.

Now, consider a different world. This second sort of world is a particularist world where some, but not all, of humanity are saved. If God were to create this second sort of world, then we might think God would have created a better world than the previous one, a world that is consistent with God's moral nature, strictly speaking. In addition to this, it would be a world consistent with the Augustinian requirement that both divine justice and divine mercy are displayed to the creation. This might be thought to be an objectively morally better sort of world than the world where every human agent is damned. Of course, a world where some people are saved rather than no people will seem to be an objectively morally better world only if we assume that, for any world God could create where n is the number of people saved, a world where $n + 1$ people are saved is an objectively morally better world. But let us assume that this is the case.

Now, here is the question: *Need God do more than this?* Must God create a world better than any of this infinite number of worlds consistent with God's benevolence, where God's justice and mercy are shown forth to all creation in the work of Christ? In other words, for our purposes, must God create an Augustinian universalist world? The answer is clear: God need not do so. The fact that God *could* do so does not mean God *must* do so. All that God has to do is act in accordance with divine nature. Creation of a particularist sort of world that is less than a universalist world is consistent with God's divine nature. But is God obliged to create a universalist world because it is objectively morally better than all other, particularist worlds (given our caveat about what, in matters of salvation, makes a world of great objective moral worth than another world)? No; God is not obliged to do more than act in a way that is consistent with the divine nature. (In fact, it may be that language of obligation does not apply to God at all.)[17] In any case, as Robert Adams has shown, God has no obligations to creatures God has not created. One can have obligations only to things that exist. If God eternally decrees to create a particularist sort of world consistent with God's benevolence, God cannot be said to have an obligation to bring about better worlds, because God cannot have an obligation to worlds and creatures that do not exist. The reasoning is as follows:

> A merely possible being cannot be (actually) wronged or treated unkindly. A being who never exists is not wronged by not being created, and there is no obligation to any possible being to bring it into existence.[18]

Now suppose, with Adams, that the following conditions apply to the world God does create:

a. None of the individual creatures in it would exist in an Augustinian universalist world.

b. None of the creatures in it has a life that is so miserable on the whole that it would be better for that creature if it had never existed.

---

17. For a defense of this claim, see Thomas V. Morris, "On Duty and Divine Goodness" reprinted in *Anselmian Explorations* (Notre Dame, IN: University of Notre Dame Press, 1987).

18. Adams, "Must God Create the Best?," 53.

c. Every individual creature in the world is at least as happy, on the whole, as it would have been in any other possible world in which it could have existed.[19]

Creation of such a world does not thereby wrong any of the creatures contained in it. Nor can God be said to be obliged to create a better world (that is, a universalist world) if, in addition to these conditions (for the purposes of our argument), the world created is consistent with divine benevolence and is a world where some number of human beings less than the total number of human beings are the object of special divine grace and are saved. In fact, I have argued that God could create a world where no one is saved and all are damned because of their sinful natures and that this is also consistent with divine benevolence (although such a world would not be consistent with traditional Augustinianism). It may well be that this world (that is, the actual world) is a particularist world. And it seems to me that such a world is consistent with divine benevolence. So, God has good reason to create a particularist world, and no obligation to create an Augustinian universalist world instead. This rebuts Augustinian universalism.

19. Ibid. (slightly adapted for present purposes).

6

Barthian Universalism?

Barth undoubtedly views all people as elect in Jesus Christ, in whom their true reality is to be found. . . . He rejects the abstract necessity of universalism in logical consequence of the election of all in Christ. . . . Nevertheless, it is not apparent why, in his view, the Holy Spirit in his ministry of calling should not positively fulfil in all individuals the one eternal will of the triune God. A gap arises here that Barth can fill only by an appeal to the divine freedom. . . . The ambivalence at this decisive point—will all be saved or not, and if not, why not?—by no means outweighs the solid merits of Barth's presentation. Nevertheless, it undoubtedly casts something of a shadow over them.
—Geoffrey Bromiley, *Introduction to the Theology of Karl Barth*

In the previous two chapters, dealing with an Augustinian version of universalism, we have already had cause to note in passing Karl Barth's doctrine of election and its apparently universalist implications. Barth's doctrine casts a long shadow over modern theological discussion of the scope of salvation. In this chapter, I want to explore his treatment of the subject of election with a little more care, as a prelude to offering a constructive argument about the scope of salvation in chapter 7, which is a species of hypothetical universalism.

Barth's doctrine of election in *Church Dogmatics* has often been thought to amount to a version of hopeful universalism. Recall that this is the view according to which all human beings may be saved, indeed we hope *will* be saved, though we cannot say definitively *must* be saved. Thus, Bruce McCormack writes, "At the end of the day, Barth's position on 'universalism' is the same as von Balthasar's. Universal salvation is something for which we ought to hope and pray but it is not something we can teach."[1] Similarly, George Hunsinger writes,

> Although Karl Barth is often labeled a "universalist," he is best understood as standing in the tradition of holy silence. If a forced option is urged between the proposition "All are saved" and the counterproposition "Not all are saved," Barth's answer in effect is: "None of the above." Barth deliberately leaves the question open, though not in a neutral fashion, but with a strong tilt towards universal hope.[2]

It is true to say that the majority of Barth scholars today who have studied this topic in detail have thought this, or something very like it. However, this was not always the case, and some of the most eminent Barth scholars of a previous generation were of the opinion that Barth's doctrine either implies universalism or is a species of universalism.[3] My own views about Barth's doctrine have developed over the past decade and are mixed. In part, this is because I think Barth's position is complicated and admits of different interpretations. (The fact that there are such different interpretations of his position

---

1. Bruce L. McCormack, "'So That He May Be Merciful to All': Karl Barth and the Problem of Universalism," in *Karl Barth and American Evangelicalism,* ed. Bruce L. McCormack and Clifford B. Anderson (Grand Rapids, MI: Eerdmans, 2011), 248. Hans Urs von Balthasar's position is set out in his little book *Dare We Hope "That All Men Be Saved"? With a Short Discourse on Hell,* trans. David Kipp and Lothar Krauth (1986, 1987; repr., San Francisco: Ignatius, 2011).

2. George Hunsinger, *Disruptive Grace: Studies in the Theology of Karl Barth* (Grand Rapids, MI: Eerdmans, 2000), 243.

3. Balthasar, in *Dare We Hope,* argues that Barth's doctrine implies universalism. So do Emil Brunner, in *The Christian Doctrine of God,* vol. 1 of *Dogmatics,* trans. Olive Wyon (London: Lutterworth, 1949), 346–53; G. C. Berkouwer, in *The Triumph of Grace in the Theology of Karl Barth,* trans. Harry R. Boer (Grand Rapids, MI: Eerdmans, 1956), 111–16 and 287–96; and Geoffrey W. Bromiley, *Introduction to the Theology of Karl Barth* (Edinburgh: T & T Clark, 1979), 97–98.

from respected Barth scholars should give any reader pause for thought.) There are, we might say, different strands to his doctrine that appear to pull in different directions, and part of the challenge for understanding Barth's doctrine from an analytic-theological point of view is that his theological method draws deeply upon philosophical and theological sensibilities at odds with those prized by analytics.

For one thing, Barth's style of writing theology is very different—not only different from analytic theology but different from much classical theology, too. When reading, say, Anselm of Canterbury or Augustine or John of Damascus, one is immediately struck by the fact that these authors inhabited a world that is, in many ways, much more sympathetic to an analytic way of thinking (broadly understood) than to the modus operandi of Barth. These classical theologians often wrote with a background in classical education, including the arts of rhetoric and logic, and prized a sort of directness and simplicity of expression that make it easy for the reader to grasp what they are trying to convey. However, were we to compare Barth's way of writing to other thinkers in the great Continental tradition of German-speaking thought of the last two hundred years, we would find a much more natural intellectual affinity. In particular, when first reading Barth, one is struck by the dialectical mode of thought. That is, he tends to begin with a thesis statement and then spells out a particular view in accordance with that statement before taking a rather different view, which at times appears to retract what he has said in the previous section of his work, and finally resolving this tension in a further section of his work. In addition, this dialectical way of writing takes Barth some time to unfold—such that the reader must often plow through a good fifty to one hundred pages of reading before she is in a position to grasp the different aspects of the dialect and begin to understand what Barth's view actually amounts to. Finally, Barth does not set out his views on a given doctrine just once before moving to the next topic, as is often the case in classical orthodox Christian theology. Instead, he returns to similar themes again and again. In fact, he remarks in one place that in commencing each part of his *Church Dogmatics,* he, as it were, began his thinking anew.

None of these observations is novel. Barth scholars of the present generation have done the theological world a great service in making plain some of the key themes and motifs in Barth's writings and helping those coming to his works for the first time to understand that reading Barth requires much more patience, and a rather different set of literary sensibilities, than they might have expected having read other theological works. John Webster's introduction to Barth makes the general point well when he speaks of Barth's *Church Dogmatics* as rather like a great piece of orchestral music, a sort of symphony, in which the author develops a leitmotif, or series of key themes to which he returns recurrently as he develops his argument in the whole work.[4] It is not so much a linear way of writing, beginning with premises and leading to a conclusion, as it is a spiral or hermeneutical circle, where the parts must be related to the whole at each point in the development of the argument, and the whole to the parts as they are developed in the body of the work. This is a much more literary way of writing theology than that found in medieval or post-Reformation-school theology. And, as Webster, Hunsinger, and others have pointed out, understanding Barth requires patience and a willingness to attend to the relationship between the thematic leitmotifs as they are developed in *Church Dogmatics* and the whole to which they correspond.[5]

---

4. See John Webster, *Barth,* 2nd ed. (London: T & T Clark, 2004).
5. See, e.g., George Hunsinger, *How to Read Karl Barth: The Shape of His Theology* (Oxford: Oxford University Press, 1991).

That said, there is good reason for trying to make clear and succinct the views Barth takes many pages of his dogmatics to expound. And, just as one might seek to understand Continental philosophers in an analytic mode (such as recent analytic work on Friedrich Nietzsche or Immanuel Kant has done), so one might seek to understand Barth from an analytic perspective, bringing the richness of his thinking into a different intellectual key, so to speak. That is what I endeavor to do in this chapter. I am not trying to shoehorn Barth into a way of doing theology alien to his own dialectical method, as if to make of him another analytic theologian. But I am trying to understand him from the perspective of analytic theology. Such transmethodological discussion can be fruitful and helpful—even vital—for the fructification of theology and as a means to greater understanding between those working with different general approaches to the dogmatic task.

To that end, in this chapter I will defend the following thesis: *that the scope of human salvation envisaged in the theology of Karl Barth either is a species of universalism or comprises several distinct, incompatible strands of doctrine that he does not finally resolve.*[6] In some respects, this lack of a clean final resolution to this doctrine on Barth's part may be due to the dialectical nature of his thought. It may also be a consequence of the fact that he was a careful reader of Scripture and believed that he was not warranted in drawing hard-and-fast conclusions about the scope of salvation from the biblical

---

6. This is not the first time I have ventured (perhaps with more chutzpah than wisdom) to write on this matter. See (in order of publication) Oliver D. Crisp, "On Barth's Denial of Universalism," *Themelios* 29 (2003): 18–29, reprinted with minor changes in *Retrieving Doctrine: Essays in Reformed Theology* (Downers Grove, IL: IVP Academic, 2011); "On the Letter and Spirit of Karl Barth's Doctrine of Election: A Reply to O'Neil," *Evangelical Quarterly* 79 (2007): 53–67; and "Barth and Jonathan Edwards on Reprobation (and Hell)," in *Engaging with Barth: Contemporary Evangelical Critiques,* ed. David Gibson and Daniel Strange (New York: T & T Clark, 2008), 300–322. For my own constructive contribution to the question of the election of Jesus Christ, see *God Incarnate: Explorations in Christology* (London: T & T Clark, 2009), chap. 2.

texts. Desiring to remain faithful to the tension in Holy Writ between the universalistic passages of place, like Colossians 1, and the particularistic passages, like Ephesians 1, Barth chose to refrain from coming down decisively on one or the other side of this apparent biblical divide. There is evidence for this sort of interpretation of Barth's work in this area in *Church Dogmatics*, and it is the conclusion to which at least several prominent contemporary Barth scholars have come on this topic.[7]

However, there are also reasons for thinking that this is not the whole story. (Given that many in the previous generation of Barth scholars thought this as well, it may be that there is something to be said for looking at this topic in a slightly different light.) I remain convinced that there are ultimately unresolved tensions in Barth's understanding of the scope of human salvation and that at least one major strand of his thought drives in the direction of universalism despite the fact that most contemporary Barth scholars seem unwilling to draw this conclusion. I will also offer some explanation as to why many Barth scholars have thought his position both internally consistent and nonuniversalist. Though I do not think this story is necessarily commensurate with all the different aspects of Barth's doctrine, it does go some way toward explaining why there has been so much heat, and not always as much light, generated by this aspect of Barth's thought.

The argument proceeds as follows. First, I shall address Barth's denial of universalism with reference to some of the recent literature on the subject. Then, I shall set out the logic of Barth's doctrine,

---

7. Thus George Hunsinger, "Hellfire and Damnation: Four Ancient and Modern Views," in *Disruptive Grace: Studies in the Theology of Karl Barth* (Grand Rapids, MI: Eerdmans, 2000); and McCormack, "'So That He May Be Merciful to All.'" Also worth noting in this connection is Tom Greggs's article "'Jesus Is Victor': Passing the Impasse of Barth on Universalism," *Scottish Journal of Theology* 60, no. 2 (2007): 196–212. I will return to Greggs's work presently. I should add that divine freedom is never far from Barth's mind when articulating reasons for his particular brand of the doctrine of election.

letting Barth speak for himself as much as possible.[8] In a final section, I offer my own explanation for why Barth's doctrine is so often thought to be nonuniversalist.

Barth's Denial of Universalism

We begin with Barth's apparent denial of universalism. Here, I offer a catena of several such denials from Barth's writings:

> It is His [God's] concern what is to be the final extent of the circle [of salvation]. If we are to respect the freedom of divine grace, we cannot venture the statement that it must and will finally be coincident with the world of man as such (as in the doctrine of the so-called *apokatastasis*). No such right or necessity can legitimately be deduced.[9]

> The Church will not then preach an *apokatastasis*, nor will it preach a powerless grace of Jesus Christ or a wickedness of men which is too powerful for it. But without any weakening of the contrast, and also without any arbitrary dualism, it will preach the overwhelming power of grace and the weakness of human wickedness in the face of it. (*CD* 2.2, p. 477)

> We should be denying or disarming . . . evil . . . and our own participation in it if, in relation to ourselves or others or all men, we were to permit ourselves to postulate a withdrawal of . . . and in this sense to expect or maintain an *apokatastasis* or universal reconciliation as the goal and end of all things. No such postulate can be made even though we appeal to the cross and resurrection of Jesus Christ. Even though theological consistency might seem to lead our thoughts and utterances most clearly in this direction, we must not arrogate to

---

8. I shall not enter into the vexed questions of whether Barth thought that God's being is constituted by God's act, and whether the Son is eternally generated for the express purpose of being the Elect One in order to save fallen humanity. Here, I am interested only in the narrower question of whether Barth taught universalism.

9. Karl Barth, *Church Dogmatics,* eds. Geoffrey W. Bromiley and Thomas F. Torrance, vol. 2, bk. 2 (Edinburgh: T & T Clark, 1957), 417. Hereinafter, this edition of the *Dogmatics* is cited parenthetically in the body of the text as *CD*, followed by volume number, part number, and pagination.

ourselves that which can be given and received only as a free gift. (*CD* 4.3, pp. 477–78)

Now, other things being equal, when someone declares unambiguously that he or she does not subscribe to a view that has been imputed to him or her, that is sufficient to settle the matter. However, other things are not equal in the case of Barth, as these citations testify. In the recent literature, Tom Greggs has pointed out that there may be some reason for thinking Barth wanted to distance himself from two problematic ideas with which he did not want to be aligned.[10] The first (as is plain from the preceding citations) is the doctrine of *apokatastasis,* or the ultimate reconciliation of all things, often associated with Origen. Barth emphatically denied that his doctrine was the same as that of Origen. At least part of the reason for doing so appears to have been a desire to avoid being identified with a doctrine that had been declared heretical. But a second concern, according to Greggs, was to avoid the reification of "universalism" as some theological principle more fundamental than Christ himself—as if "universalism," rather than unification with Christ, were the most basic theological concern. Related to this, Greggs argues that Barth eschewed the reduction of his view to some sort of christological principle. I take it that the idea with which Greggs is working is something like this: The election of Christ is not about mere assent to some theological notion that secures one's salvation. Election concerns a relationship between (in order of importance) Christ, humanity, the community, and the individual united to him. It is not just a concept that we are free to manipulate as we please.

It is natural for a Christian theologian to want to avoid being labeled as a heretic. In his volume on Barth's and Origen's doctrines

---

10. See Greggs, "'Jesus Is Victor.'"

of salvation, Greggs points out several important ways in which the respective doctrines of Barth and Origen differ, despite some structural similarities.[11] Assuming Greggs's analysis is broadly correct, then, whether or not Barth's doctrine entails *apokatastasis,* it is not the same as the doctrine espoused by Origen. But the other two claims Greggs makes are less easy to adjudicate. Why think that any careful, nuanced analysis of Barth's doctrine would reduce it to some sort of abstract principle? What would it mean to do such a thing?

Suppose a physicist explains to me how the formula $E = mc^2$ encapsulates the physics needed to construct an atomic bomb. Surely it would be perverse to think the physicist was guilty of *reducing* certain physical constants in the universe to an abstract principle, or that she was guilty of reducing to a mere concept the physics informing the creation of an atomic bomb. Such thinking would surely be met with incredulous stares—and with good reason. How, then, does the careful analysis of Barth's position yield a sort of illegitimate abstracting of his thinking to a concept or principle, such as Greggs claims? It is difficult to see. Surely any doctrine is a notion or concept of some sort that (usually) includes further notions and concepts. And, in one way of thinking about such things, a notion or concept is merely an idea, a shorthand description of something. It would be crass to mistake such a thing for that which it refers to. This would be to confuse the sign with the thing signified, or the sense of a thing with that to which it refers.

Perhaps this concern is a simple case of theological confusion. Even if that is true, there is still a deeper theological concern here that is less easy to solve. This is that, if Greggs is right, Barth seems to have been mistaken about the precise nature of the problem his doctrine of election faces. The issue is not whether his readers had

11. See Tom Greggs, *Barth, Origen, and Universal Salvation: Restoring Particularity* (Oxford: Oxford University Press, 2009).

mistaken his view for some sort of "lifeless" abstract principle rather than something more "substantial" or "real"—namely, the person of Christ.[12] The real problem has to do with whether the logic of Barth's position entails a doctrine of universalism. If the claim is that, by focusing on universalism as the most pressing issue, one mistakes the fact that, for Barth, union with Christ is the most fundamental matter, then this is a piece of theological obfuscation.

Suppose that a passenger wants to know whether or not a lifeboat is capacious enough to hold all the survivors aboard a stricken vessel. To reply that he needs to understand that the number of those who can be stowed onboard the lifeboat is not the fundamental issue but the fact that the passengers need to be on the lifeboat is, would hardly be thought an adequate response. But this is precisely the sort of reasoning Greggs enjoins upon those worrying about the scope of election in Barth's dogmatics.

So it seems that Barth's denial of universalism is not the last word to be said on the subject. There is good reason to think that Barth had political reasons for wanting to distance himself from a doctrine of universalism, reasons to do with being tarred with the same brush as Origen.[13] This is understandable enough. However, it also seems that some of the further reasons he gives for thinking his doctrine is not "reducible" to universalism are, to be blunt, less than convincing

---

12. I pass over the obvious difficulties such a dichotomy presumes for the sake of the larger point at issue.
13. See *CD* 4.3.1, p. 478, where Barth says this: "If for a moment we accept the unfalsified truth of the reality which even now so forcefully limits the perverted human situation, does it not point plainly in the direction of the work of a truly eternal divine patience and deliverance and therefore of an *apokatastasis* [Origen's doctrine of universalism] or universal reconciliation? If we are certainly forbidden to count on this as though we had a claim to it . . . we are surely commanded the more definitely to hope and pray for it . . . to hope and pray cautiously and yet distinctly that, in spite of everything which may seem quite conclusively to proclaim the opposite, His compassion should not fail, and that in accordance with His mercy which is 'new every morning' He 'will not cast us off forever' (La. 3.22., ff.)." Here, Barth clearly points to the presumption of Origen's doctrine while holding out the hope, though not the necessity, of universal salvation.

if Greggs's argument is right. What is required is an analysis of where Barth's doctrine actually leads, what its logical form is, and what this entails and implies. It is this task to which we now turn.

Barth's Universalism

Contrary to the received view of Reformed orthodoxy, God does not, according to Barth, decree to elect some of humanity and reject others. For Barth, there must be no decree lying behind a putative covenant of redemption by which the Father ordains—by a sheer act of will—the election of some of humanity and the reprobation of the remainder that is then brought into effect by the Son in his work of redemption. Barth is utterly opposed to this deliverance of the Reformed tradition, sometimes called the *decretum absolutum* (absolute decree), which he thinks is the underlying flaw in Calvin's doctrine of election:

> How can we have assurance in respect of our own election except by the Word of God? And how can even the Word of God give us assurance on this point if this Word, if this Jesus Christ, is not really the electing God, not the election itself, not our election, but only an elected means whereby the electing God—electing elsewhere and in some other way—executes that which he has decreed concerning those whom He has—elsewhere and in some other way—elected? The fact that Calvin in particular not only did not answer but did not even perceive this question is the decisive objection which we have to bring against his whole doctrine of predestination. The electing God of Calvin is a *Deus nudus absconditus*. (CD 2.2, p. 111)

Barth is also opposed to the consequence of this *decretum absolutum*, seen in the bifurcation of election in Reformed theology. God does not elect some number of human beings for salvation; God elects Christ. As Barth has it, "[I]n its simplest and most comprehensive form the dogma of predestination consists, then, in the assertion that the divine predestination is the election of Jesus Christ" (CD 2.2, p. 103). Christ is the Elect One. He is also the Reprobate One, the judge judged in our place and the one who takes our sin upon himself—the sin of humanity in toto—being reprobated for us:

> In this one man Jesus, God puts at the head and in the place of all other men the One who has the same power as Himself. . . . The rejection which all men incurred, the wrath of God under which all men lie, the death which all men must die, God in His love for men transfers from all eternity to Him in whom He loves and elects them, and whom He elects at their head and in their place. . . . Indeed, the very obedience which was exacted of Him and attained by Him was His willingness to take upon Himself the divine rejection of all others and to suffer that which they ought to have suffered. . . . He, the Elect, is appointed to check and defeat Satan on behalf of all those that are elected "in Him," on behalf of the descendants and confederates of Adam now beloved of God. (CD 2.2, p. 123)

Moreover, "That the elected man Jesus had to suffer and die means no more and no less than that in becoming man God makes himself responsible for man who became His enemy, and that He takes upon Himself all the consequences of man's action—his rejection and death" (CD 2.2, p. 124).

This is underlined in Barth's discussion of supra- and infralapsarianism.[14] As is well known, Barth opts for a supralapsarian view of the divine decrees. But he resists the traditional assimilation of supralapsarianism to a *decretum absolutum* coupled with a doctrine of double predestination. Instead, he weds his doctrine of Christ,

---

14. Supra- and infralapsarianism are the two major views in Protestant orthodoxy concerning the logical ordering of the divine decrees. According to Barth (CD 2.2, p. 142), supralapsarianism has to do with God's ordaining the salvation of some and the damnation of others prior to (usually understood in the tradition to mean conceptually or logically prior to, not temporally prior to) God's decision to create the world or to redeem it—hence the "supra-," which refers to the fact that the *decretum absolutum* takes place "prior to" or "before" the decree to the fall. By contrast, infralapsarianism, according to Barth, begins with the decree to create and preserve humanity despite the fall. Only subsequent to this decree does God ordain the election of some and the reprobation of others; hence "infra-" (after the fall) (CD 2.2, pp. 143–44).

the Elect and Reprobate One, to supralapsarianism. This results in God's decreeing the salvation of humanity in and through Christ, the Elect human being: "This foreordination of elected man is God's eternal election of grace, the content of all the blessings which from all eternity and before the work of creation was ever begun God intended and determined in Himself for man, for humanity, for each individual, and for all creation." So sure is Barth of this that he says a little later in the same passage, "It remains to the individual only to grasp the promise which is given in the one Elect, and to seek and find his salvation, not as a private end, but as a participation in the victory and blessedness of this other, the Elect of God" (*CD* 2.2, p. 142).[15]

Thus, as is well known, Barth ingeniously inverts the traditional Reformed doctrine of the double decree: God's eternal counsels do not fork at the point of election, designating eternal life for some and eternal damnation for others. Rather, damnation and election are focused on the person of Christ alone. Human beings are, in Barth's way of thinking (although not in Barth's language), only *derivatively* elect. We might say that human beings as a whole are elect because of Christ the Elect One; and no human being is reprobate, because Christ is the only Reprobate One. Perhaps better, we might say that Christ stands in our place as the Reprobate One so that we do not have to be cast away from God's presence. What needs to be emphasized here is that Barth states that *all humanity* is derivatively elect in Christ. No human being is outside the scope of this divine act:

---

15. Later in his discussion of the one Elect, Barth even goes as far as to say, "The exchange which took place on Golgotha, when God chose as His throne the malefactor's cross, when the Son of God bore what the son of man ought to have borne, took place once and for all in fulfilment of God's eternal will, and it can never be reversed. There is no condemnation—literally none—for those that are in Christ Jesus" (*CD* 2.2, p. 167). And, of course, as Barth has already labored to show us, this means there can be no condemnation for any human being, because all human beings are somehow derivatively elect in Christ, the Elect One.

This, then, is the message with which the elect community (as the circumference of the elect man, Jesus of Nazareth) has to approach every man—the promise, that he, too, is an elect man. It is fully aware of his perverted choice. It is fully aware of his godlessness. . . . It is fully aware, too, of the eternal condemnation of the man who is isolated over against God, which is unfailingly exhibited by the godlessness of every such man. . . . It knows of the wrath and judgment and punishment of God in which the rejection of the man isolated over and against God takes its course. . . . It knows that God, by the decree He made in the beginning of all His works and ways, has taken upon Himself the rejection merited by the man isolated in relation to Him; and on the basis of this decree of His the only truly rejected man is His own Son; that God's rejection has taken its course and been fulfilled and reached its goal, with all that that involves, against this One, so that it can no longer fall on other men or be their concern. The concern of other men is still the sin and guilt of their godlessness—and it is serious and severe enough. Their concern is still the suffering of the existence which they have prepared for themselves by their godlessness (in the shadow of that which the One has suffered for them)—and it is bitter enough to have to suffer this existence. Their concern is still to be aware of the threat of their rejection. But it cannot now be their concern to suffer the execution of this threat, to suffer the eternal damnation which their godlessness deserves. Their desire and their undertaking are pointless in so far as their only end can be to make them rejected. And this is the very goal which the godless cannot reach, because it has already been taken away by the eternally decreed offering of the Son of God to suffer in place of the godless, and cannot any longer be their goal. (CD 2.2, pp. 318–19)

Nor, as this passage shows, is it truly possible for a human being to be reprobate, because Christ has atoned for our sin by becoming the Reprobate One in our place. And this act of Christ is not merely a means by which God makes *possible* our inclusion in election; it is an act that ensures that the derivative election of all human beings via the work of the Elect One, Christ, has already been realized. All humanity is already elect in Christ, the Elect One. This election is not merely a potential election but an actual one—that is, it is an election that God has already brought about on the basis of supralapsarianism.[16] God's *decretum absolutum* is not to elect some and reject others, it is to (derivatively) elect all humanity "in" the one Elect, Christ. But the election of Christ is certain—God has decreed it from before the foundation of the world, in Barth's way of thinking. And all of humanity is derivatively elect in Christ, so no human being is derivatively nonelect.[17] This means that any attempt to live as if this election were not already achieved in and through the work of Christ is an "impossible possibility." It makes no sense. (In this regard, recall *CD* 2.2, pp. 318–19, where Barth says that damnation "is the very goal which the godless cannot reach, because it has already been taken away by the eternally decreed offering of the Son of God to suffer in the place of the godless, and cannot any longer be their goal.")[18] Moreover, and importantly for the matter in hand, for Barth, Christ's work is appropriated now not by repentance and salvation (the traditional Reformation model of conversion) but by an agent's coming to realize that he or she is already saved *now*, by the prior act of God in Christ *then*, at the cross. In this regard, Barth comments, "This, then, is the message with which the elect community (as the circumference of the elect man, Jesus of Nazareth) has to approach every man—the promise, that he, too, is an elect man" (*CD* 2.2, p. 318). Note the unconditional nature of Barth's formula

16. This is not to suggest that Barth's adherence to supralapsarianism commits him to his particular doctrine of election, or vice versa. My point is just that this is how things stand in Barth's account. Nor, I should add, am I implying that infralapsarianism would yield a merely "potential" election. The question of the potentiality or actuality of election is distinct from the question of whether God ordains that God's decrees are organized in a supra- or infralapsarian fashion.

17. This is conceded even by theologians who want to speak of some sort of "space" in which, in Barth's reckoning, God allows God's creatures freedom to respond to this election. So, for instance, Colin Gunton says, "That God has destined all for reconciliation with himself need not preclude the eschatological space—that is to say, the time and freedom—for the way in which this predestiny works itself out." Colin E. Gunton, *Theology through the Theologians* (Edinburgh: T & T Clark, 1996), 101.

18. Geoffrey Bromiley comments on this: "The gospel declares that the individual is already elected in Jesus Christ, who bore his merited rejection." Bromiley, *Introduction*, 95 (emphasis added).

here. As George Hunsinger points out, "[I]n Barth's understanding, God has already freely included us [in salvation]." Hence, "it falls to us henceforth freely to receive our inclusion as the gift it is proclaimed to be."[19]

But clearly, this can be the case only if the agent concerned is in some sense *already* saved by the work of Christ. If I have a large debt with my tailor that, unbeknownst to me, my friend paid off when he was measured for a new suit a year ago, then I am free of debt from that moment onward, whether or not I know I am free of it. And when my friend tells me he has paid my debt, I come to realize, so to speak, that I am debt-free now because of the prior action of my friend a year ago. But for the whole year between my friend's paying the debt and my coming to know the debt was paid, I no longer had a debt with my tailor even though I was unaware of that fact. It would make little sense to say I need only realize that I am now debt-free because of the prior beneficent act of my friend if that act was only a matter of his offering to pay my debt if I were to *ask* him to do so. But it would make perfect sense to say this if he had in actual fact already paid my debt a year ago *unbeknownst* to me at that time. In a similar way, Barth's understanding of election must mean that Christ has paid my debt not just potentially—offering to free me from my debt if I am willing—but actually or really: I am free of debt because of what Christ has already done on my behalf. For Barth, then, the election of Jesus Christ has this immediate effect: it means that when God creates human beings, they are already, as it were, objects of God's divine grace because of God's election of Christ and derivative election of the whole of humanity "in" Christ.[20] Given Barth's view,

---

19. Hunsinger, *How To Read Karl Barth*, 130–31.

20. This, I should say, is my extrapolation from what Barth says, not what Barth actually says, although I am not alone in making this point. (See, for instance, Colin Gunton, "Karl Barth's Doctrine of Election as Part of His Doctrine of God," in *Theology through the Theologians*, 91–93, 101.) Of course, this raises an important question for the consistency of Barth's

all that remains to be changed regarding my relationship to God in the present is an *epistemic* matter (a matter of what I know and understand my relationship to God in Christ to be), not an *ontological* one (a matter of whether I am among the [derivatively] elect or not, which has already been decided through the decision of Christ to become the Elect One). In this regard, Barth's doctrine echoes the justification-in-eternity view discussed in chapter 2.

In an earlier essay on Barth's doctrine of election, I argued that this position leads to universalism (or, alternatively, incoherence), whether Barth thinks human beings have what we might call a "strong" free will, that is, a doctrine of human free will consistent with libertarianism, or a "weak" free will, that is, a doctrine of free will consistent with compatibilism. According to most libertarians, a fundamental reason why a person is said to be free with respect to a particular action is that the person in question is able to refrain from choosing that course of action, and his or her free act is not caused or otherwise necessitated by an antecedent act (either temporally or logically antecedent) either of the moral agent him- or herself or of some outside cause or agency. And, to the extent that that person is free to do a particular action, he or she is morally responsible for the choice made. According to most traditional versions of compatibilism, human beings are free with respect to a particular action to the extent that they are not hindered from choosing what they want to do or prevented from choosing what they want to do. Such actions, unlike libertarian free acts, are caused either by prior choices of the moral agent (not necessarily temporally prior choices

supralapsarianism. If, logically, prior to the creation Christ is the Elect and Reprobate One, how can he be elect or reprobate without reference to some object of election or reprobation? For no object of election or reprobation can be in view at the "moment" when God ordains Christ's election, according to the ordering of the decrees set forth in supralapsarianism, because the decree to create is conceptually "after" or consequent to the decree to elect Christ. For discussion of Barth's supralapsarian doctrine, see Edwin Christian van Driel, *Incarnation Anyway: Arguments for Supralapsarian Christology* (New York: Oxford University Press, 2008).

and perhaps including several different causal factors that give rise to the choice made) or by the moral agent in concert with some other causal factor or agency, such as God.[21] And, to the extent that that person is free to do a particular action, he or she is morally responsible for the choice made. (Compatibilists also argue that moral agents could be morally responsible for acts they commit even if they have no alternative option open to them. But we need not enter into this here, although it is an important difference from libertarian accounts of freedom.)[22]

If human moral freedom consists in some version of compatibilism, then, applied to Barth's views, human beings are all elect in Christ and will all be saved. Indeed, this is *inevitable*, given the prior free act of election in Christ, the Elect One. However, if human moral freedom reflects a version of libertarianism that applies to choices involving human salvation,[23] then, applied to Barth's doctrine of election, human beings are all derivatively elect in Christ as a matter of fact. Yet (presumably) human beings would be able to "opt out" of their election. At times, Barth suggests something like this "opt-out" version of election in passages like the following:

> If he [the believer] believes in Him [Christ], he knows and grasps his own righteousness as one which is alien to him, as the righteousness of this other, who is justified man in his place, for him. He will miss his

---

21. In fact, matters are much more complicated than this thumbnail sketch allows. But, for present purposes, these very rough and ready characterizations will suffice. For one thing, some contemporary compatibilists think that a virtue of their position is that it requires a doctrine of free will "weak" enough to be consistent with determinism if determinism proves true. It is not a requirement of compatibilism that determinism is true, however. Others maintain that moral responsibility is the more fundamental issue and that it can be had without "free will" in the historic sense of that term. For a helpful and up-to-date overview of the contemporary philosophical literature on this, see Kevin Timpe, *Free Will: Sourcehood and Its Alternatives,* 2nd. ed. (London: Bloomsbury, 2013).

22. I am referring to Harry Frankfurt's famous principle of alternate possibilities, which has been much discussed in recent analytic philosophy. See his essays in Frankfurt, *The Importance of What We Care About* (Cambridge: Cambridge University Press, 1988).

23. This caveat is important, given our earlier discussion of libertarian Calvinism.

own righteousness, he will fall from it, if he thinks he can and should know and grasp and realise it in his own acts and achievements, or in his faith and the result of it. He will be jeopardising, indeed he will already have lost, the forgiveness of his sins, his life as a child of God, his hope of eternal life, if he ever thinks he can and should seek and find these things anywhere but at the place where as the act and work of God they are real as the forgiveness of his sins, as his divine sonship, as his hope, anywhere but in the one Jesus Christ. (*CD* 4.1, p. 631)

But clearly, this has to be understood in the context of Barth's claim that derivative election is accomplished in Christ, the Elect One. So no one can *begin* life outside the number of the derivatively elect, although some may "opt out" of this group of humanity (and into the number of the nonelect?) by rejecting the work of Christ. The problem is that this does not seem to make sense when taken together with what he says about the impossibility of opting out of election elsewhere in *Church Dogmatics* because election has already been accomplished through the person and work of Christ. Recall, for example, the passage cited earlier:

[I]t cannot now be their concern [that is, the concern of "other men," as Barth puts it, presumably those who do not profess Christian faith] to suffer the execution of this threat [of damnation], to suffer the eternal damnation which their godlessness deserves. Their desire and their undertaking are pointless in so far as their only end can be to make them rejected. And this is the goal that the godless cannot reach, because it has already been taken away by the eternally decreed offering of the Son of God to suffer in place of the godless, and cannot any longer be their goal. (*CD* 2.2, p. 319)

So, those wishing to defend the view that Barth's doctrine is consistent must do one of two things: They must affirm that election in Christ is conditional in some way, contrary to what Barth says in a number of important passages in *CD* 2.2 where he deals with election but in keeping with some things he says elsewhere in *CD* 2.2

and, later, in *CD* 4. This leaves open the door to one nonuniversalist construal of his doctrine. Alternatively, they may affirm with Barth that election in Christ is a completed matter, not merely something that, it is hoped, may finally apply to all of humanity. But then some sense has to be made of Barth's assertion that he is not committed to universalism, without thereby falling into inconsistency. However, clearly, defenders of Barth cannot affirm both these sorts of passages in his *CD*, on pain of contradiction.[24]

A Barthian Story of Election

Up to this point, we have simply rehearsed the two ways in which Barth's doctrine has been read. And, as I have just said, much depends on whether we take Barth at his word, and which passages in his corpus we privilege in attempting to understand his doctrine in the round. However, what if we were to "see past" the problematic language in which Barth expresses himself in *CD* 2.2 to try to offer a more charitable account of what he might be getting at. Could we then tell a story that takes seriously much of Barth's account, setting to one side the *letter* of some of what Barth says but retaining the *spirit* of much of his stated doctrine? I think we can.[25]

First, let us return to Barth's supralapsarianism and his inversion of the double decree of traditional Calvinism. In the conceptual scheme of the divine decrees (according to Barth), the first divine fiat has to

24. My point here is just that affirming both that election is a closed matter (all have been saved through the election and atonement of Christ, and therefore all will inevitably be saved) and that election is still an open matter (some people may not be finally saved, for all we know, despite their being derivatively elect because of Christ) implies a contradiction. Yet this is just what Barth says in different passages in *CD* 2.2, as we have seen.

25. Of course, this is a hazardous task. The very way in which I have set this out in terms of the "letter" and "spirit" of Barth's doctrine will be objectionable to some. But I think that the account this section lays out may be what Barth was aiming at in *CD* 2.2. If it turns out that this story does not even represent the putative spirit of Barth's account, it may still be a theologically interesting way of thinking about election, inspired by Barth's thinking on this matter, that is consistent and nonuniversalist.

do with the Father electing the Son as the Elect One. As we have seen, all humanity is derivatively elect "in" the Son.

Second, in the course of setting forth God's decrees, God ordains that human beings (or, at least, the human beings God will create) all have libertarian freedom. All of humanity is derivatively elect in Christ, so that all humans are born elect, but *remaining in this state is conditional upon each human's not finally opting to reject Christ.* This condition—what we might call the default position for this spirit-not-letter version of Barth's doctrine—is deliberately framed in as broad a fashion as possible.[26] Plausibly, only those who at the Last Judgment continue to reject Christ will be cast off, and even then, this condition may be construed so as to allow for some sort of "second-chance" doctrine postmortem, in hell. (I say it *might* be construed this way, not that it *has to* be construed in this way or even that Barth would construe it this way.) At the very least, the proviso concerning the finality of a person's rejection of Christ has to be taken seriously in this reckoning. If all human beings are elect but may freely reject the derivatively elect status bestowed upon them, then some may continue to reject Christ forever and be lost. But they may not. And, although there are ways of cashing this out in terms of a hopeful universalism where, it is hoped, all of humanity will eventually be saved (contingent upon the free choices of the individuals who are the objects of salvation), this need not be how this way of thinking about election actually obtains. But it is certainly an eschatologically optimistic vision of election, and it fits with what Barth and his defenders have said about the hope, but not the certainty, that all of humanity will eventually be saved.

Third, Barth speaks of Israel and the church as the (derivatively) elect community whose mission it is to proclaim the fact that all

---

26. It also sounds rather like one aspect of Karl Rahner's doctrine of anonymous Christians.

human beings are already elect "in" Christ. This is more difficult to unpack. After all, does this mean simply explaining to non-Christians that they are already elect and just need to see that this is the case (which, to all intents and purposes, is justification in eternity by another name)? This seems to sit rather ill with the New Testament emphasis on repentance and faith as the normal means by which salvation is applied to fallen individuals (for instance, in Acts 2:38). But let us assume some sense can be made of this commensurate with Scripture. The (derivatively) elect community is the catalyst used by Providence for "activating" or "awakening" what we might call the "sleepers"—that is, those who are unaware of their derivatively elect status in Christ. Those who do not hear the gospel, like those who reject their election, have an uncertain status in this account, but it may be that they, too, are saved unless they actively reject God when they encounter God (however it is that they do encounter God) in this life or, perhaps, postmortem (depending on what one makes of the finality of death in matters of salvation). So, in this view, the church has a reason to carry out its great commission—the "awakening" of theological "sleepers"—and has reason to hope that all will finally be saved, although it cannot be certain that this will be the final outcome of salvation.

It must be said that this way of thinking about Barth's doctrine of election makes sense of much of what he says in various parts of CD 2.2 and, I think importantly, takes Barth at his word with respect to both his denial of universalism and his eschatological optimism. Yet it is still the case that the actual account we have of Barth's doctrine of election in CD 2.2 presents this reading with a number of serious problems, which have to do with the ambiguity of Barth's language and the fact that he does seem to say contradictory things about the nature and scope of election in different places in CD 2.2. The most serious of these problems for this spirit-not-letter account of Barth's doctrine is that, at times, Barth speaks in language that, taken at face value, means the derivative election of humanity is an event that is complete and that cannot be rescinded by any human action now. In Christ, all humanity is (derivatively) elect, and Christ's death and resurrection ensure that all of humanity is saved. So, this spirit-not-letter account of Barth's doctrine has to set to one side those passages where Barth speaks unequivocally about the fact that all of humanity is elect and can do nothing to place itself beyond that election in Christ. Nevertheless, the spirit-not-letter account of Barth's views offers one plausible explanation of Barth's doctrine (given certain important qualifications) that is consistent and nonuniversalist. However, those who have attended to what Barth *actually says* in *CD* 2.2 could be forgiven for not seeing this, when what Barth writes in that volume of his dogmatics is couched in language that is obscure and at times occludes, or even appears at times to contradict, what he intends to convey (assuming this story, or something very like it, is what Barth intended to convey).

Conclusion

The aim of this chapter has been modest: to show that if one reads Barth's *Church Dogmatics,* and in particular volume 2, book 2, with attention to what Barth actually says about election and tries to develop an argument from this, one can find the outline of several different accounts, one of which seems to be universalist. However, if we look to the spirit of Barth's account—and put to one side the apparent inconsistencies in what he actually says in search of a deeper underlying theme—an account of election can be had that is internally consistent and that does not necessarily imply universalism. What I am suggesting is that Barth's way of doing theology (at least, in the case of his doctrine of election) is rather like a story told by a brilliant raconteur. It is full of big ideas and bold statements, which, if they are analyzed carefully, do not always seem to fit together into one seamless whole. But if we sit back and try to grasp the larger picture the raconteur tells, ignoring the infelicities in his telling of it, we will grasp what he intends to convey—and will see that what he intends to communicate to us, unlike the way he sometimes expresses himself, is perfectly intelligible.

None of this means that what Barth actually says about election is either coherent or nonuniversalist. But it does mean that an argument that looks beyond the letter to the spirit of Barth's account, taking seriously the problems this involves, may be able to present a doctrine of election that is consistent, nonuniversalist, and theologically interesting. This is true even if the argument offered here is not Barth's doctrine as such but a peroration on Barth's thinking, a distinct but related account of election inspired by the great Swiss theologian. Of course, whether such a doctrine is true is another matter entirely.

7

Hypothetical Universalism

It demonstrates also the infinite love of God towards the human race, who willingly sent his own Son to redeem miserable mortals. . . . It must also be observed, that the Apostle does not say we have redemption by the Son of God, but in him. For by Christ the whole world is said to be redeemed, inasmuch as he offered and gave a sufficient ransom for all; but in him the elect and faithful alone have effectual redemption, because they alone are in him.

—Bishop John Davenant, *An Exposition of the Epistle of St. Paul to the Colossians*

Calvinism is often thought to be synonymous with a particular doctrine of double predestination, according to which God eternally ordains the salvation of a small remnant of humanity, and damns the rest, by means of the salvific work of Christ. This is commonly believed to go hand in hand with a particular view of the scope of Christ's atoning work: that it is accomplished on behalf of, and applied to, the elect, and only them—what is often, and unfortunately, called the doctrine of "limited" atonement. On both counts, this is to identify a broad tradition of Christian theology with one particular doctrine of election and the scope of redemption held by many of its adherents, but by no means all. It would be like conflating Marxism with socialism, or Theravada Buddhism with

Buddhism as a whole. Recent historiographical work has begun to show that early Reformed theology tolerated much greater doctrinal breadth than some popular pictures of it would suggest.[1]

Hypothetical Universalism and the Reformed Symbols

One of the most interesting recent developments in this area has been work done on the doctrine of hypothetical universalism, or what in the older theological literature is sometimes called "Calvinistic universalism."[2] As we shall see, there are different versions of this doctrine, but they share in common the claim that the work of Christ is universal in its sufficiency but applied to an elect number less than the total number of fallen humanity; hence *hypothetical universalism*. This in turn draws on an ancient, catholic distinction found in discussion of the scope of Christ's atoning work that goes

1. To give just one example of this from Richard Muller, whose work has made an important contribution to "broadening out" our understanding of early Reformed theology: "[T]he Reformed tradition . . . is a highly diverse tradition and, in addition, was rather diverse in its origins. Nonetheless, the diversity of the older Reformed tradition was not a prominent subject of discussion in the older literature on 'Calvinism.' The appearance of diversity in the Reformed tradition . . . identifies a significant line of argument in the on-going work of examining and reassessing the development of seventeenth century Protestant thought." Muller, "Diversity in the Reformed Tradition," in *Drawn into Controversie: Reformed Theological Diversity and Debates within Seventeenth-Century British Puritanism*, ed. Michael A. G. Haykin and Mark Jones, Reformed Historical Theology 17 (Göttingen, Ger.: Vandenhoeck & Ruprecht, 2011), 12. Similar sentiments are expressed by W. Robert Godfrey in "Reformed Thought on the Extent of the Atonement to 1618," *Westminster Theological Journal* 37 (1975): 133–71.
2. The most interesting and lively contribution to the recent historiographical debate about this doctrine can be found in Jonathan D. Moore, *English Hypothetical Universalism: John Preston and the Softening of Reformed Theology* (Grand Rapids, MI: Eerdmans, 2007). Other useful resources include Moore, "The Extent of the Atonement: English Hypothetical Universalism versus Particular Redemption," in Haykin and Jones, *Drawn into Controversie*, 124–61; Robert Letham, *The Westminster Assembly: Reading Its Theology in Historical Context* (Phillipsburg, NJ: Presbyterian and Reformed, 2009), 58–61, 177–82; and G. Michael Thomas, *The Extent of the Atonement: A Dilemma for Reformed Theology from Calvin to the Consensus (1536–1675)*, Studies in Christian History and Thought (Milton Keynes, UK: Paternoster, 1997). The phrase "Calvinistic universalism" is sometimes used in nineteenth-century discussions of the doctrine. See, e.g., William Cunningham, *Historical Theology: A Review of the Principal Doctrinal Discussions in the Christian Church since the Apostolic Age,* 3rd ed. (Edinburgh: T & T Clark, 1870), 2:360–70.

back at least as far as Peter Lombard, with whom it is usually identified. This is the so-called sufficiency–efficiency distinction. We can state it thus: *Christ offers himself for all humanity with respect to the sufficiency of his work but for the elect alone with regard to its efficacy, because he brought about salvation only for the predestined.*[3]The distinction is sometimes accused of being too porous to be of much theological use, because it is consistent with both the doctrine of definite atonement (according to which God intends the work of Christ to be only for the elect) and the Arminian doctrine (according to which Christ dies in principle for every individual, and election depends on foreseen faith).[4] However, it has had a considerable vogue in medieval and post-Reformation theology—perhaps *because* the terms *sufficient* and *efficient* are not given a precise scope. Be that as it may, it is certainly a distinction that has informed historic discussion of hypothetical universalism. In fact, one might argue that hypothetical universalism is simply the extrapolation of one obvious way of understanding this distinction. This is a matter to which we shall return.

Hypothetical universalism is often thought to be heretical, or at least unorthodox, as far as the Reformed tradition goes. This claim is more than a little odd, given that there is arguably a significant

3. Adapted from Peter Lombard, *The Sentences,* vol. 3, *On the Incarnation of the Word,* trans. Giulio Silano (Toronto: Pontifical Institute of Medieval Studies, 2008), 20.5, p. 86. In the first chapter of his work *A Dissertation on the Death of Christ* (1650), Bishop John Davenant argues that the core claim of hypothetical universalism goes back to the Fathers and can be found in the work of such divines as Clement of Alexandria, Origen, Augustine of Hippo, and Augustine's disciple Prosper. An English translation of the work can be found appended to the second volume of Davenant's *Exposition of the Epistle of St. Paul to the Colossians,* ed. and trans. Josiah Allport, 2 vols. (London: Hamilton, Adams, 1832). The *Dissertation* has recently been reissued as a stand-alone monograph by Quinta Press (Weston Rhyn, UK, 2006).

4. Raymond Blacketer is one recent example of this line of criticism in his (somewhat partisan) defense of the history of the doctrine of definite atonement. See his "Definite Atonement in Historical Perspective," in *The Glory of the Atonement: Biblical, Theological, and Practical Perspectives,* ed. Charles E. Hill and Frank A. James III (Downers Grove, IL: IVP Academic, 2004), 311.

strand of hypothetical universalism in Reformed theology from its inception. As Richard Muller has recently pointed out,

> Given that there was a significant hypothetical universalist trajectory in the Reformed tradition from its beginnings, it is arguably less than useful to describe its continuance [that is, the continuance of hypothetical universalism in post-Reformation Reformed thought] as a softening of the tradition. More importantly, the presence of various forms of hypothetical universalism as well as various approaches to a more particularistic definition [of the work of Christ] renders it rather problematic to describe the tradition as "on the whole" particularistic and thereby to identify hypothetical universalism as a dissident, subordinate stream of the tradition, rather than as one significant stream (or, perhaps two!) among others, having equal claim to confessional orthodoxy.[5]

In fact, hypothetical universalism has never been repudiated by a Reformed synod or council. The French theologians of the Academy of Saumur, where one version of the doctrine flourished in the seventeenth century, were never formally condemned for their views on this matter.[6] The only confessional symbol that does take issue with hypothetical universalism in its Saumurian guise is the Formula Consensus Helvetica (1675). But this is a late document, written in large part by the Swiss theologian Johann Heinrich Heidegger, and its influence was short-lived.[7] It is not a subordinate standard for any

---

5. Muller, "Diversity in the Reformed Tradition," 25. According to Muller, early Reformed theologians who held to a doctrine of universal atonement include Heinrich Bullinger (1504–1575), Wolfgang Musculus (1497–1563), Zacharias Ursinus (1534–1583), and Girolamo Zanchi (1516–1590).

6. As Muller remarks, "Amyraldian hypothetical universalism can be recognized as belonging to the internal diversity of the Reformed tradition itself." Earlier in the same passage, he writes, "The French Synods, while objecting to some of the formulations of Amyraut and Testard, refrained from condemning their views and it was left to the Formula Consensus Helvetica, a document of limited geographical reach and short-lived use, to disapprove the doctrine—yet without identifying it as a heresy" (ibid., 19).

7. Canon 6 of the Formula, which is directed against the Saumurian theologians, reads as follows: "Wherefore, we can not agree with the opinion of those who teach: 1) that God, moved by philanthropy, or a kind of special love for the fallen of the human race, did, in a kind of conditioned willing, first moving of pity, as they call it, or inefficacious desire, determine the

Reformed communion, and even in its criticism of the doctrine does not label it heretical. It is not beyond the bounds of confessional orthodoxy in the Reformed tradition. In this way, it is quite different from, say, the Remonstrant doctrines that called for the condemnations of the Synod of Dort. The Three Forms of Unity—the Belgic Confession, the Heidelberg Catechism, and the Canons of the Synod of Dort—as well as the Anglican Articles of Religion, which do have the status of subordinate standards or confessions for many Reformed and Anglican communions, are consistent with hypothetical universalism.[8]

Of these symbols, the condemnations of Dort have the most pointed things to say about the scope of Christ's atonement. However, and contrary to some popular presentations on the matter, there is no good reason to think that Dort affirmed a doctrine of atonement that excludes hypothetical universalism. In fact, some of the most prominent delegates at the synod, including the German Reformed Martinius, and several members of the British delegation,

---

salvation of all, conditionally, i.e., if they would believe, 2) that he appointed Christ Mediator for all and each of the fallen; and 3) that, at length, certain ones whom he regarded, not simply as sinners in the first Adam, but as redeemed in the second Adam, he elected, that is, he determined graciously to bestow on these, in time, the saving gift of faith; and in this sole act election properly so called is complete. For these and all other similar teachings are in no way insignificant deviations from the proper teaching concerning divine election." See Martin I. Klauber, "The Helvetic Formula Consensus (1675): An Introduction and Translation," *Trinity Journal* 11 (1990): 103–23. Cf. the remarks of Philip Schaff on the theological and historical context of this symbol in *The Creeds of Christendom: With a History and Critical Notes*, 6th ed., vol. 1, *The History of Creeds* (Grand Rapids, MI: Baker, 1983), 477–89. As we shall see, the objections raised in the Formula do not have purchase with other versions of hypothetical universalism, which the symbol does not even address.

8. See the Heidelberg Catechism answer to question 37: "What dost thou understand by the word Suffered? [in the creed]," to which the response given is "[H]e bore, in body and soul, the wrath of God against the sin of the whole human race, in order that by his passion, as the only atoning sacrifice, he might redeem our body and soul." Translation in Schaff, *Creeds of Christendom*, vol. 3, *The Evangelical Protestant Creeds*, 319. Similarly, the twenty-first of the Thirty-Nine Articles of the Church of England reads, "The Offering of Christ once made, is the perfect redemption, propiciation, and satisfaction for all the sinnes of the whole worlde, both originall and actuall." Schaff, *Creeds of Christendom*, 3:507. The relevant article of the Belgic Confession, article 21, is ambiguous on the scope of the atonement.

including its leader, Bishop John Davenant, were in favor of hypothetical universalism.[9] This can be seen in the relevant article of the synod, 2.8, "Christ's Death and Human Redemption through It," which deals with the scope of the atonement thus:

> For it was the entirely free plan and very gracious will and intention of God the Father that the enlivening and saving effectiveness of his Son's costly death should work itself out in all the elect, in order that God might grant justifying faith to them only and thereby lead them without fail to salvation. In other words, it was God's will that Christ through the blood of the cross (by which he confirmed the new covenant) should effectively redeem from every people, tribe, nation, and language all those and only those who were chosen from eternity to salvation and given to him by the Father; that Christ should grant them faith (which, like the Holy Spirit's other saving gifts, he acquired for them by his death). It was also God's will that Christ should cleanse them by his blood from all their sins, both original and actual, whether committed before or after their coming to faith; that he should faithfully preserve them to the very end; and that he should finally present them to himself, a glorious people, without spot or wrinkle.[10]

Clearly, this article applies the benefits of Christ's work only to those with faith, whom God has elected. Christ's work is said to "work itself out in all the elect, in order that God might grant justifying faith to them only and thereby lead them without fail to salvation." But this is entirely consistent with the claim that the work of Christ is sufficient for the salvation of all humanity in principle, though it is effectual only for the elect who are given faith. As Jonathan Moore points out,

9. For discussion, see Thomas, *Extent of the Atonement;* and Anthony Milton ed., *The British Delegation and the Synod of Dort (1618–1619),* Church of England Record Society 13 (Woodbridge, UK: Boydell, 2005), especially part 6, which reproduces the text of George Carleton et al., *The Collegiate Suffrage of the Divines of Great Britaine: Concerning the Five Articles Controverted in the Low Countries* (London: Milbourne, 1629). See also Nicholas Tyack, "The British Delegation at the Synod of Dort" in *Anti-Calvinists: The Rise of English Arminianism, ca. 1590–1640* (Oxford: Oxford University Press, 1987), 99.

10. The Canons of Dort, reproduced in English translation in *Ecumenical Creeds and Reformed Confessions* (Grand Rapids, MI: CRC, 1988), 130–31.

"[A]s it stands, what the Canons teach here is that Christ's effectual redemptive work was 'only' for the elect." He goes on: "This leaves the door open—even if it is only a back door—for any subscriber to hold privately to an *ineffectual* redemptive work for the non-elect, or, to put it differently, Christ dying for the non-elect sufficiently but not efficiently—precisely what a hypothetical universalist usage of the Lombardian formula entailed."[11] In short, the relevant canon of the Synod of Dort does not exclude Reformed theologians persuaded by the hypothetical universalist doctrine. This is precisely why British delegates like Bishop Davenant and Bishop Ward were able to sign on to the articles.

The doctrine of Davenant and a number of other Anglican divines represents a strand of historic hypothetical universalism, which developed in England independently of, and earlier than, the Amyraldian version. Although it informed theological debate in the early-modern period of English theology, it was not censured in synods and was not repudiated by the major post-Reformation symbol of Great Britain after the Articles of Religion, namely, the Westminster Confession.[12] This is significant, given the influence of the Westminster Confession in subsequent Presbyterianism as a subordinate doctrinal standard. Chapter 8.5, of theConfession, entitled "Of Christ the Mediator," states,

> The Lord Jesus, by His perfect obedience, and sacrifice of Himself, which He through the eternal Spirit, once offered up unto God, has fully satisfied the justice of His Father; and purchased, not only reconciliation,

---

11. Moore, "Extent of the Atonement," 146.
12. This is the conclusion reached by Jonathan Moore in ibid. He does so via a careful analysis of the relevant passages of the Westminster Confession, showing that it does not exclude hypothetical universalism and that the doctrine was not regarded as synonymous with Amyraldianism. See also Lee Gatiss, "'Shades of Opinion within a Generic Calvinism': The Particular Redemption Debate at the Westminster Assembly," *Reformed Theological Review* 69, no. 2 (2010): 101–18.

but an everlasting inheritance in the kingdom of heaven, for those whom the Father has given unto Him.

But this is commensurate with hypothetical universalism, because one could claim that Christ's work is sufficient for the world but efficacious for only "those whom the Father has given" to Christ. Section 8 of the same chapter reads,

> To all those for whom Christ has purchased redemption, He does certainly and effectually apply and communicate the same; making intercession for them, and revealing unto them, in and by the word, the mysteries of salvation; effectually persuading them by His Spirit to believe and obey, and governing their hearts by His word and Spirit.[13]

On the face of it, this appears to require a doctrine of definite atonement. However, as Moore points out, the first sentence is still porous enough to admit of a hypothetical universalist reading, even if it is not entirely natural. The claim that "all those for whom Christ has purchased redemption" have salvation "certainly and effectually" applied to them is consistent with the notion that effectual redemption is restricted to the elect. But this in turn is commensurate with hypothetical universalism.[14]

There are other worries lurking in the Westminster Confession. Two further sections merit some comment. First, there is the third chapter on the divine decrees. A potential problem lies in the claim of chapter 3.6 to the effect that "[n]either are any other redeemed by Christ, effectually called, justified, adopted, sanctified, and saved, but the elect only." But here, as in other contested passages, the hypothetical universalist can claim that redemption in this context is clearly meant to refer to the effectual calling of God that is reserved

---

13. There are many editions of the Confession. I have consulted *The Confession of Faith and Larger Catechism, Shorter Catechism, Director of Public Worship, Presbyterial Church Government* (Edinburgh: Blackwood, 1969).
14. Moore, "Extent of the Atonement," 151.

only for the elect. Then there is chapter 29.2, "Of the Lord's Supper," which speaks of Christ's "only sacrifice," being "the alone propitiation for all the sins of His elect." However, this holds no terror for the hypothetical universalist either, provided (as before) she glosses this passage as a reference to the effectual work of Christ, not to its intrinsic sufficiency for the whole world. Given that the immediate context is the appropriate reception of the sacramental elements in the Eucharist, this interpretation seems entirely appropriate; for only the elect receive the elements in faith on the basis of the "alone propitiation" of Christ for their sins.

Having said this, there are a number of problems with hypothetical universalism that are less easy to dismiss. Some of these have been the subject of discussion in this recent historical-theological literature. However, there has not been any attempt (as far as I am aware) to offer a constructive account of the doctrine. That is what I shall set forth here. The idea is not to endorse the doctrine but to show that it is a viable theological option for those in the Reformed tradition, which should be taken much more seriously than it is in current systematic theology. We might call this task "theological clarification." It involves setting forth a doctrine in the best light and attempting to account for objections that have been raised against it, in order to understand and explain its importance as a contribution to Christian theology.[15]

---

15. Scott MacDonald recommends this strategy of "clarification" to philosophical theologians. He writes that philosophical clarification is "not primarily concerned with . . . epistemic justification." It "is concerned instead with understanding, developing, systematizing, and explaining it. It is possible for [the philosophical theologian] to do all these things without raising the issue of its truth or her justification for holding it. The fact is that a very large part of philosophy has nothing directly to do with the truth or justification of certain theories or propositions. . . . Hence, clarification of theological matters is a legitimate task for the philosopher." Scott MacDonald, "What Is Philosophical Theology?," in *Arguing about Religion*, ed. Kevin Timpe (New York: Routledge, 2009), 24. I say that a similar strategy can be developed along systematic theological lines, *mutatis mutandis*.

Two Versions of Hypothetical Universalism

As has already been intimated, there is no single doctrine of hypothetical universalism; there are different species of the same genus.[16] In the historic seventeenth-century discussion of the subject, the backdrop was the (sometimes) heated debate about the ordering of the divine decrees in Reformed theology, as well as the issue of the scope of divine grace. There were those who took a supralapsarian position and those who opted for infralapsarianism. Very roughly, supralapsarianism is the view according to which the decree to elect some number of humanity logically precedes the decree to create a world of free creatures. So, the ordering of the divine decrees in this way of thinking is typically something like this: election, creation, fall, redemption. The infralapsarians took the view that the decree to elect some number of humanity to salvation must be logically consequent to the decree to create a world of free creatures. Hence, in their way of thinking, the divine decrees were thought to be organized in the following sequence: creation, fall, election, redemption. Note that in this infralapsarian way of thinking, God elects from a mass of fallen humanity, whereas in supralapsarianism, God elects independent of a decree to create a world where human beings will fall.

In this theological context, different versions of hypothetical universalism arose, of which we shall briefly consider two that are arguably the most prominent and that have received the most treatment in the recent literature. The first, which flourished prior to the second and more famous version of the doctrine, was developed by a group of Anglican divines in the later sixteenth century, including John Preston, Bishop John Davenant, and Archbishop

---

16. This was not always appreciated, and in some older literature "Amyraldianism" is conflated with hypothetical universalism. See, e.g., the discussion of A. A. Hodge in *The Atonement* (Philadelphia: Presbyterian Board of Publication, 1867), 375–80.

James Ussher of Armagh. They stayed within the parameters set by the supralapsarian–infralapsarian discussion of the divine decrees, adding that Christ had died for all, obtaining a conditional salvation for those who believe in him and have his work applied to them. Following Jonathan Moore's recent work in this area, let us call this version of the doctrine "English hypothetical universalism," or just "the English version" for short.

By contrast, the second group of hypothetical universalists (commonly thought to be synonymous with hypothetical universalism) were centered upon the French Reformed Academy at Saumur and the teachings of the Scottish theologian John Cameron. His disciples there, most notably Moïse Amyraut, whose name became synonymous with the Saumur doctrine, offered a revision to the supralapsarian–infralapsarian discussion. They claimed that God decreed the election of some human beings logically subsequent to the decree to elect Christ the mediator of salvation; in which case the Amyraldian ordering of the decrees is something like this: creation, fall, redemption, election. This ordering of the decrees was the same as that advocated by Jacob Arminius and the Remonstrants, who claimed that God elected individuals on the basis of foreknowledge, not merely by God's good pleasure and will. The Amyraldians did not concede this to the Arminians. Instead, they argued that there are two distinct phases in eternal election. The first is a decree to save all humanity by the work of Christ. However, this initial decree is ineffectual, because God sees that not all humanity will have faith. So God decrees that some of the mass of fallen humanity who have the gift of faith will be saved through the work of Christ. Although this version of the doctrine is usually known as Amyraldianism, it should probably be called "Scottish hypothetical universalism," or "the Scottish version," because it originates with John Cameron, not his disciple Amyraut. That is how we shall refer to it in what follows.

I shall avoid using the term *Amyraldianism* altogether, because it unhelpfully confuses hypothetical universalism with the Saumur version of the doctrine.[17]

Hypothetical universalism is sometimes accused of bordering on Arminianism, or even of being Arminianism "in disguise." As I see it, such accusations boil down to one of two sorts of objection. Either x significantly overlaps y in content, so that it is easy to confuse the two positions (even if they are formally distinct); or x is materially equivalent to y. That is, the content of x is identical to the content of y. Naturally, the latter claim is the more worrisome. However, hypothetical universalism is not equivalent to Arminianism and does not imply it. Nevertheless, the two views have sometimes been confused. In order to avoid this, it will be useful to distinguish them at the outset.

A. A. Hodge's criticism is representative of this sort of concern. He states that "[t]he serious objection" to hypothetical universalism "is *it necessarily involves the use of language which properly and by common usage is significant of Arminian error.*" He goes on: "Its use generally marks a state of transition from comparative orthodoxy to more serious error. It often covers a secret sympathy with heresies not distinctly avowed."[18] The recent historical work done on this doctrine to which we have already made reference demonstrates

---

17. Amyraut's best-known work, *Brief traitte de la predestination et de ses principales dépendances* (Saumur, Fr.: Lesnier & Debordes, 1634), has been translated into English by Richard Lum as "Brief Treatise on Predestination and Its Dependent Principles" (PhD diss., Dallas Theological Seminary, 1985). Also of note is the subsequent elaboration and biblical underpinning of the theology of the *Brief traitte* in Amyraut, *Six sermons de la nature, estendue, necessite, dispensation, et efficace de l'evangile* (Saumur, Fr.: Girard & de Lerpiniere, 1636). The classic modern treatment of Amyraut and his milieu is Brian G. Armstrong's study *Calvinism and the Amyraut Heresy: Protestant Scholasticism and Humanism in Seventeenth Century France* (Madison, WI: University of Wisconsin Press, 1969). Several aspects of this work have been the subject of some dispute in subsequent historiography. A more recent and extremely thorough treatment of the controversy generated by the Saumur theology is F. P. van Stam, *The Controversy over the Theology of Saumur, 1635–1650: Disrupting Debates among the Huguenots in Complicated Circumstances* (Amsterdam: APA-Holland University Press, 1988).

that Hodge's latter assertion is manifestly false. It is just not the case that hypothetical universalism has historically been the gateway from some Reformed consensus on the scope of atonement to Arminianism. In fact, hypothetical universalism is an ancient doctrine that predates the Reformation and that can be found in the work of a number of early Reformed theologians as well. It is precisely this mistaken view of some primitive orthodoxy threatened by later theological compromise that is at issue in the recent historical literature on the topic. But what of Hodge's claim that hypothetical universalism "necessarily involves" language that "is significant of Arminian error"? This, too, is mistaken, as even a cursory glance at the difference between the Arminian and the hypothetical universalist schemes of atonement shows.

In outlining his position on predestination in his *Declaration of Sentiments*, Jacob Arminius writes, "God decreed to save and to damn certain particular persons. This decree has its foundations in divine foreknowledge, through which God has known from all eternity those individuals who through the established means of his prevenient grace would come to faith and believe, and through his subsequent sustaining grace would persevere in the faith. Likewise, in divine foreknowledge, God knew those who would not believe and persevere."[19] Like the hypothetical universalists, Arminius conceived of the atonement as universal in scope: Christ's work is sufficient in

---

18. Hodge, *Atonement*, 379 (original emphasis). Interestingly, in his recent treatment of the atonement, the British Anglican theologian Lee Gatiss argues the opposite: "[T]he generally Calvinistic substructure of the position [i.e., hypothetical universalism] ought to be acknowledged, defended (by its advocates), and spoken of more than it usually is. Otherwise, Reformed communities in which the only thing young theologians pick up is that being classically Reformed on this issue is for some reason disapproved of, could easily degenerate into Arminianism within a generation." Gatiss, *For Us and for Our Salvation: "Limited Atonement" in the Bible, Doctrine, History, and Ministry*, Latimer Studies 78 (London: Latimer Trust, 2012), 99.

19. Jacob Arminius, *Arminius and His Declaration of Sentiments: An Annotated Translation with Introduction and Theological Commentary*, ed. and trans. W. Stephen Gunter (Waco, TX: Baylor University Press, 2012), 135.

principle for all humanity. And, like the hypothetical universalists, the Arminians agreed that the atonement is applied only to those who have faith. However, it is just here that the two schemes diverge. Whereas the hypothetical universalists claimed that God effectually applies the work of Christ only to those whom God has eternally elected according to God's good pleasure and will, the Arminians claimed that God elects those "individuals who through the established means of his prevenient grace would come to faith and believe" and persevere in the faith. In other words, the Arminian scheme allows that God's election *depends on foreseen faith*, whereas the hypothetical universalist scheme claims that God elects *independent of any knowledge God has concerning foreseen faith.*[20] To claim, as Hodge does, that the hypothetical universalist position uses language that implies Arminianism or otherwise leads to it is to mischaracterize the situation. Although they agree on some important issues about the scope of Christ's work, they have different views on the question of the means by which God applies the benefits of Christ's work to the elect.[21] With this made tolerably clear, we may turn to the consideration of hypothetical universalism itself.

English Hypothetical Universalism

In his discussion of "Calvinistic universalism" (that is, hypothetical universalism), the nineteenth-century Scottish historical theologian William Cunningham characterizes the view as follows:

---

20. Two of Arminius's recent interpreters, Keith Stanglin and Thomas McCall, maintain that, for this reason, Arminius's position can fairly be described as "conditional predestination." See Stanglin and McCall, *Jacob Arminius: Theologian of Grace* (New York: Oxford University Press, 2012), 134.

21. I say this as one committed to greater understanding between Arminians and Reformed. I am not interested in perpetuating the historic antipathy between Reformed and Arminian theologians that has been the cause of so much unhappiness between fellow Christians. My only concern here is getting the different positions clear as part of the remit of "theological clarification."

[T]hey [Calvinist universalists] try to show that we should conceive of God as *first* decreeing to send His Son into the world to suffer and die for all men, so as to make the salvation of all men possible, and to lay a foundation for tendering it to them all; and then, foreseeing that all men would reject this provision, if left to themselves, decreeing to give to some men, chosen from the human race in general, faith and repentance, by which *their* salvation might be secured.[22]

In this way of thinking, hypothetical universalism is a doctrine having primarily to do with the ordering of the divine decrees respecting salvation. There is a first ineffectual decree of universal salvation provided through the work of Christ. Because individuals will reject this offer (having no faith), there is a consequent effectual decree to elect some to eternal life by means of the same work of Christ. However, in the English version of the doctrine, there is no change to the sequence of decrees as traditionally envisaged. In fact, theologians like John Davenant conceived of hypothetical universalism as a doctrine that sits within a conventional infralapsarian scheme. The focus is not so much on reordering God's intentions in creation and redemption to reflect a hypothetically universalist position as it is a matter of emphasizing the relation between election and faith. The elect, in this way of thinking, are those God provides with the gift of faith so that they can respond appropriately to Christ's saving work. Those for whom Christ died in principle but who are not given the gift of faith are not reconciled to God.

Perhaps the most sophisticated and sustained treatment of the English version of the doctrine is given in John Davenant's *Dissertation on the Death of Christ* (*Dissertatio de Morte Christi*), first published in 1650.[23] The *Dissertation* is structured around four

---

22. Cunningham, *Historical Theology*, 2:362.
23. I shall be using the Allport translation of Davenant's *Dissertation* in the body of the text, the reference to which can be found in footnote 3. Citations are given in the body of the text as

substantial theses, or "propositions," as Davenant refers to them. Given their importance in the argument, I cite them here in full:

1. The death of Christ is represented in holy Scripture as an universal remedy, by the ordinance of God, and the nature of the thing itself, applicable for salvation to all and every individual of mankind. (*Dissertation*, 340–41) [Let us call this the "universal-atonement thesis."]

2. The death of Christ is the universal cause of the salvation of mankind, and Christ himself is acknowledged to have died for all men sufficiently, and not by reason of the mere sufficiency or of the intrinsic value, according to which the death of Christ is a price more than sufficient for redeeming a thousand worlds; but by reason of the Evangelical covenant confirmed with the whole human race through the merit of his death, and of the divine ordination depending upon it, according to which, under the possible condition of faith, remission of sins and eternal life is decreed to be set before every mortal man who will believe it, on account of the merits of Christ. (*Dissertation*, 401–2) [Call this the "sufficiency–efficiency thesis."]

3. The death or passion of Christ, as the universal cause of the salvation of mankind, hath, by the act of its oblation, so far rendered God the Father pacified and reconciled to the human race, that he can truly be said to be ready to receive into favour any man whatsoever, as soon as he shall believe in Christ; yet the aforesaid death of Christ does not place any one, and least of all adults, in a state of grace, of actual reconciliation, or of

Dissertation, followed by page reference. Also of relevance here is Davenant's *Animadversions: Written by the Right Reverend Father in God, John Lord Bishop of Sarisbury upon a Treatise Intituled God's Love to Mankind* (London: Partridge, 1641). Here, Davenant sets out his doctrine of predestination and infralapsarianism with some care. Moore discusses Davenant's outputs in *English Hypothetical Universalism*, 187–88.

salvation, before he believes. (*Dissertation*, 440–41) [Call this the "anti-eternal-justification thesis."]

4. The death of Christ being granted to be applicable to all men on condition of faith, it is consistent with the goodness and justice of God to supply or to deny, either to nations or to individuals, the means of application, and that according to the good pleasure of his own will, not according to the disparity of human wills. (*Dissertation*, 475) [Call this the "predestination thesis."]

To these four is added a fifth in the final chapter of the *Dissertation*:

5. The death of Christ, from the special design of God the Father, who from eternity ordained and accepted that sacrifice; and of Christ, who offered it in the fullness of time to God the Father; was destined for some certain persons, whom the Scripture calls the elect, and for them alone, so as to be effectually and infallibly applied to the obtaining of eternal life. (*Dissertation*, 516) [This we shall dub the "effectual-atonement thesis."]

Let us consider each of these theses in more detail, beginning with some brief remarks about the anti-eternal-justification thesis.

Regarding the Anti-Eternal-Justification Thesis

There are two things to be said about this aspect of Davenant's case. First, it is largely concerned with the question of whether the elect are justified in eternity, from eternity, or in history, matters that we have already considered in detail in chapter 2.[24] For this reason, we will not deal with it again in detail here. Second, eternal justification is not

---

24. Davenant returned to this topic in *A Treatise on Justification; or the Disputatio de justitia habituali et actuali, of the Right,* trans. Josiah Allport, 2 vols. (1634; repr., London: Hamilton, Adams, 1844–46).

an essential component of Davenant's positive case for hypothetical universalism. This means that we can set it to one side without weakening or doing violence to his position.

Regarding the Sufficiency–Efficiency Thesis

This is at the heart of Davenant's case, running like a golden thread through much of the rest of the work. It is this thesis upon which the first and third theses depend in important respects. The first thesis is just a statement of the universal-atonement doctrine, which Davenant spends a great deal of time elaborating and defending against various objections in the second chapter of the *Dissertation*. The fourth of Davenant's "propositions" we have termed the predestination thesis. This is the corollary to the universal-atonement thesis in that it spells out how it is that only some human beings are saved. These are the number of humans God decides will be given faith in order to benefit from the work of Christ, according to God's good pleasure and will.

This raises one of the most serious objections to hypothetical universalism. We might call this the "ordination–accomplishment objection." It goes like this: What God ordains, God accomplishes. Nothing can frustrate God's will; God always achieves the end God designs. Yet it appears, in the hypothetical universalist view, that the goal of the salvation of fallen humanity is not achieved, though God designs it. For if the atonement is sufficient for the salvation of all fallen human beings and God ordains that this is the case, why is it not also efficacious for all?

To this, Davenant responds as follows. The hypothetical universalist is committed to the claim not that God intended the salvation of each and every individual through the satisfaction of Christ but only that God "appointed, willed, and ordained that the death of his Son should be, and should be esteemed, a ransom of such a kind that it might be offered and applied to all men individually. And this God evidently accomplished" (*Dissertation,* 391). In other words, God ordains and intends that the satisfaction of Christ be a means of salvation that is truly sufficient for all but conditional upon faith. That is its sufficiency.

To make his position clearer, Davenant distinguishes between a "mere sufficiency" and an "ordained sufficiency" (*Dissertation*, 402–3). Mere sufficiency has to do with the intrinsic value of a particular act. Suppose Christ's work has an infinite value in principle and is independent of any intention of God in applying the work of Christ to a particular number. In that case, it has a mere sufficiency to atone for all human sin because of its value. But clearly, this does no work in explaining God's intention in the atonement, that is, whether it is intended for the salvation of all fallen humans, for only some, or for none.

By contrast, an ordained sufficiency has to do with the intention informing the use of a particular thing. Suppose a man incurs a debt of 1,000 talents, and his friend has a wealth much greater than this. The friend could easily pay off the debt. The question is whether the friend intends to direct the requisite amount of his wealth to this purpose. Such ordained sufficiency can be either absolute or conditional, according to Davenant (*Dissertation*, 403). Absolute sufficiency obtains when there is a fixed price for redemption that, once fulfilled, is automatically remitted. Conditional sufficiency obtains when there is a fixed price for redemption that includes an additional condition that must be satisfied before the redemption is delivered. Davenant remarks: "When we say that Christ died sufficiently for all, we do not understand the mere sufficiency of the thing with a defect of the oblation as to the greater part of mankind, but that ordained sufficiency, which has the intent and act of offering joined to it, and that for all; but with the conditional, and not the absolute ordination which we have expressed" (*Dissertation*, 403–4 [in italics in the original]).

It is this conditional ordained sufficiency that applies in the case of the atonement. It is not a mere intrinsic sufficiency, such as those who defend a definite atonement claim. In other words, it is not only that Christ's death is in principle and independent of any actual divine intention sufficient to atone for all human sin because it has an infinite value, being the work of the God-man. Although this is true and may even be a necessary condition of the atonement, it is not a sufficient condition. To it must be added the following: God has ordained that the infinite sufficiency of the satisfaction of Christ is truly given for all people. We might say that it has been accomplished for the salvation of all human beings. However, the benefits of Christ can be effectually applied to fallen human beings only where the condition of faith is met. Hence, the atonement involves a conditional ordained sufficiency (*Dissertation*, 409, 412). As Davenant puts it earlier in the *Dissertation*,

> [W]e do not affirm that the death of Christ at the moment of his dissolution, was actually applied to all and every individual of mankind, nor that after his oblation it was infallibly to be applied, but that, according to the appointment of God, it is applicable to all. For God hath ordained that it should be applicable to every individual through faith, but he hath not determined to give that faith to every individual, but which it may be infallibly applied. Why he should give this medium of application to some and not give it to others, ought not to be inquired, since it cannot be solved; but must be referred to the secret will of God. (*Dissertation*, 343)

It is important to see that this way of construing the sufficiency of Christ's work means that the application of what Christ has accomplished in his oblation for the elect is entirely due to the divine will. It cannot be that Christ's work is intended only for an elect; it is for the whole world. This is its conditional ordained sufficiency. But if his work in and of itself is ordained to be conditionally sufficient for all, then its efficacy for the elect alone must be due to the divine will, not to the work of Christ as such. This is consistent with what Davenant says elsewhere, in his *Animadversions*: "Predestination is an eternal decree or purpose of God, in time, causing effectual grace in all those whom he hath chosen, and by this effectual grace bringing then infallibly to glory."[25] Moreover, "The grace prepared for the elect in God's eternal predestination, and bestowed upon them in the temporal dispensation, so causeth their belief, repentance, perseverance, as that it imposeth no necessity or violent coaction upon the wills of men, but causeth their free and voluntary endeavours."[26]

Regarding the Effectual-Atonement Thesis

The effectual-atonement thesis rounds out the core claims of Davenant's hypothetical universalism. It underlines the fact that the condition of faith requisite for redemption is a divine gift given only to the elect. In this manner, the atonement is said to be effectual for a particular number, though it is ordained as conditionally sufficient for all humanity.

This thesis raises (at least) two further objections. The first of these we shall call the "divine-benevolence objection": How does the hypothetical universalist claim that God provides an atonement that

---

25. Davenant, *Animadversions*, 8 (given as the first proposition in his argument).
26. Ibid., 11 (given as the third proposition of his argument). Davenant does think that Christ has a "double will" in his satisfaction, willing that his death has regard to all fallen humanity in one sense and to the elect in particular in another sense. But this is consistent with the point being made here about the scope of election depending upon the divine will alone, rather than upon other, christological considerations. For useful discussion of this, see Moore, *English Hypothetical Universalism*, 191–96.

is ordained to be conditionally sufficient for all of humanity make God more benevolent than God would be under the conditions of a definite-atonement doctrine? As Roger Nicole puts it,

> To proffer a blessing contingent upon the fulfillment of an unrealizable condition is altogether futile. On the hypothetical-universalists' own showing, since no one has faith but those to whom it is efficaciously given by God, a universal redemption on condition of faith is not a blessing which issues in any concrete advantage to the non-elect. In this light the vaunted benevolence of God toward all mankind appears as nugatory.[27]

To this, the defender of Davenant's position can respond as follows. An important motivation (perhaps the most important motivation) for defenders of hypothetical universalism like Davenant is the desire to do justice to two sorts of data in Scripture. On the one hand, there are those passages which speak of the scope of salvation in universalizing terms: "[F]or God so loved the world that he gave his only Son, that whosoever believes in him shall not perish but have everlasting life" (John 3:16). On the other hand, Scripture is clear that God elects some to life: "[H]e chose us in him before the foundation of the world, that we should be holy and blameless before him. In love he predestined us for adoption as sons through Jesus Christ, according to the purpose of his will" (Eph. 1:4-5). The hypothetical universalist attempts to hold both sorts of data together in one scheme, where faith is what distinguishes the elect from the reprobate, so that God may be said to have provided a satisfaction in Christ sufficient for all, though efficient only for the elect.

It could be argued that the definite-atonement scheme beloved of theologians like Nicole fails the biblical-soteriology test, because it must presume that the New Testament passages that speak in

---

27. Roger Nicole, "The Case for Definite Atonement," *Bulletin of the Evangelical Theological Society* 10, no. 4 (1967): 203.

apparently universal terms about the scope of Christ's work are actually making claims about some number less than the whole world. Taken at face value, the definite-atonement view does seem to be laboring against the current of biblical soteriology in an important respect. So, one motivation for adopting a hypothetical universalist argument is that it preserves the biblical tension between those passages bespeaking a universal atonement and others that speak in terms of a particular number of elect according to the good pleasure and will of God; in which case one concrete advantage of a hypothetical universalist argument is that it better tracks the biblical witness.

Critics of hypothetical universalism like Nicole regard the notion of a conditional ordained sufficiency in the atonement as a mistake. Universal redemption on condition of faith "is not a blessing which issues in any concrete advantage to the non-elect." It makes the divine benevolence presented in the doctrine of universal atonement appear "nugatory." But from a biblical-theological point of view, defenders of hypothetical universalism like Davenant appear to hold the high ground. It is hardly a *more* benevolent picture of the Deity that presumes that God's intention in the atonement is wholly focused on the elect and that interprets the universalist-sounding passages of the New Testament accordingly. Nicole's position, and the definite-atonement doctrine of others like him, takes a principled hermeneutical position on these universalist-sounding biblical passages; I am not denying that. A good case can be made for the definite-atonement doctrine on biblical grounds. But a good case can also be made for the hypothetical universalist position. In both, certain hermeneutical decisions are made about which texts ought to be privileged in one's understanding of biblical soteriology, or, at least, how the different sorts of biblical data should be weighted. Those defending the definite-atonement position think that the particularist passages are somehow more theologically fundamental than the universalist-sounding ones. The latter should be understood in light of the former, for God's purposes are not confounded by creaturely actions and God accomplishes all God set out to do in creation. Hypothetical universalism presents readers of the biblical texts with a different way of thinking about the same material. Rather than privileging one set of passages over another, why not let them stand in tension?

We have already seen that this represents an important strand of Barth's thinking on the matter. Rather than seeking to find a hermeneutical framework that reduces the tension between these two different sorts of biblical data, the hypothetical universalist in company with Barth at this juncture can claim that we should simply take both sorts of biblical material at face value and find a way of making sense of them both, despite the soteriological tension that this creates. This is not to say that the biblical material is paradoxical or contradictory. Rather, it is to suggest that there is a sense in which the atonement is universal in scope as well as a sense in which God provides the atonement as the means by which to save the elect. The genius of the hypothetical universalist view is that it provides a state of affairs in which both these things are compossible. This is no minor matter. All the options on the scope of atonement have to deal with problematic biblical texts that do not fit neatly into the scheme in question. One important advantage the hypothetical universalist position has over potential rivals is that it requires much less by way of exegetical gymnastics than some alternative views, because it treats both the universal-sounding and particularist-sounding biblical texts with equal seriousness.

There is a further objection to the effectual-atonement thesis. It is, in many ways, the most intractable problem facing the doctrine. We can put it like this: How are those passed over by divine grace and without saving faith morally responsible for their preterition? It appears that they are not morally responsible, because their salvation is not a choice they are capable of making (absent divine grace). Call this the "moral-responsibility objection."

Davenant addresses this issue directly in the *Dissertation*. He argues that God commonly provides things for certain creatures that God knows will not benefit them, including the gifts given to the angels that fell, and to Adam in his state of righteousness: "It is not therefore foreign to Divine wisdom to appoint and ordain means applicable to a certain end, although he may understand that the application would be hindered by some intervening obstacle, which he had not determined to remove" (*Dissertation*, 369–70). God provided the angels with rectitude and holiness, knowing that they would fall; and God provided righteousness for Adam, knowing he would rebel and not be confirmed in his original estate. If it is asked why God would provide an atonement for all humanity that is not effectual for some, Davenant replies that "from hence the good-will, mercy, and justice of God may appear more conspicuous, whilst that remedy which, from the ordination of God, is applicable to every one for salvation, is applied nevertheless only to certain persons. . . . [I]t is not applied to others . . . through their own wickedness" (*Dissertation*, 370).

However, would it not be grossly immoral for one person to provide a benefit to another who is known to be incapable of attaining it, only to blame that beneficiary for not attaining it? Why would this be different in the case of God and God's creatures, the relevant changes having been made? Davenant himself provides an example later in the same chapter of the *Dissertation* that makes this concern abundantly clear. He says this:

> [I]f a king's son should suffer death for all who were guilty of treason, on this condition, that all should be absolved who were willing to humble themselves as suppliants before the king's throne, and faithfully

promise obedience for the future; but he should design to obtain this in addition from his father for some of them, that on account of the merit of his death he would deign to persuade them to this submission and obedience, and having thus persuaded them, would not only absolve them, but also advance them to the highest honours: who does not perceive that death would have been endured for all, and yet all were not loved in the highest and greatest degree? (*Dissertation,* 394)

Davenant goes on to affirm that God does not love all God's creatures equally, because God does not provide them with equal benefits: the elect are provided with faith for their salvation; the rest are not. Elsewhere, in his response to the Gallican controversy (that is, the Continental controversy regarding the Scottish version of hypothetical universalism), Davenant admits that God intends to provide atonement that is sufficient for all in a general will but confirms this in the elect by faith in a specific act of will.[28]

It appears that Davenant's position is equivalent to the claim that God provides an atonement conditionally sufficient for all humanity, knowing that no human being will be able to avail him- or herself of its benefits without faith, which is a divine gift. Instead of providing a reason for thinking that those who are outside the scope of election are nevertheless culpable for failing to avail themselves of Christ's benefits in the atonement, Davenant's doctrine actually underlines the fact that this universal-atonement doctrine does no work in getting God off the hook, so to speak. Rather, it demonstrates that

28. John Davenant, *On the Controversy among the French Divines of the Reformed Church concerning the Gracious and Saving Will of God towards Sinful Men,* reprinted in Davenant, *Exposition,* 2:561–69. According to Muller, Davenant's distinction between a general and a specific willing in the atonement draws on the distinction between the *voluntas beneplaciti,* or ultimate will of God to save the elect, and the *voluntas signi sive praecepti,* the preceptive will of God that involves the universal proclamation of the gospel and the ordained sufficiency of the atoning work of Christ. See Muller, "Davenant and Du Moulin: Variant Approaches to Hypothetical Universalism," in *Calvin and the Reformed Tradition: On the Work of Christ and the Order of Salvation* (Grand Rapids, MI: Baker Academic, 2012), 157.

God could have applied to all the saving benefits of Christ but did not.

Defending English Hypothetical Universalism

But perhaps the defender of English hypothetical universalism can regroup without having to embrace Augustinian universalism. We have seen that Davenant defends something like the following reasoning: according to the sufficiency–efficiency principle (due to Lombard), Christ offers himself for all humanity with respect to the sufficiency of the ransom but for the elect alone with regard to its efficiency, because it effects salvation for the predestined alone. On the basis of this assumption, Davenant argues as follows:

1. The atonement is sufficient for all of humanity, upon the condition of faith.
2. God intends the work of Christ to bring about the salvation of all those who have faith.
3. Faith is a divine gift.
4. Normally, fallen human beings obtain salvation through Christ by means of the interposition of divine grace logically prior to salvation, producing faith.[29]
5. God provides faith for the elect.

Now, recall that, according to Davenant, God ordained that the death of God's Son should be a ransom of such a kind that it *might be offered* and applied to all human beings individually. Its sufficiency is conditional upon faith. Like that of many historic theological

---

29. The caveat "normally" is inserted because there may be classes of fallen humans who are saved without faith, such as the severely mentally disabled and infants who die before the age of discernment. Like Thomas Aquinas, whom he cited with approval, Davenant allows that infants may be saved without the need for a decision of faith; see *Dissertation*, 446–47. See also his treatise on baptismal regeneration, *Baptismal Regeneration and the Final Perseverance of the Saints*, trans. Josiah Allport (London: Macintosh, 1864).

compatibilists, Davenant's argument seems to turn on a conditional analysis of human freedom. By this I mean something like the following: *Saying S could have done* x *rather than* y *is equivalent to saying S would have done* x *rather than* y *if he had chosen* x *rather than* y. However, this is a failure as an analysis that supports the freedom of S to do *x* rather than *y;* for, as Kevin Timpe has recently pointed out, in this way of thinking, "[t]he conditional attributing to an agent the ability to do otherwise . . . could be true even when there is nothing the agent could do to fulfill the antecedent of the conditional. But if there is no way the agent could fulfill the antecedent of the conditional, then the agent couldn't in fact do what the conditional says the agent could do."[30] This seems absurd. Yet it is just this sort of worry that lies behind the moral-responsibility objection to Davenant's hypothetical universalism. Transpose the logical form of the conditional analysis onto Davenant's reasoning, and the issue comes into focus: *The nonelect could have availed themselves of the benefits of the work of Christ sufficient for their salvation, but did not; they would have availed themselves of the benefits of the work of Christ if they had chosen to do so.* This is consistent with Davenant's argument for hypothetical universalism. But plainly, the nonelect cannot fulfill the antecedent of the conditional, because they are not given the gift of faith. It is this theological sleight of hand that motivates the moral-responsibility objection. Davenant's argument appears to offer a real concession to the nonelect. The atonement is sufficient for their sin in a nontrivial sense. It is not merely intrinsically sufficient but also conditionally sufficient. Yet because the nonelect are incapable of fulfilling the condition of faith, the sufficiency of the atonement to which Davenant appeals is

---

30. Kevin Timpe, *Free Will: Sourcehood and Its Alternatives,* 2nd ed. (London: Bloomsbury, 2013), 75.

irrelevant to the question of the moral responsibility of the nonelect. If they cannot avail themselves of the benefits of the work of Christ because they lack faith, then the claim that they would have availed themselves of the benefits of Christ had they chosen to do so is an empty gesture. They could not avail themselves of Christ's work, so they would not have done so.

Happily, all is not lost for the defender of English hypothetical universalism. One promising alternative involves decoupling moral responsibility from the idea that free will requires the ability to do otherwise at the moment of choice when it comes to the case of saving faith. There are several strategies the hypothetical universalist could adopt here, utilizing some helpful work in the recent metaphysics of free-will literature. The first involves adapting Princeton philosopher Harry Frankfurt's analysis of moral responsibility absent a principle of alternate possibilities.[31] Frankfurt's position has several components. First, he distinguishes between first- and second-order desires and judgments. Take the following example. Jones may have conflicting first-order desires (or multiple first-order desires). Suppose he desires to drink a large glass of beer but also desires to drive home that evening. Next, suppose he has a second-order desire to desire to desire to remain sober (in order that he may drive home that evening). Because he has this second-order desire, his first-order desires will be ordered accordingly in a hierarchy of desires, the higher-order desires ordering and meshing with the lower-order ones. The result is that Jones chooses to refrain from drinking the alcohol so as to remain sober and drive home that night, despite his penchant for a pint of beer. In this example, although Jones has some conflict in his first-order desires, this is

31. The locus classicus is Harry Frankfurt, "Alternate Possibilities and Moral Responsibility," *Journal of Philosophy* 66 (1969): 829–39. This has generated a voluminous literature on Frankfurt-style counterexamples that continues unabated.

resolved through the structure of the hierarchy of desires via the overriding second-order desire. According to the Frankfurtian, when a person acts in this way according to a hierarchy of desires that is properly ordered, he acts *wholeheartedly*, identifying with one line of desires and judgments. This blocks an infinite regress of desires and judgments.[32]

But what if a person acts according to an ordered structure of desires because he has been manipulated to do so? What if Jones were hypnotized by his friend Smith prior to the evening's drinking, in order to prevent Jones from having too many beers and being unable to drive home? The implanted suggestion is what gives rise to the desire to desire to remain sober. Jones is not forced or coerced into making the decision he does. Nevertheless, it seems that this counts against his being truly responsible for his choice, even if the choice he makes does not require alternate possibilities. Frankfurt thinks that this is not a significant problem for his position, because he regards the origin of the conditions for choice as irrelevant to the question of moral responsibility. He writes, "[T]he degree to which [a person's] choice is autonomous and the degree to which he acts freely do not depend on the origin of the conditions which lead him to choose and act as he does."[33] In short, Jones is morally responsible for refraining from drunk driving if he chooses wholeheartedly, and under no coercion or compulsion. The fact that he chooses to choose as he does because of hypnotic suggestion does not absolve him of responsibility.

The second strategy involves adopting something like John Martin Fischer and Mark Ravizza's sophisticated refinement of a compatibilist account of moral responsibility.[34] According to their

---

32. For a helpful presentation of the issues on which this paragraph relies, see Timpe, *Free Will*.
33. Harry Frankfurt, *The Importance of What We Care About* (Cambridge: Cambridge University Press, 1988), 46.

view, what is required here is a two-stage process. First, one must show via Frankfurt-inspired thought experiments that alternate possibilities are irrelevant to the ascription of moral responsibility. Then, one can turn to the question of whether causal determinism in itself and independent of considerations regarding alternate possibilities actually threatens moral responsibility. This two-stage process delivers what they call semicompatibilism, the view according to which moral responsibility requires not alternate possibilities but only something much weaker—what Fischer calls "guidance control,"[35] consistent with the truth of causal determinism. Guidance control issues from the agent herself, who is the source of her action. Such control must also be responsive to reasons for doing what one is doing. To return to the case of Jones, he has guidance control if he is the source of his choice to refrain from drunk driving, and he makes the choice he does knowing that there are good reasons for preferring the course of action he takes, namely, that it is immoral and dangerous to get behind the wheel when inebriated. Suppose that, unknown to Jones, Smith has arranged that whatever Jones decides to drink, the barman will give Jones only a nonalcoholic beverage. Then, even though Jones cannot actually decide to drink too much beer, because he will not be served an alcoholic drink, he is still responsible for making the choice he does if it issues according to mechanisms within Jones himself that are responsible to reasons.

Unlike the first Frankfurtian strategy, the second (Fischer-Ravizza) one allows that the source of the desires that inform choice are relevant to the question of moral responsibility. If Jones chooses as he does because Smith hypnotizes him, then that counts against Jones's moral responsibility for the choice he makes. The history behind

---

34. See John Martin Fischer and Mark Ravizza, *Responsibility and Control: A Theory of Moral Responsibility* (Cambridge: Cambridge University Press, 1999).
35. John Martin Fischer, "Frankfurt-Type Examples and Semi-Compatibilism," in *The Oxford Handbook of Free Will,* ed. Robert Kane (Oxford: Oxford University Press, 2002), 291.

the hierarchy of desires and judgments is important in ascertaining responsibility. This is supposed to help to avoid problems raised by cases of manipulation.

If one can be morally responsible for certain actions absent the ability to do otherwise, as per Frankfurt's analysis or semicompatibilism, then the defender of a Davenant-style hypothetical universalism has the raw materials with which to form a theological argument for the conclusion that the nonelect are morally responsible for not availing themselves of the benefits of Christ's atonement even if it was not in their power to do so. Here is an outline of how that might go.

All orthodox Christians agree that faith is a divine gift; one cannot "attain" to faith through hard work or human effort; that is Pelagianism. Augustinians maintain that there is nothing fallen human beings can do to prepare themselves in order to be more likely to be recipients of faith, for salvation is according to the good pleasure and will of God, not on the basis of any foreseen merit in the individual concerned. So, according to the logic of Augustinianism, no fallen human can merit salvation, and none can bring about her own salvation through moral exertion. Those who are not elect, according to the Augustinian way of thinking, are incapable of doing anything to alter that status. God has ordained who will be saved and who will be passed over. So, all Augustinians share in common the problem that, in the Augustinian scheme of salvation, the nonelect can never do anything to change the fact that God has ordained that they are passed over when it comes to divine saving grace. This much can be said *ad hominem* to those defenders of particular atonement who take issue with hypothetical universalism.

So, the particular problem in view with respect to Davenant's position is not that God passes over some and elects others; that is a problem common to all versions of Augustinianism, including hypothetical universalism. The problem has to do with the fact that provision of a conditionally sufficient atonement seems like an empty gesture: Christ dies to save a large proportion of the human race who are incapable of availing themselves of the benefits of his saving work. Although in one respect salvation is really offered to the nonelect (for Christ really does die to atone for their sins), it is not an offer that any member of the nonelect can ever take up, on account of the fact that none of them are given the gift of faith.

But can the nonelect be morally responsible for not availing themselves of the work of Christ if they cannot avail themselves of his work in the absence of faith? Perhaps they can. Consider the following reasoning, using Jones as our nonelect everyman:

1. Because of God's decree, there is no possibility of Jones gaining or being granted saving faith.
2. Jones is unaware that he cannot gain faith.
3. Jones hears the gospel call according to which Christ died for his sins.
4. Jones refuses this call and remains in his sin.

Now, Jones could not have chosen salvation, because he is not elect. Nevertheless, according to hypothetical universalism, Christ truly died for his sin. The fact that Jones could not fail to refuse the gospel call (because he is nonelect) even though he is not aware of this fact does not mean he has no moral responsibility for refusing the call. He is responsible for his choice even though, as a matter of fact, there was no alternative open to him. For he made the choice; no one else did. And he chose as he did. He wholeheartedly identified with the choice to refuse the gospel call. We might put it like this: where there are two (or more) moral alternatives from which to choose and a person chooses one rather than the other for good reason and without being coerced or forced to choose one over the other, the fact that the alternative not chosen and was, in fact, not a live option for that individual at the moment of choice does not necessarily impugn moral responsibility for the choice actually made. For, irrespective of whether the alternative was actually an open one (that is, one that Jones could have opted for), *Jones* made the choice he did. He thought about it and decided to refuse the gospel call. For this he is morally responsible.

If Jones were manipulated into making the choice he did (by being hypnotized, say), then we would probably think this compromises his responsibility. However, if he is the source of his choice and is responsive to reasons for doing what he did, then this may well be sufficient for his being responsible. In the case envisaged, it looks like Jones is the source of his choice: he decides to refuse the gospel call. It is true that he could not have chosen to respond positively to that call, because he is not elect. But the appeal here does not depend on the sort of conditional analysis that we have already seen is problematic (that is, an analysis of the following form: Jones *could* have availed himself of the benefits of the work of Christ sufficient for his salvation, but did not; he *would* have availed himself of the benefits of the work of Christ if he had chosen to do so). Instead, it depends on the following claims culled from the contemporary debate about the metaphysics of free will: (a) plausibly, alternate possibilities are irrelevant to the ascription of moral responsibility in the case of Jones's refusal of the gospel, because Jones is the source of his choice and is not coerced in making the choice he does, a choice that he is wholehearted in making; and (b) theological determinism in itself and independent of considerations regarding alternate possibilities offers no threat to moral responsibility.

In sum, it seems that the English hypothetical universalist, like many other Augustinians, can claim that the nonelect are morally responsible for failing to choose Christ, even though they are constitutionally incapable of choosing Christ. However, on the question of why God provides an atonement for all humanity if many are not given the gift of faith and therefore are incapable of availing themselves of the benefits of Christ's work, the English hypothetical universalist seems to be in some difficulty. Like Davenant, the appeal to Scripture may be a decisive move at this point: if God reveals that Christ's work is conditionally sufficient for all but efficacious only for those with faith who are elect, then this is an important theological constraint on what we can say about the scope of atonement. Perhaps the appeal to authority is a way of blocking further discussion of this, but it is not an entirely satisfactory response to this concern.

One reason why it is not entirely satisfactory is that Davenant does not think Christ's work is efficacious only for those with faith. He allows that there are certain limited cases where God may provide salvation absent faith, such as infant baptismal regeneration. To this we may add other well-known limited cases to which we have referred previously, for example, the severely mentally impaired. Are such persons simply damned on account of the fact that they are incapable of forming faith? Though possible according to the logic of Davenant's position, this seems extremely harsh, even incongruous, given the nature of God. If there are such limited cases that do not require faith, then we may wonder why God does not extend these instances to other potentially worthy recipients, such as those who, through no fault of their own, have never heard the gospel and therefore have never had an opportunity to form faith. This is surely a matter to which contemporary hypothetical universalists should address themselves.

The Promise of Hypothetical Universalism

In offering a theological clarification of one brand of hypothetical universalism, the English version found in the work of John Davenant, I have attempted to do several things. First, I have tried to remove certain mistaken views about the doctrine that have obscured its importance in recent Reformed theology. Chief among these is the conflation of Amyraldianism with the doctrine of hypothetical universalism. This usually goes along with a way of thinking about the Reformed understanding of the scope of atonement that privileges definite-atonement doctrines and treats hypothetical universalism as either unorthodoxy or the eccentric preserve of a few theologians now largely forgotten.

In fact, if divines like Davenant are to be believed (and, as I have shown, the recent historical-theological literature supports this conclusion), the doctrine has a long history in the Christian tradition and was arguably present in Reformed theology from the outset. Rather than being an aberration, hypothetical universalism is a notion that united many early Reformed thinkers with their catholic heritage. It preserved what was nonnegotiable, namely, the doctrine of divine election, without the associated costs of the definite-atonement doctrine. And, most important for thinkers like Davenant, it provided a better, more plausible way of holding to the universalistic-sounding and particularistic-sounding passages of Scripture. According to the hypothetical universalist, Christ really does die for the sins of the world, in keeping with Scripture. His death is ordained as a conditionally sufficient satisfaction for human sin, that is, the sin of all fallen humanity. Those who have faith are redeemed. Yet God provides this gift to the elect alone. What is more (and important for righty understanding the shape of the doctrine), the English version of hypothetical universalism does not require any change to the sequence of divine decrees. It is rooted in a clear understanding of the biblical texts and is commensurate with major Reformed symbols like the Thirty-Nine Articles, the Canons of the Synod of Dort, and even the Westminster Confession (which postdated Davenant's treatment of the subject).

In addition, I have attempted to set out and defend Davenant's version of the doctrine against several common objections to it. These are that it is equivalent to or implies Arminianism; the ordination–accomplishment objection; the divine-benevolence objection; and the moral-responsibility objection. Davenant's version of the doctrine appears to have sufficient resources to meet all but the last of these concerns. In the case of the last one, the problems that remain for hypothetical universalism are ones that are shared in common with other versions of Augustinianism, including those that advocate for a definite-atonement doctrine. This, I submit, is a not insignificant conclusion. Although this does not show that hypothetical universalism is more plausible than its chief rival in Reformed thought on the scope of atonement (namely, the definite-atonement view), it does show that it has the resources to meet the most serious objections to it in all but one case. What is more, it does not seem that the hypothetical universalist is any worse off in accounting for human moral responsibility for salvation than other Augustinians who take a definite-atonement line. For these reasons, it seems that the English version of hypothetical universalism deserves greater attention than it currently enjoys. It may also be that further work on the different versions of hypothetical universalism extant in early-modern theology would provide more resources for a constructive version of the doctrine suitable to the contemporary theological climate.

8

The Double-Payment Objection

> It was the will of God that Christ by the blood of the cross, whereby he confirmed the new covenant, should effectually redeem out of every people, tribe, nation, and language, all those, and those only, who were from eternity chosen to salvation, and given to Him by the Father; that he should confer upon them faith, which, together with all the other saving gifts of the Holy Spirit, he purchased for them by his death; should purge them from all sin, both original and actual, whether committed before or after believing; and having faithfully preserved them even to the end, should at last bring them free from every spot and blemish to the enjoyment of glory in his own presence forever.
>
> —Canons of the Synod of Dort, 2.8

We have already had cause to discuss the definite-atonement view (hereinafter, DA) in passing in the previous chapters. It states that Christ's work atones for a particular number of human beings less than the total number. One indirect means by which to argue for the DA depends on showing how the general- or universal-atonement view, which is the historic alternative doctrine of atonement, suffers from a significant problem that the DA does not. This problem has to do with the fact that, in the universal-atonement view (hereinafter, UA), Christ dies to purchase redemption for all humanity, yet some fallen humans die without faith and are punished in hell everlastingly. This looks like a significant problem for defenders of UA, such as hypothetical universalists (and Arminians and Roman Catholics as well).[1] For, on the face of it, this means that Christ dies for the sins of those damned to hell for the punishment of those very same sins. As with the legal doctrine of double jeopardy, it seems monumentally unjust that punishment be served for the same sins twice over. Defenders of the DA do not face this difficulty, because they maintain that Christ dies only for his elect. He does not actually pay the penalty for the sin of those who are damned. This, in outline, is the double-payment objection to the UA.

This chapter is a sequel to chapter 7. It provides an argument for the conclusion that the double-payment objection fails. Like a number of the previous chapters, it is an exercise in theological retrieval. As Kathryn Tanner puts it, knowledge of Christianity "in other times and places is a way . . . of expanding the range of imaginative possibilities for theological construction in any one time and place, a way of expanding the resources with which one can work."[2] Through paying attention to the work of several historic Reformed theologians, we shall seek to retrieve certain concepts and ideas as resources for constructive contemporary theology. I argue that the double-payment objection does not provide a sound basis for the rejection of UA. Such reasoning does not show that the UA is the right account of the scope of the atonement; that would have to be argued for on separate grounds, and I offer no such argument here. Nevertheless, if the reasoning of what follows is correct, one important objection to the logic of UA (namely, the double-payment objection) is unsound and should be rejected. I regard this conclusion

1. "Jesus, the Son of God, freely suffered death for us in complete and free submission to the will of God, his Father. By his death he has conquered death, and so opened the possibility of salvation to all men." *Catechism of the Catholic Church*, 1019, the Holy See, http://www.vatican.va/archive/ENG0015/__P2J.HTM.
2. Kathryn Tanner, *Jesus, Humanity, and the Trinity: A Brief Systematic Theology* (Minneapolis: Fortress Press, 2001), xviii.

as a sort of ground-clearing exercise in soteriology. By our removing objections and arguments that are wide of their mark, those working on the doctrine of atonement today should have a clearer picture of where the real dogmatic issues lie.

The chapter falls into four parts. The first analyzes several distinctions that are needed in order to apprehend the shape of the objection and its importance for the doctrine of atonement. A second section sets out the argument in detail. Then, the third section deals with some of the most important attempts to rebut the double-payment objection. A final, summary section draws the different threads together and indicates the dogmatic significance of the failure of the double-payment objection.

Some Terminological Distinctions

Christians believe that God's desire is to provide salvation for humanity (1 Tim. 2:4-6; 1 John 3:16); that God brings this about through the work of Christ in the atonement (John 3:16); that Christ's work has the power to remit all human sin (1 Pet. 1:18-19; Heb. 8:18); and that the normal means by which this is applied to the believer is by faith (Rom. 3:21-25; Eph. 2:8-9). On these matters, there is very little disagreement in the tradition. But on the question of the intention of God in bringing about the atonement, opinions diverge.

In order to tease out some of the subtle conceptual issues that this question of divine intention raises, we need to turn in the first instance to two closely related pairs of theological distinctions that often crop up in historic discussion of this topic. The first is the sufficiency–efficiency distinction, which we have already met in chapter 7. The second is the accomplished–applied distinction. Getting a clearer picture of what these distinctions entail will provide a helpful conceptual framework for the subject matter of this chapter.

Let us consider them in turn, beginning with the sufficiency–efficiency distinction.

As we noted in discussing hypothetical universalism, in much Western catholic theology, the atoning work of Christ is said to be sufficient for the salvation of all human beings but efficient only for the salvation of those whom Christ came to save, that is, his elect. This is the sufficiency–efficiency distinction.[3] Is it a distinction without a difference? It might be thought so. On the face of it, if a condition or group of conditions is sufficient for a particular end, then it (or they) would appear to be efficient for that end, provided that "efficient" is understood to mean something like "all that is required in order for this end to obtain." However, that is not the only way to understand the word *efficient* in this context. A second way to construe it is as the effectual bringing about of a particular end.[4]

In this way of thinking, if a condition or group of conditions is sufficient for some end, then nothing more, in principle, is required in order for that end to be achieved, provided the condition or conditions in question are met. Alternatively, if a condition or group of conditions is efficient for some end, then (so one might think) it

---

3. Cf. Charles Hodge: "In view of the effects which the death of Christ produces in the relation of all mankind to God, it has in all ages been customary with Augustinians to say that Christ died 'sufficienter pro omnibus, efficaciter tantum pro electis'; sufficiently for all, efficaciously only for the elect." *Systematic Theology* (1871; repr., Grand Rapids, MI: Eerdmans, 1940), 2:545–46. Discussion of the Lombard's distinction is a staple of historic Reformed accounts of the topic. See, e.g., Heinrich Heppe, *Reformed Dogmatics*, trans. G. T. Thomson (1861; repr., London: Collins, 1950), 475–79.

4. This seems more in keeping with the Aristotelian notion of an efficient cause. Alan C. Clifford points out that an "element of ambiguity in the term 'sufficient' permitted all schools to attach their own meaning to it." Clifford, *Atonement and Justification: English Evangelical Theology, 1640–1790; An Evaluation* (Oxford: Oxford University Press, 1990), 74. This meant that those who adopted an Arminian as well as those who endorsed a Calvinist doctrine of the atonement could use the distinction in support of their own views about a universal and definite atonement, respectively. The same is true for those who adopt a doctrine of hypothetical universalism, such as Clifford himself. Disambiguating that to which "sufficiency" refers is vital in order for this distinction to be of use in discussions of the scope of the atonement.

is *not* just that, in principle, the condition or conditions necessary for the bringing about of that end have been met. The condition or conditions will effectually or actually bring about the end in question; there is no possibility that the end in question will not be brought about. Divine intentionality must also be at work in the atonement, too, so that the work of Christ is efficient in this second sense insofar as God intends it for the particular end God does.

However, this way of construing matters does not seem to be conceptually fine-grained enough. For one thing, there are different ways the notion of "sufficiency" can be construed in this context.[5] For this reason, let us distinguish between two different sorts of sufficiency, on the one hand, and efficiency, on the other. We can put it like this: If some condition x is, in principle, sufficient for some end E, then x is intrinsically sufficient for E. If x is in fact sufficient for some end E, where some agent G intends that the intrinsic sufficiency of E has a particular application, then x is extrinsically sufficient for E. If x actually brings about or otherwise ensures that E obtains (where G intends that x brings about E), then x is efficient for the bringing about of E. Note that an intrinsic sufficiency does not entail an extrinsic sufficiency. A particular thing could be, in principle, sufficient to some end E but not actually or in fact sufficient for E, because it is not applied to E. So, I could, in principle, have the means by which to vaccinate a whole populace from a deadly disease (intrinsic sufficiency), but I may intend that only a fraction of the

---

5. Sometimes the different ways of parsing "sufficiency" in the sufficiency–efficiency distinction can lead the unwary astray. For instance, in a discussion of the Saumur theologian Moïse Amyraut, Willem van Asselt remarks that whereas "Amyraut posited that Christ hypothetically died for all, the Dort theologians taught that the sacrifice of Christ was sufficient for all but efficient only for the elect. According to the Dort theologians, therefore, Christ died only for the elect." Asselt, *Introduction to Reformed Scholasticism* (Grand Rapids, MI: Reformation Heritage, 2011), 151. But assent to the sufficiency–efficiency distinction does not imply that Christ died only for the elect, which is why Amyraut could legitimately claim to hold views consistent with the Synod of Dort.

population be actually treated with the vaccine (extrinsic sufficiency). By contrast, if x is efficient for E, then x brings about E. So, the difference between extrinsic sufficiency and plain efficiency (in this way of discriminating between sufficiency and efficiency) is rather like saying I intend to vaccinate a fraction of the populace (extrinsic sufficiency), whereupon I go about ensuring that this is the case, actually vaccinating that number (that is, efficiently carrying out what I intended).

If we apply these ideas to the atonement, Christ's work is intrinsically sufficient, provided it is, in principle, able to save every fallen human being. In this way of thinking, the sufficiency of the atonement has no direct reference to the actual intent or extent of Christ's work—that is, to what God wills. It pertains only to the intrinsic merit of the person and work of Christ in atoning for sin. Usually this is thought to be an infinite merit, which is how we shall understand it.[6] Contrast this with the idea that Christ's work is extrinsically sufficient for the sin of all fallen humans. Those who defend the DA understand the sufficiency of Christ's work for fallen humanity only in the sense of an intrinsic sufficiency, whereas advocates of UA think of it as being both intrinsically and extrinsically sufficient. That is, according to the DA, the atonement is, in principle, sufficient to save all sinners because it generates an infinite merit. But God does not intend it to save all from sin. By contrast, according to defender of the UA, the atonement is, in principle, sufficient to save all sinners because it is infinitely

6. There is a historic debate about this matter, following from Duns Scotus's claim that Christ's work has no intrinsic value but only the value God assigns it. For one recent account of this, see my essay "On the Value and Necessity of the Work of Jesus Christ," in *The God of Salvation: Soteriology in Theological Perspective*, ed. Ivor J. Davidson and Murray A. Rae (Aldershot, UK: Ashgate, 2010), chap. 7. There is also a related historic debate about whether Christ's atonement is an exact equivalent to the penalty due for human sin or merely a suitable equivalent to it. But this need not detain us. For present purposes, we only need to allow that it is a work of infinite merit, whether that infinite merit is an exact or a suitable equivalent to the demerit of human sin.

meritorious, and God intends it to remove any legal obstacle to salvation, thereby providing the means by which all human beings may be saved. In this way, the distinction being made here between intrinsic and extrinsic sufficiency is similar to the distinction we saw Davenant deploy in chapter 7 between sufficiency in principle and a conditional, ordained sufficiency.

We come to the accomplished–applied distinction. Here, the work of Christ is regarded slightly differently, in terms of the merit it actually generates for the accomplishment of salvation and the application of that merit to those who are beneficiaries of Christ's work. Once again, the divine intention in salvation is at the forefront in this distinction. Both what Christ accomplishes in the atonement and how it is applied to those for whom he came to die have to do with the divine intention regarding those whom Christ saves. In other words, both accomplishment and application are about the concrete actuality of what is brought about in the atonement. Neither aspect refers to the value of Christ's work independent of, or abstracted from, those for whom it is intended, as is the case with the intrinsic sufficiency of the atonement. To illustrate: If I have accomplished the production of the vaccine, then it is ready to be administered. All that remains is for me to actually perform the vaccinations, applying the benefits of the medicine to those I treat.

There is clearly some conceptual overlap between our two pairs of distinctions. For instance, the efficiency component of the sufficiency–efficiency distinction has to do with the actual number of those to whom Christ's work is applied. But they are also different in important respects. The sufficiency–efficiency distinction has to do with the difference between the power of Christ's work independent of the purpose for which God intends it, and the purpose given divine intention. The accomplishment–application distinction works within the context of what God has ordained concerning the atonement.

It accomplishes its purpose and is applied to those for whom God intends it.

With these two distinctions in mind, we turn to analyze the double-payment objection in more detail.

The Double-Payment Objection Examined

There are a number of ways to provide reasons for thinking that the DA is the right way to conceive the scope of Christ's saving work. One strategy involves giving positive reasons for thinking that this doctrine is a better account of the work of Christ than any of the alternatives to it. This is not the only way of proceeding, however. In general, a doctrine can be indirectly argued for by showing that the alternatives to it have significant drawbacks that it does not share. Such reasoning is only as strong as the objections it provides to the alternative accounts of the same data. What is more, an objection to one alternative does not necessarily provide an objection to other viable alternatives to the view being defended. If I argue that democracy is a better political theory than an absolute monarchy because absolute monarchy does not provide for the political representation of the views of the general populace, this may be a reason for thinking there is a significant political drawback to absolute monarchy from which democracy does not suffer. That may be a good reason for preferring democracy to absolute monarchy; but it does not show that democracy is to be preferred over, say, socialism. That would need to be argued for on separate grounds, because socialism does not appear susceptible to the objection that it fails to provide for the political representation of the views of the general populace. Such reasoning has the following form: where A and B are both arguments for some particular view, C, B has a significant drawback that A does not have. Therefore, A is to be preferred over B as an argument for C, ceteris paribus.

The double-payment objection is an argument like this. It depends on showing that the main alternative to a DA, namely, UA, suffers from a significant structural problem to which the DA is immune. This provides a reason for thinking that the DA is to be preferred to a UA, other things being equal. However, it does not necessarily provide a reason for thinking the DA is preferable to all other views of the scope of the atonement. That would require a different sort of argument, one that is more comprehensive than the double-payment objection, taking into consideration all logically possible alternatives.[7] Nevertheless, given that DA and UA are arguably the two live options for the majority of historic Christian theology, this argumentative strategy is an important one. It may not be the only argument, or even the most important argument, that lends support to DA; but if the reasoning of this chapter is valid and sound, then the defender of DA cannot use the double-payment objection to provide a reason for thinking his view is preferable to the major historic alternative, that is, UA.[8]

Those who defend UA claim that Christ actually dies for all the sins of all humanity. His death really pays the price for the sin of the whole world. To return to our earlier distinction, according to UA, Christ's work is intrinsically and extrinsically sufficient for salvation.

7. The atonement could be definite or particular in scope (in the sense of particularity assumed in the DA), universal in scope, indefinite in scope, or completely ineffectual. A comprehensive discussion of the scope of atonement would have to account for all of these logically possible alternatives.

8. The double-payment objection has a long history in theological discussion. Gottschalk appears to be the first theologian to use it in the Middle Ages as a means by which to argue for the superiority of a definite atonement. It is also hinted at by Calvin, who says, "[S]ince Christ, by expiating their [humanity's] sins, has anticipated the judgment of God, and by His intercession not only abolishes death, but also covers our sins in oblivion, so that no account is taken of them . . . so there remains no condemnation, when the laws have been satisfied and the penalty already paid." John Calvin, *Institutes of the Christian Religion*, ed. John T. McNeill, trans. Ford Lewis Battles (1559; repr., Philadelphia: Westminster, 1960), 184–85 (emphasis added).

However, it is efficacious only for those who turn to Christ in faith. As Jacob Arminius, quoting Prosper of Aquitaine, puts it,

"He who says that the savior was not crucified for the redemption of the whole world, has regard, not to the virtue of the sacrament, but to the case of unbelievers, since the blood of Jesus Christ is the price paid for the whole world. To that precious ransom they are strangers, who, either being delighted with their captivity, have no wish to be redeemed, or, after they have been redeemed, return to the same servitude."

Moreover,

"With respect both to the magnitude and potency of the price, and with respect to the one general cause of mankind, the blood of Christ is the redemption of the whole world. But those who pass through this life without the faith of Christ, and without the sacrament of regeneration, are utter strangers to redemption."[9]

Now, suppose Arminius is right and Christ's death actually pays the penalty due for the sin of all fallen human beings. That is, suppose Christ's death is both intrinsically and extrinsically sufficient for the penalty due for human sin. Yet not all human beings are saved, for not all human beings have faith in Christ. Those who die without saving faith go to hell, where they are punished for their wickedness everlastingly. However, this generates a problem of double payment; for if the sin of those suffering in hell has already been atoned for by the work of Christ, then it appears unjust for God to require the punishment of the sinner in hell as well. This amounts to atoning for the same sins twice over, once in the person of Christ on the cross and a second time in the person of the unrepentant sinner in hell. But this is surely intolerable; such a double payment would be monumentally

9. Jacob Arminius, "Apology against Thirty-One Theological Articles: Article XII," in *The Works of Arminius*, trans. James Nichols (Grand Rapids, MI: Baker, 1986), 2:9–10. The citation is from Prosper of Aquitaine's *Ad objectiones Gallorum calumniantium*.

unjust. God is not unjust. So the atonement cannot be universal in the sense Arminius thinks it is. The upshot is that there is a significant problem with the logic of UA not shared by the doctrine of DA. Other things being equal, this is an important reason for preferring the DA to the UA.

There are two ways to avoid this double-payment objection. The first is to opt for universalism.[10] In this case, God intends that the intrinsically infinitely sufficient work of Christ be extrinsically sufficient for the salvation of all humanity. The redemption accomplished in his life and death is applied to all fallen humans, with the result that all are saved. Historically, the vast majority of Christian theologians have rejected universalism on the grounds that this is not the teaching of Scripture and ecclesiastical tradition (creeds, confessions, and so forth), as we have already had cause to note earlier in this study.[11] That leaves the option of restricting the scope of atonement, as per the DA. Then, Christ's work is intrinsically but not extrinsically sufficient for all human sin, and the atonement he accomplishes is effectually applied only to the elect in the purposes of God. The rest of humanity is passed over by divine grace. They do not have Christ's work applied to them, so they must suffer the penal consequences of their sin by being everlastingly punished in hell. As Augustus Montague Toplady memorably put it in his hymn "From Whence This Fear and Unbelief," "Payment God cannot twice demand / First at my wounded Surety's hand / And then again at mine."

---

10. Obviously, the doctrine of universalism is not synonymous with the doctrine of universal atonement.

11. See chapter 4 in particular. Whether universalism is theologically permissible is currently the subject of some debate. See, for example, Gregory MacDonald, *The Evangelical Universalist*, 2nd ed. (Eugene, OR: Cascade, 2012); and Robin A. Parry and Christopher H. Partridge, eds., *Universalism: The Current Debate* (Grand Rapids, MI: Eerdmans, 2004).

Assessing the Double-Payment Objection

We are now in a position to assess the effectiveness of the double-payment objection against the UA. Before examining some of the main counterarguments to the double-payment objection, it would be helpful to set forth a further theological distinction that informs many of the attempts to "push back" against the double-payment objection. This has to do with the difference between "pecuniary satisfaction" and "forensic satisfaction."

Pecuniary and Forensic Satisfaction

The nineteenth-century Princeton theologian Charles Hodge offers a particularly clear examination of this distinction. According to Hodge, pecuniary satisfaction is a kind of purely commercial transaction between two parties. One example would be paying a fine for a parking ticket. It does not matter who pays the fine, whether it is the perpetrator or someone else. What matters is that the fine is paid. The law is blind to the question of who it is that actually hands the fine over to the relevant authorities. Once the fine is paid, the person who has incurred the fine is no longer indebted. The transaction—the paying of the fine—automatically remits the debt. But, says Hodge, the same conditions do not apply to a case of what he calls forensic satisfaction. In that case, satisfaction for a debt does not necessarily liberate the debtor, because there is a connection between the perpetrator and the remittance of culpability that is not present in pecuniary satisfaction and that demands discretionary judgment.[12]

---

12. Hodge, *Systematic Theology*, 2:557. Cf. his earlier discussion of pecuniary satisfaction on p. 470. The distinction between forensic and pecuniary satisfaction is found elsewhere in nineteenth-century Reformed theology as well. See, e.g., Robert L. Dabney, *Christ Our Penal Substitute* (1898; repr., Harrisonburg, VA: Sprinkle, 1985), 33–34.

Hodge thinks that the atonement is an instance of forensic rather than pecuniary satisfaction. It does not automatically release the sinner from culpability for her sin, nor does it automatically bring about her redemption. For if the atonement is forensic in nature, then, in addition to its accomplishment in the purposes of God, the Holy Spirit must also apply its benefits to the sinner. It is vital to see that this distinction between pecuniary satisfaction and forensic satisfaction turns on whether the benefits of the atonement are automatically applied to those for whom Christ dies or applied only at the discretion of God and according to God's purposes. If the atonement is pecuniary in nature, there is no reason why the benefits of Christ's satisfaction should not be automatically applied to those for whose sin his work atones. It is a kind of transaction between God the Father and God the Son. But if it is forensic in nature, there is an element of divine discretion that obtains so that the benefits of Christ's work do not necessary apply ipso facto. In Hodge's way of thinking, if the atonement is forensic in nature, then there is nothing unjust in God's choosing to pass over some sinners, punishing their sin in hell, for the atonement does not grant any automatic means of salvation.[13] Hodge writes,

> It is a matter of justice that the blessings which Christ intended to secure for his people should actually be bestowed upon them. This follows for two reasons: first, they were promised to Him as the reward of his obedience and sufferings. God covenanted with Christ that if He fulfilled the conditions imposed, if He made satisfaction for the sins of his people, they should be saved. It follows, secondly, from the nature of a satisfaction. If the claims of justice are satisfied they cannot be again enforced. . . . This is what the Scriptures teach when they say that Christ gave Himself for a ransom. When a ransom is paid and accepted, the deliverance of the captive is a matter of justice. . . . So in the case of the

13. However, had God intended a forensic satisfaction to atone for all humanity, it would have done. It is just that, if the atonement is forensic in nature, it does not necessarily apply to all humanity—the scope of atonement depends on divine ordination.

satisfaction of Christ. Justice demands the salvation of his people. That is his reward. It is He who has acquired this claim on the justice of God; his people have no such claim except through Him. Besides, it is the nature of a satisfaction that it answers all the ends of punishment. What reason can there be for the infliction of the penalty for which satisfaction has been rendered?[14]

Those who defend UA often accuse DA partisans of being susceptible to the charge that their doctrine of atonement ought to be pecuniary in nature, or even that it implies a pecuniary atonement. For, according to the DA, God intends that Christ's infinitely meritorious work accomplish salvation for the elect alone—to which it is applied. But why are the benefits of Christ's work not automatic in their application, given the logic of the DA? If Christ dies to save only the elect, it would appear that there is a commercial element to the atonement. Christ dies to save the elect; his death (somehow) brings about the salvation of the elect. It is a sort of transaction between God the Father and God the Son. But once a commercial transaction is complete, the exchange for which the transaction was established should follow ipso facto. Yet Hodge and defenders of DA deny this. Why?

The main reason turns once again on the claim that the application of what Christ has accomplished in the atonement depends on divine discretion. Although God intends that Christ's work accomplish atonement only for the sins of the elect, it does not follow from this fact alone that in virtue of accomplishing this work, the benefits of atonement are immediately transferred to those for whom Christ dies.[15] The application of Christ's benefits normally depends upon the exercise of faith through the secret working of the Holy Spirit.[16] It is not as if Christ's work automatically transforms the elect,

14. Hodge, *Systematic Theology*, 2:472.
15. Cf. Thomas F. Torrance, who makes this case against the universalism of John A. T. Robinson in "Universalism or Election?," *Scottish Journal of Theology* 2 (1949): 310–18.

regenerating them at the very moment the crucifixion is finished. Although the atonement is the means by which God will bring about the regeneration of God's elect, the realization of this goal requires the further work of the Holy Spirit in conversion.[17] It is the difference between purchasing the vaccine for some number of individuals and actually inoculating those individuals. The mere purchase of the vaccine does not in and of itself inoculate anyone.

UA, Forensic Atonement, and Double Payment

So, it would seem that the DA doctrine does not require a commercial or pecuniary understanding of the atonement. But clearly, the UA does not demand this either, for the UA stipulates that Christ's atonement does not actually atone for anybody without the requirement of faith. So, neither the DA nor UA implies a pecuniary atonement; both are commensurate with a forensic atonement.

Does this have any implications for the double-payment objection to the UA? Let us turn to the nineteenth-century American Southern Presbyterian theologian Robert Dabney for an answer to this question. In the course of comments about the satisfaction of Christ in his Lectures on Theology, he says this:

> Nor would we attach any force to the argument, that if Christ made penal satisfaction for the sins of all, justice would forbid any to be punished. To urge this argument surrenders virtually the very ground on which the first Socinian objection was refuted, and is incompatible with the facts that God chastises justified believers, and holds elect unbelievers subject to wrath till they believe. Christ's satisfaction is

16. The caveat "normally" is important. We have noted in previous chapters that there may be situations in which a person is saved without conscious faith in Christ, e.g., those who die in infancy and the severely mentally impaired.
17. Christ's work is proleptically effectual for those who died before Christ, i.e., Old Testament saints. After the completion of Christ's earthly work, it is applied to those appointed for salvation by the Holy Spirit, so that Christ's work is effectual across time at many different moments and for many different people.

not a pecuniary equivalent, but only such a one as enables the Father, consistently with His attributes, to pardon, if in His mercy He sees fit. The whole avails of the satisfaction to a given man is suspended on His belief [sic]. There would be no injustice to the man, if he remaining an unbeliever, his guilt were punished twice over, first in his Savior, and then in Him.[18]

The "first Socinian objection" to which Dabney refers is the claim—which we have already touched upon—that Christ's satisfaction ought to release sinners from debt if it truly pays for sin. For once the price for sin is paid, it would be immoral and unjust for God to withhold the benefits of that transaction from those for whom it is made. Like Hodge, Dabney maintains that this Socinian objection would go through if Christ's satisfaction were pecuniary or commercial in nature. If, in other words, Christ's work were merely the automatic payment for all human sin, then all those for whom Christ died would be immediately released from their culpability before God, just as the person who has incurred a fine is immediately released from culpability for that fine as soon as it is paid by his friend. But, Dabney observes, this is not how the satisfaction of Christ works—either according to the DA or according to the UA. It is not a merely commercial or automatic transaction between God and the mass of fallen humanity. It is a forensic satisfaction, which requires some divine judgment in order to be applied. It does not imply an automatic transfer of benefits from Christ to fallen humans; "it is not ipso facto in this commercial sense," as Dabney puts it earlier in his discussion of atonement.[19]

This suggests that the distinction between pecuniary and forensic satisfaction undercuts the double-payment objection. Recall that, according to the UA view, the application of Christ's work to the

18. Robert L. Dabney, *Systematic Theology* (1871; repr., Edinburgh: Banner of Truth, 1985), 521.
19. Ibid., 504.

sinner depends upon a response of faith. Although the atonement is universal in scope, its effectiveness is not. So, it does not fall prey to the worry about the atonement's becoming a commercial transaction between God the Father and God the Son, which should apply automatically to those for whom Christ dies. But if that is right, then the double-payment objection has little force against UA, because it does not admit an automatic transference of the benefits of Christ once the atonement has been achieved. This is what Dabney is getting at when he says that there "would be no injustice to the man, if he remaining an unbeliever, his guilt were punished twice over, first in his Saviour, and then in Him." There would be injustice if atonement is commercial in nature, for then there would be no impediment to the benefits of atonement being automatically applied to the sinner, with the result that all of humanity would be immediately saved. However, there is nothing immoral in the defender of UA claiming that Christ's death atones for the sin of all humanity but that some humans are punished for their sin in hell. For, in the UA scheme, the damned are those who refuse Christ. They are offered pardon, but they prefer to remain outside the ambit of salvation procured for them by Christ's work. Hence, they are justly punished for their sins in hell despite the fact that Christ has atoned for their sin at the cross, for they refuse to avail themselves of what Christ has done for them. It is as if the stock of vaccine purchased for the whole community, upon being made available, is refused by some. There is vaccine enough for all, but some still refuse the free offer of medication and die as a consequence.

This is a significant counterargument to the double-payment objection. It effectively circumvents John Owen's famous trilemma of unbelief:

> God imposed his wrath due unto, and Christ underwent the pains of hell for, either all the sins of all men, or all the sins of some men, or some

sins of all men. If the last, some sins of all men, then have all men some sins to answer for, and so shall no man be saved. . . . If the second, this is it which we affirm, that Christ in their stead and room suffered for all the sins of all the elect in the world. If the first, why, then, are not all freed from the punishment of all their sins? You will say, "Because of their unbelief; they will not believe." But this unbelief, is it a sin, or is it not? If not, why should they be punished for it? If it be, then Christ underwent punishment for it or not. If so, why must that hinder them more than their other sins for which he died from partaking of the fruit of his death? If he did not, then he did not die for all their sins. Let them choose which part they will.[20]

Dabney's discussion demonstrates that if faith is a condition that must be met in order for the benefits of the atonement to be applied to an individual, then Christ's atonement cannot be a commercial satisfaction. It does not provide an automatic redemption for sin; faith is an additional requirement that must be exercised prior to the application of redemption. Note that this is true irrespective of Owen's point about Christ's work atoning for unbelief, which the defender of UA can accommodate as a trivial consequence of a truly universal atonement. Even if unbelief is dealt with at the cross, according to the UA, faith is still required for the application of the atonement that has been accomplished. In this case, there is no double-payment objection to answer, because those who are damned have simply not exercised the faith requisite for redemption. Christ dies for their sin, all right—including their unbelief; but if they do not have the faith necessary to have the benefits of his death applied to them, then they suffer the just punishment for their sin regardless.

We have already noted that this sort of reasoning can be found in the work of John Davenant, one of the Anglican defenders of hypothetical universalism. Davenant has much to say on the question of the necessity of faith for the application of atonement. Given

---

20. John Owen, "The Death of Death in the Death of Christ," in *The Works of John Owen*, ed. William H. Goold (1850–53; repr., Edinburgh: Banner of Truth, 1967), 10:173–74.

the importance of this counterargument to the double-payment objection, we quote him at length:

> [T]his universal redemption, satisfaction, or expiation performed by the death of Christ, brings nothing more than an universal cause of salvation to be confirmed and granted to the human race by the Divine ordination; the benefit of which every individual may enjoy through faith required by the Gospel. We therefore call Christ the Redeemer of the world, and teach that he made satisfaction for the sins not of some, but of the whole world, not because that on account of the payment of this price for the sins of the human race, all mankind individually are to be immediately delivered from captivity and death, but because by virtue of the payment of this price, all men individually may and ought to be delivered from death, and, in fact, are to be delivered according to the tenor of the evangelical covenant, that is, if they repent and believe in this Redeemer.

To the claim that UA is unjust because it means Christ atones for all human sin yet damns some to hell, he replies thus:

> That this would indeed be most unjust, if we ourselves had paid this price to God, or if our Surety, Jesus Christ, had so offered to God his blood as a satisfactory price, that without any other intervening condition, all men should be immediately absolved through the offering of the oblation made by him; or, finally, if God himself had covenanted with Christ when he died, that he would give faith to every individual, and all those other things which regard the infallible application of this sacrifice which was offered up for the human race. But since God himself of his own accord provided that this price should be paid to himself, it was in his own power to annex conditions, which being performed, this death should be advantageous to any man, not being performed it should not profit any man. Therefore no injustice is done to those persons who are punished by God after the ransom was accepted for the sins of the human race, because they offered nothing to God as a satisfaction for their sins, nor performed that condition, without the performance of which God willed not that this satisfactory price should benefit any individual. . . .

We ought not, therefore, to deny that the offering of Christ once made is a perfect satisfaction for the sins, not of some men only, but of all; yet so that he who is simply said to have died for all, promises remission of sin through his death and salvation conditionally, and will perform it to those alone who believe.[21]

Davenant offers an illustration of what he means.[22] Suppose some men commit high treason and are condemned to death. However, the king's son discharges the debt of these men by being punished in their place. Though he has become their substitute in this matter, it does not follow that those for whose sin he suffers are automatically released from the death penalty upon atonement being offered. For the king commands that the atonement made by his son shall be applied only to those traitors who willingly repent of their treason and serve the royal household faithfully henceforth. There is nothing unjust in such an arrangement, urges Davenant. And, as with the atonement of Christ, the application of the benefits purchased by the work of the prince as substitute is contingent upon penitence and faith. So, even if Christ's work atones for all human sin, including unbelief, its application still depends upon the exercise of faith.

In sum: The defender of UA is not guilty of endorsing a double payment for sin, because (a) those who hold to the UA doctrine conceive the atonement as forensic in nature, so that God must apply the accomplished work of Christ to the elect, and (b) this application (normally)[23] requires faith. Without faith, the sinner is justly damned in hell for failing to avail himself of Christ's work.

This leads to a final point. As all participants to this debate agree, faith is a divine gift (Eph. 2:8). So the reason why not all are saved,

---

21. John Davenant, "A Dissertation on the Death of Christ," in *An Exposition of the Epistle of St. Paul to the Colossians* (London: Hamilton, Adams, 1832), 2:374–77.

22. Cited in the previous chapter.

23. Here, as previously, I insert the parenthetical qualification to allow for certain special cases where salvation appears to be possible in the absence of personal faith.

although Christ's work does indeed atone for all human sin, including the sin of unbelief, is that not all are given the gift of faith. In other words, the defender of UA can resist the slide to universalism by appealing to the divine mystery of election. God gives faith to some and they are saved. God passes over others, according to God's good pleasure and will. We are not given to understand why this is the case, but it is the clear teaching of Scripture that this is how God arranges things (see, for example, Deut. 29:29; Prov. 16:33; Eph. 1:5, 11; Rom. 8:28-29; Luke 12:32; and Acts 13:48).

Summary and Conclusion

Let us take stock. It seems that the defender of UA has the resources to meet the double-payment objection. Owen is right to think Christ's work atones for all sin, unbelief included. But he is mistaken in thinking that if Christ's work atones for all human sin, including the sin of unbelief, there is no impediment to the salvation of all human sinners. Faith is a condition of the application of the redemption accomplished by Christ. This, as Davenant and Dabney make clear, is a perfectly just arrangement; in which case, even if UA obtains, there is no doctrine of double payment to answer. This does not necessarily mean that UA is the right way of conceiving the scope of atonement, of course. One might believe that the double-payment objection is a poor argument against UA while also thinking that there are other good reasons for remaining a defender of DA. Nevertheless, if this reasoning is sound, then the double-payment objection fails. Given that this is widely regarded as the most damning objection to UA, this is not an insignificant conclusion. Advocates of DA must look elsewhere for resources with which to defend their view against those convinced that the atonement is universal in scope.

Conclusion

> The Reformed faith impels persons to confess their faith as part of the
> ecumenical church, the whole people of God. . . . Reformed churches
> are a portion of the full household of faith. . . . Though some Reformed
> bodies have tended to become more narrow and almost assume that their
> formulations are the only means of expressing God's truth, this impulse
> runs counters to the genuine heartbeat of Reformed faith. Reformed
> faith is open to God's Spirit, who may encounter us at any time in any
> place.
> —Donald McKim, *Introducing the Reformed Faith*

In the first of his 1898 Stone Lectures, the great Dutch Reformed
statesman Abraham Kuyper argues that there are different ways in
which the term *Calvinism* has been used.[1] There is its deployment as
a sectarian name, used to disparage a particular theological position.
There is its confessional guise, as something almost synonymous
with a particular defining doctrine, namely, predestination. There is
the denominational use among some Baptists ("Calvinistic Baptists")
and Methodists of the Whitefieldian stripe ("Calvinistic Methodists").
This is particularly strange given that during Calvin's lifetime, "no
Reformed Church ever dreamed of naming a Church of Christ after

---

1. Abraham Kuyper, "Calvinism a Life-System," in *Lectures on Calvinism, The Stone Lectures of 1898* (Grand Rapids, MI: Eerdmans, 1961), 9–40. "Life-system" is Kuyper's attempt to Anglicize the German word *Weltanshauung*, which is more commonly translated "worldview."

any man."[2] Then there is the use of *Calvinism* as a scientific term in a historical, philosophical, or political sense, which was current in the German scholarship at the end of the nineteenth century, when the Stone Lectures were originally delivered, at Princeton Theological Seminary. Each of these designations has its limitations, as Kuyper points out. It has been worn as a badge of pride as much as it has been a term of abuse. The idea that Calvinism is equivalent to some "central dogma" that defines all those who adhere to its tenets has been shown in the recent historiographical work on Reformation and post-Reformation Reformed theology by scholars like Willem van Asselt, Carl Trueman, and Richard Muller to be without historical foundation. Indeed, this recent work has challenged the usefulness of the term *Calvinism* as a denominational epithet, because this use associates a broad confessional tradition with the work of one man in a way that is ahistorical. Better to refer to the Reformed churches than the Calvinistic ones. However, *Calvinism* is so deeply ingrained that it is unlikely to be entirely displaced and, in any case, does serve some purposes even if only to distinguish the tenor of the theology that was adopted by a range of different churches and denominations after the Reformation that did not consider themselves Lutheran or Socinian. Kuyper remarks, "In a given sense, therefore, it may be said that the entire field which in the end was covered by the Reformation, so far as it was not Lutheran and not Socinian, was dominated in principle by Calvinism. Even the Baptists applied for shelter at the tents of the Calvinists."[3] This seems right.

Nevertheless, it has been the burden of this book that *Calvinism* is still regarded too narrowly, even among those cognizant of the recent historical-theological reassessment of the shape and character of the early Reformed tradition. Although *Calvinism* is not so frequently

2. Ibid.,13.
3. Ibid., 16.

regarded as another name for "rigid predestinarianism" these days, it is still often associated with a fairly tightly connected set of doctrines that are usually summed up in the tulip acronym. Some myths still persist: that the Reformed exercise an antiexperiential religion; that they all hold to a doctrine of double predestination; that they are theological determinists, effectively denying human freedom; that the internal logic of their views about divine ordination should drive them to embrace universalism; and that they regard the atonement as definite in scope and intended for a particular number of people, the elect, so that the vast majority of the human race is simply damned without any chance of salvation.[4]

In each of these cases, we have seen that the myth is not the whole story. There is a softer face to Calvinism; the Reformed tradition truly is a confessionalism that tolerates doctrinal plurality within certain parameters. In several of these cases (though not all), its confessionalism is more like a centered set than a bounded one, defined by sharing things in common rather than by excluding marginal views. This is even true of the Reformed confessions themselves, which have sometimes (and mistakenly) been thought of as making nice distinctions that constrain their adherents rather than providing a dogmatic framework within which Christian freedom may be exercised.

There is a sense in which the purposes of God are all "yea and amen." God has ordained all that comes to pass — a deliverance of Scripture so plain it is difficult to see how it can be elided. However, this in and of itself is consistent with one of several different views about the relationship between God's plans and human freedom, as we have seen in chapters 2 and 3. In fact, there is reason to think that

---

4. For a useful recent attempt to rebut some of the more persistent myths about Calvinism, see Kenneth J. Stewart, *Ten Myths about Calvinism: Recovering the Breadth of the Reformed Tradition* (Downers Grove, IL: IVP Academic, 2011).

one can be both a "Calvinist" and a libertarian about human freedom, and that this does not go against the grain of the major confessions of the Reformed faith but is consistent with them. Although one could be an Augustinian and a universalist, and although Augustinianism as a theological stream might be thought to press in the direction of universalism, given certain assumptions about God's purposes in creation and salvation, there are resources within the Reformed branch of Augustinianism with which to resist the pull toward this conclusion for principled theological reasons. What is more, the scope of atonement need not be conceived of as "limited." There is a venerable tradition in Reformed theology (now largely forgotten, or treated as the eccentricity of a small minority) that thinks of the atonement as universal in its ordained, conditional sufficiency, though it is efficacious only for the elect. It turns out that the major objection to the doctrine of universal atonement—that regarding the problem of a double payment—is a failure. There is scope within Reformed confessionalism, including the Canons of Dort and the Westminster Confession, for a doctrine of hypothetical universalism.

But make no mistake: this is not the whole story either. I have not claimed that these attempts to redress the balance in Reformed theology in favor of a more generous orthodoxy and a more charitable reading of the major confessions provide a *complete* account of Reformed approaches to the question of the scope of salvation. The aim here has been much more modest: to commend to those within and without the ambit of the Reformed community a way of looking at several central and defining doctrines of Calvinistic theology that broadens out what is regarded as appropriately Reformed doctrine.

To some, this will signal a worrying declension, as if Reformed theology required a much more rigid adherence not only to particular confessions but also to a particular way of interpreting key tenets of those confessions. However, as I have already made plain in the course of this book, it seems to me that confessional and creedal documents are primarily about confessing the faith once delivered to the saints. They also serve to help the faithful see that certain notions are damaging to one's spiritual health, because they are theologically unorthodox. Clearly, saying what the faith is and denying certain errors are perfectly consistent with allowing more than one particular theological interpretation of a given doctrine the space to flourish. Thus, the ancient fathers of the church did not set out in detail what the divine persons or essences were in respect to the Trinity, though they did confess that God is one and yet subsists in three persons, and they did take care to exclude certain mistaken ways of understanding the divine nature, such as tritheism or modalism. But this leaves a lot of room for different models of the Trinity to flourish, and history testifies to the theological riches and doctrinal plurality that has followed on the heels of this decision.

In a similar manner, the Reformed confessions restate the faith and rebut errors. They are more detailed in some of their statements than the ancient creeds, but that is to be expected in confessional documents that represent a particular theological expression of the Christian tradition. Nevertheless, as the arguments of this book concerning things like libertarian Calvinism and hypothetical universalism have attempted to show, even where a line is taken in a particular confession, there is more "wiggle room" than has often been thought to exist. Or at least there is reason to think that greater doctrinal plurality has been regarded as acceptable in these instances, as the work of a number of eminent divines of previous generations testifies. In retrieving their views, or using their doctrines as a point of departure for contemporary theological construction, we have been able to show the virtues of this broader confessionalism.

In his introduction to the Reformed faith, Donald McKim points out that the Reformed tradition is one family of the Christian

Church: "Though diversities abound, important common ingredients mark us as brothers and sisters in the Reformed family. These 'family resemblances' are discovered in the ways in which we find that our faith is best nourished, our understandings of the Scriptures and theology best articulated, and our Christian lives best focused."[5] Too often in recent theology, Reformed divines have presented their own tradition as something much narrower than it actually is. A small section of the spectrum of views on several nodal theological topics are commonly presented as the only live options, or even as the only dogmatically tolerable ones within the bounds of theological orthodoxy as understood by confessional Calvinists. If this volume goes some way toward redressing that balance and challenging Reformed thinkers to look again at the wealth and diversity of the tradition to which they belong, then it will have succeeded in the task for which its author sent it out into the world. That would be a theological softening of the right sort; a recognition that the themes it contains are not deviant forms of Calvinism after all.

5. Donald McKim, *Introducing the Reformed Faith* (Louisville, KY: Westminster John Knox, 2001), 2.

Works Cited and Consulted

Adams, Marilyn McCord. "Hell and the God of Justice." *Religious Studies* 11 (1974): 433–47.

Adams, Robert M. *The Virtue of Faith.* New York: Oxford University Press, 1987.

Adams, Robert Merrihew and Marilyn McCord Adams, eds. *The Problem of Evil.* Oxford: Oxford University Press, 1990.

Ames, William. *The Marrow of Theology.* Translated by John D. Eusden. Boston: Pilgrim, 1968.

Amyraut, Moïse. "Brief Treatise on Predestination and Its Dependent Principles." Translated by Richard Lum. PhD diss., Dallas Theological Seminary, 1985. Originally published as *Brief traitte de la predestination et de ses principales dépendances.* Saumur, Fr.: Lesnier & Debordes, 1634.

———. *Six sermons de la nature, estendue, necessite, dispensation, et efficace de l'evangile.* Saumur, Fr.: Girard & de Lerpiniere, 1636.

Anselm of Canterbury. *St. Anselm: Basic Writings.* Translated by S. N. Deane. 2nd ed. (La Salle, IL: Open Court, 1962).

Aquinas, Thomas. *Summa Contra Gentiles.* Edited by Anton Pegis et al. 4 vols. Notre Dame, IN: University of Notre Dame Press, 1991.

Arminius, Jacob. "Apology against Thirty-One Theological Articles: Article XII." In *The Works of Arminius,* translated by James Nichols. Vol. 2. Grand Rapids, MI: Baker, 1986.

———. *Arminius and His Declaration of Sentiments: An Annotated Translation with Introduction and Theological Commentary.* Edited and translated by W. Stephen Gunter. Waco, TX: Baylor University Press, 2012.

Armstrong, Brian G. *Calvinism and the Amyraut Heresy: Protestant Scholasticism and Humanism in Seventeenth Century France.* Madison, WI: University of Wisconsin Press, 1969.

Asselt, Willem van. *Introduction to Reformed Scholasticism.* Grand Rapids, MI: Reformation Heritage, 2011.

Asselt, Willem van, J. Martin Bac, and Roelf T. te Velde, eds. *Reformed Thought on Freedom: The Concept of Free Choice in Early Modern Reformed Theology.* Grand Rapids: Baker Academic, 2010.

Augustine, Aurelius. *City of God.* Translated by Henry Bettenson. Harmondsworth, UK: Penguin, 1972.

———. *Enchiridion.* Translated by Ernst Evans. London: SPCK, 1953.

Balthasar, Hans Urs von. *Dare We Hope "That All Men Be Saved"? With a Short Discourse on Hell.* Translated by David Kipp and Lothar Krauth. 1986, 1987. Reprint, San Francisco: Ignatius, 2011.

Barth, Karl. *Church Dogmatics.* Edited by Geoffrey W. Bromiley and Thomas F. Torrance. 5 vols. in 13 pts. Edinburgh: T & T Clark, 1956–75.

———. *Dogmatics in Outline.* Translated by G. T. Thomson. London: SCM, 1949.

Bauckham, Richard. "Universalism: A Historic Survey." *Themelios* 4, no. 2 (1978): 47–54.

Bebbington, David. *Evangelicalism in Modern Britain: A History from the 1730s to the 1980s.* London: Routledge, 1989.

Beck, A. J., and Antonie Vos. "Conceptual Patterns Related to Reformed Scholasticism." *Nederlands Theologisch Tijdschrift* 57 (2003): 223–33.

Berkhof, Hendrikus. *Christian Faith: An Introduction to the Study of the Faith.* Translated by Sierd Woudstra. Grand Rapids, MI: Eerdmans, 1979.

Berkhof, Louis. *Systematic Theology.* Edinburgh: Banner of Truth, 1958.

Berkouwer, G. C. *Faith and Justification.* Translated by Lewis B. Smedes. Grand Rapids, MI: Eerdmans, 1954.

———. *The Triumph of Grace in the Theology of Karl Barth.* Translated by Harry R. Boer. Grand Rapids, MI: Eerdmans, 1956.

Blacketer, Raymond. "Definite Atonement in Historical Perspective." In *The Glory of the Atonement: Biblical, Theological, and Practical Perspectives,* edited by Charles E. Hill and Frank A. James III, 304–23. Downers Grove, IL: IVP Academic, 2004.

Boersma, Hans. *A Hot Pepper Corn: Richard Baxter's Doctrine of Justification in Its Seventeenth-Century Context of Controversy.* Vancouver, BC: Regent College Publishing, 2004.

Boettner, Lorainne. *The Reformed Doctrine of Predestination.* Philadelphia: Presbyterian and Reformed, 1932.

Bonda, Jan. *The One Purpose of God: An Answer to the Doctrine of Eternal Punishment.* Grand Rapids, MI: Eerdmans, 1998.

Bromiley, Geoffrey W. *Introduction to the Theology of Karl Barth.* Edinburgh: T & T Clark, 1979.

Brunner, Emil. *Dogmatics.* Translated by Olive Wyon. Vol. 1, *The Christian Doctrine of God.* London: Lutterworth, 1949.

Calvin, John. *Institutes of the Christian Religion.* Edited by John T. McNeill. Translated by Ford Lewis Battles. 1559. Reprint, Philadelphia: Westminster, 1960.

Cameron, Nigel M. de S., ed. *Universalism and the Doctrine of Hell.* Carlisle, UK: Paternoster, 1992.

Carleton, George, et al., *The Collegiate Suffrage of the Divines of Great Britaine: Concerning the Five Articles Controverted in the Low Countries.* London: Milbourne, 1629. Reprinted in Milton, *The British Delegation and the Synod of Dort.*

Carroll, Lewis. *Through the Looking-Glass: And What Alice Found There.* London: Macmillan, 1871.

Catechism of the Catholic Church, located at http://www.vatican.va/archive/ENG0015/_INDEX.HTM (last accessed June 2014).

Chapman, Mark. *Anglicanism: A Very Short Introduction.* Oxford: Oxford University Press, 2006.

———. *Anglican Theology.* London: T & T Clark, 2012.

Clifford, Alan C. *Atonement and Justification: English Evangelical Theology, 1640–1790; An Evaluation.* Oxford: Oxford University Press, 1990.

Colquhoun, John. *Sermons, Chiefly on Doctrinal Subjects.* Edinburgh: Collie, 1836.

Colwell, John. "The Contemporaneity of the Divine Decision: Reflections on Barth's Denial of Universalism." In Cameron, *Universalism and the Doctrine of Hell.*

The Confession of Faith and Larger Catechism, Shorter Catechism, Directory of Public Worship, Presbyterial Church Government. Edinburgh: Blackwood, 1969.

Couenhoeven, Jesse. *Stricken by Sin, Cured by Christ: Agency, Necessity, and Culpability in Augustinian Theology.* New York: Oxford University Press, 2013.

Crisp, Oliver D. "Barth and Jonathan Edwards on Reprobation (and Hell)." In *Engaging with Barth: Contemporary Evangelical Critiques,* edited by David Gibson and Daniel Strange, 300–322. New York: T & T Clark, 2008.

———. "Desiderata for Models of the Hypostatic Union." In *Christology Ancient and Modern: Explorations in Constructive Dogmatics,* edited by Oliver D. Crisp and Fred Sanders. Grand Rapids, MI: Zondervan Academic, 2012.

———. "Divine Retribution: A Defence." *Sophia* 42 (2003): 35–52.

———. *God Incarnate: Explorations in Christology.* London: T & T Clark, 2009.

———. "On Barth's Denial of Universalism." *Themelios* 29 (2003): 18–29.

———. "On the Letter and Spirit of Karl Barth's Doctrine of Election: A Reply to O'Neil." *Evangelical Quarterly* 79 (2007): 53–67.

———. "On the Value and Necessity of the Work of Jesus Christ." In *The God of Salvation: Soteriology in Theological Perspective,* edited by Ivor J. Davidson and Murray A. Rae. Aldershot, UK: Ashgate, 2010.

———. *Retrieving Doctrine: Essays in Reformed Theology.* Downers Grove, IL: IVP Academic, 2011.

Cunningham, William. "Calvinism and the Doctrine of Philosophical Necessity" (1862). In *The Reformers and the Theology of the Reformation,* 471–599. Edinburgh: Banner of Truth, 1989.

———. *Historical Theology: A Review of the Principal Doctrinal Discussions in the Christian Church since the Apostolic Age.* 3rd ed. Vol. 2. Edinburgh: T & T Clark, 1870.

Dabney, Robert L. *Christ Our Penal Substitute.* 1898. Reprint, Harrisonburg, VA: Sprinkle, 1985.

———. *Systematic Theology.* 1871. Reprint, Edinburgh: Banner of Truth, 1985.

Davenant, John. *Animadversions: Written by the Right Reverend Father in God, John Lord Bishop of Sarisbury upon a Treatise Intituled God's Love to Mankind.* London: Partridge, 1641.

———. *Baptismal Regeneration and the Final Perseverance of the Saints.* Translated by Josiah Allport. London: Macintosh, 1864.

———. *A Dissertation on the Death of Christ.* In *An Exposition of the Epistle of St. Paul to the Colossians,* edited and translated by Josiah Allport. 2 vols. London: Hamilton, Adams, 1832.

———. *A Treatise on Justification; or the Disputatio de justitia habituali et actuali.* Translated by Josiah Allport. 2 vols. 1634. Reprint, London: Hamilton, Adams, 1844–46.

Davis, Stephen T. "Universalism, Hell, and the Fate of the Ignorant." *Modern Theology* 6, no. 2 (1990): 173–86.

Dempsey, Michael T., ed. *Trinity and Election in Contemporary Theology.* Grand Rapids, MI: Eerdmans, 2011.

Driel, Edwin Christian van. *Incarnation Anyway: Arguments for Supralapsarian Christology.* New York: Oxford University Press, 2008.

Ecumenical Creeds and Reformed Confessions. Grand Rapids, MI: CRC, 1988.

Edwards, Jonathan. "The Eternity of Hell Torments." In *The Works of Jonathan Edwards,* edited by Edward Hickman. Vol. 2. 1834. Reprint, Edinburgh: Banner of Truth, 1988.

———. *Ethical Writings,* edited by Paul Ramsey. Vol. 8 of *The Works of Jonathan Edwards,* edited by Perry Miller. New Haven, CT: Yale University Press, 1989.

————. *Freedom of the Will,* edited by Paul Ramsey. Vol. 1 of *The Works of Jonathan Edwards,* edited by Perry Miller. New Haven, CT: Yale University Press, 1957.

————. *The "Miscellanies"(Entry Nos. a–z, aa–zz, 1–500),* edited by Thomas A. Schafer. Vol. 13 of *The Works of Jonathan Edwards,* edited by Perry Miller. New Haven, CT: Yale University Press, 1994.

————. "Personal Narrative." In *A Jonathan Edwards Reader,* edited by John E. Smith, Harry S. Stout, and Kenneth P. Minkema. New Haven, CT: Yale University Press, 1995.

————. *Religious Affections,* edited by John E. Smith. Vol. 2 of *The Works of Jonathan Edwards,* edited by Perry Miller. New Haven, CT: Yale University Press, 1959.

Ehrlich, Dror. "Some Further Reflections regarding the Talbott–Crisp Debate on the Augustinian Concept of Everlasting Punishment." *Religious Studies* 47 (2011): 23–40.

Fischer, John Martin. "Frankfurt-Type Examples and Semi-Compatibilism." In *The Oxford Handbook of Free Will,* edited by Robert Kane, 281–308. Oxford: Oxford University Press, 2002.

————, and Mark Ravizza, *Responsibility and Control: A Theory of Moral Responsibility* (Cambridge: Cambridge University Press, 1999).

————, Robert Kane, Derk Pereboom, and Manuel Vargas. *Four Views on Free Will.* Malden, MA: Blackwell, 2007.

Frankfurt, Harry. "Alternate Possibilities and Moral Responsibility." *Journal of Philosophy* 66 (1969): 829–39.

————. *The Importance of What We Care About.* Cambridge: Cambridge University Press, 1988.

Gatiss, Lee. *For Us and for Our Salvation: "Limited Atonement" in the Bible, Doctrine, History, and Ministry.* Latimer Studies 78. London: Latimer Trust, 2012.

————. "'Shades of Opinion within a Generic Calvinism': The Particular Redemption Debate at the Westminster Assembly." *Reformed Theological Review* 69, no. 2 (2010): 101–18.

Gibson, David, and Jonathan Gibson, eds. *From Heaven He Came and Sought Her: Definite Atonement in Historical, Biblical, Theological, and Pastoral Perspective.* Wheaton, IL: Crossway, 2013.

Gill, John. *A Body of Doctrinal Divinity.* London, 1769.

Girardeau, John L. *The Will in Its Theological Relations.* Columbia, SC: Duffie, 1891.

Godfrey, W. Robert. "Reformed Thought on the Extent of the Atonement to 1618." *Westminster Theological Journal* 37 (1975): 133–71.

Greggs, Tom. *Barth, Origen, and Universal Salvation: Restoring Particularity.* Oxford: Oxford University Press, 2009.

———. "'Jesus Is Victor': Passing the Impasse of Barth on Universalism." *Scottish Journal of Theology* 60, no. 2 (2007): 196–212.

Gunton, Colin E. "Salvation." In Webster, *Cambridge Companion to Karl Barth.*

———. *Theology through the Theologians.* Edinburgh: T & T Clark, 1996.

Hart, Trevor. "Universalism: Two Distinct Types." In Cameron, *Universalism and the Doctrine of Hell.*

Hastie, William. *The Theology of the Reformed Church in Its Fundamental Principles.* Edinburgh: T & T Clark, 1904.

Haykin, Michael A. G., and Mark Jones, eds. *Drawn into Controversie: Reformed Theological Diversity and Debates within Seventeenth-Century British Puritanism.* Reformed Historical Theology 17. Göttingen, Ger.: Vandenhoeck & Ruprecht, 2011.

Haykin, Michael A. G., and Kenneth J. Stewart, eds. *The Advent of Evangelicalism: Exploring Historical Continuities.* Nashville, TN: B & H, 2008.

Helm, Paul. "Are They Few That Be Saved?" In Cameron, *Universalism and the Doctrine of Hell.*

———. *Faith with Reason.* Oxford: Oxford University Press, 2000.

———. "Reformed Thought on Freedom: Some Further Thoughts." *Journal of Reformed Theology* 4, no. 3 (2010): 185–207.

———. "'Structural Indifference' and Compatibilism in Reformed Orthodoxy." *Journal of Reformed Theology* 5, no. 2 (2011): 184–205.

————. "Synchronic Contingency Again." *Nederlands Theologisch Tijdschrift* 57 (2003): 234–38.

————. "Synchronic Contingency in Reformed Scholasticism: A Note of Caution." *Nederlands Theologisch Tijdschrift* 57 (2003): 207–22.

Heppe, Heinrich. *Reformed Dogmatics.* Translated by G. T. Thomson. 1861. Reprint, London: Collins, 1950.

Hick, John. *Death and Eternal Life.* London: Collins, 1976.

Hickman, Louise. "Love Is All and God Is Love: Universalism in Peter Sterry (1613–1672) and Jeremiah White (1630–1707)." In *"All Will Be Well": Explorations in Universalism and Christian Theology, from Origen to Moltmann,* edited by Gregory MacDonald, 95–115. Eugene, OR: Cascade, 2011.

Hodge, A. A. *The Atonement.* Philadelphia: Presbyterian Board of Publication, 1867.

Hodge, Charles. *Systematic Theology.* Vol. 2. 1871. Reprint, Grand Rapids, MI: Eerdmans, 1940.

Hoeksema, Herman. *Reformed Dogmatics.* 1966. Reprint, Grand Rapids, MI: Reformed Free Publishing Association, 1973.

Hunsinger, George. *Disruptive Grace: Studies in the Theology of Karl Barth.* Grand Rapids, MI: Eerdmans, 2000.

————. *How to Read Karl Barth: The Shape of His Theology.* Oxford: Oxford University Press, 1991.

————. "A Tale of Two Simultaneities: Justification and Sanctification in Calvin and Barth." In *Conversing with Barth,* edited by John C. McDowell and Mike Higton, 68–89. Aldershot, UK: Ashgate, 2004.

Jersak, Brad. *Her Gates Will Never Be Shut: Hope, Hell, and the New Jerusalem.* Eugene, OR: Wipf & Stock, 2010.

Klauber, Martin I. "The Helvetic Formula Consensus (1675): An Introduction and Translation." *Trinity Journal* 11 (1990): 103–23.

————. *The Problem of Hell.* New York: Oxford University Press, 1993.

Kuyper, Abraham. *Lectures on Calvinism, The Stone Lectures of 1898.* Grand Rapids, MI: Eerdmans, 1961.

———. *The Work of the Holy Spirit.* Translated by Henri de Vries. Vol. 2. 1900. Reprint, Grand Rapids, MI: Eerdmans, 1946.

Kvanvig, Jonathan L. *Destiny and Deliberation: Essays in Philosophical Theology.* Oxford: Oxford University Press, 2011.

———. *The Problem of Hell.* New York: Oxford University Press, 1993.

Letham, Robert. *The Westminster Assembly: Reading Its Theology in Historical Context.* Phillipsburg, NJ: Presbyterian & Reformed, 2009.

Lombard, Peter. *On the Incarnation of the Word.* Vol. 3 of *The Sentences,* translated by Giulio Silano. Toronto: Pontifical Institute of Medieval Studies, 2008.

Ludlow, Morwenna. "Universal Salvation and a Soteriology of Divine Punishment." *Scottish Journal of Theology* 53 (2000): 449–71.

MacDonald, Gregory. *The Evangelical Universalist.* 2nd ed. Eugene, OR: Cascade, 2012.

MacDonald, Scott. "What Is Philosophical Theology?" In *Arguing about Religion,* edited by Kevin Timpe, 17–29. New York: Routledge, 2009.

Marshall, I. Howard. "The New Testament Does Not Teach Universal Salvation." In Cameron, *Universalism and the Doctrine of Hell.*

McCormack, Bruce L. "Grace and Being: The Role of God's Gracious Election in Karl Barth's Theological Ontology." In *Orthodox and Modern: Studies in the Theology of Karl Barth.* Grand Rapids, MI: Baker Academic, 2008. Originally published in *The Cambridge Companion to Karl Barth,* edited by John Webster. Cambridge: Cambridge University Press, 2000.

———. "'So That He May Be Merciful to All': Karl Barth and the Problem of Universalism." in *Karl Barth and American Evangelicalism,* edited by Bruce L. McCormack and Clifford B. Anderson, 227–49. Grand Rapids, MI: Eerdmans, 2011.

McDonald, Suzanne. *Re-Imaging Election: Divine Election as Representing God to Others and Others to God.* Grand Rapids, MI: Eerdmans, 2010.

McKim, Donald. *Introducing the Reformed Faith.* Louisville, KY: Westminster John Knox, 2001.

Milton, Anthony, ed. *The British Delegation and the Synod of Dort (1618–1619)*. Church of England Record Society 13. Woodbridge, UK: Boydell, 2005.

Moore, Jonathan D. *English Hypothetical Universalism: John Preston and the Softening of Reformed Theology*. Grand Rapids, MI: Eerdmans, 2007.

———. "The Extent of the Atonement: English Hypothetical Universalism versus Particular Redemption." In Haykin and Jones, *Drawn into Controversie*, 124–61.

Morris, Thomas V. *Anselmian Explorations*. Notre Dame, IN: University of Notre Dame Press, 1987.

Mouw, Richard J. *Calvinism in the Las Vegas Airport*. Grand Rapids, MI: Zondervan, 2004.

Muller, Richard A. *Calvin and the Reformed Tradition: On the Work of Christ and the Order of Salvation*. Grand Rapids, MI: Baker Academic, 2012.

———. "Diversity in the Reformed Tradition." In Haykin and Jones, *Drawn into Controversie*.

———. *God, Creation, and Providence in the Theology of Jacob Arminius*. Grand Rapids, MI: Baker, 1991.

———. "Jonathan Edwards and the Absence of Free Choice: A Parting of the Ways in the Reformed Tradition." *Jonathan Edwards Studies* 1, no. 1 (2011). http://jestudies.yale.edu/index.php/journal/article/view/63.

Nicole, Roger. "The Case for Definite Atonement." *Bulletin of the Evangelical Theological Society* 10, no. 4 (1967): 199–207.

Olson, Roger. *Arminian Theology: Myths and Realities*. Downers Grove, IL: Intervarsity, 2006.

Owen, John. *The Death of Death in the Death of Christ*. In *The Works of John Owen*, edited by William H. Goold. Vol. 10. 1850–53. Reprint, Edinburgh: Banner of Truth, 1967.

Parry, Robin A., and Christopher H. Partridge, eds. *Universal Salvation? The Current Debate*. Grand Rapids, MI: Eerdmans, 2004.

Plantinga, Alvin. *The Nature of Necessity*. Oxford: Oxford University Press, 1974.

Rahner, Karl. "Religious Inclusivism." In *Philosophy of Religion: Selected Readings,* edited by Michael Peterson et al. 4th ed. New York: Oxford University Press, 2010.

Reitan, Eric, and John Kronen. *God's Final Victory: A Comparative Philosophical Case for Universalism.* New York: Bloomsbury, 2011.

Rogers, Katherin A. *Perfect Being Theology.* Edinburgh: Edinburgh University Press, 1998.

Rowe, William L. *Can God Be Free?* Oxford: Oxford University Press, 2004.

———. "Evil and the Theistic Hypothesis: A Response to Wykstra." In Adams and Adams, *Problem of Evil.*

Schaff, Philip. *The Creeds of Christendom: With a History and Critical Notes.* 6th ed. 3 vols. 1931. Reprint, Grand Rapids, MI: Baker, 1983.

Schleiermacher, Friedrich. *The Christian Faith.* 1830. Reprint, Edinburgh: T & T Clark, 1999.

Sessions, William Lad. *The Concept of Faith.* Ithaca, NY: Cornell University Press, 1994.

Seymour, Charles. "Hell, Justice, and Freedom." *International Journal for Philosophy of Religion* 43 (1998): 69–86.

Sonderegger, Katherine. "Called to Salvation in Christ: Justification and Predestination." In *What Is Justification About? Reformed Contributions to an Ecumenical Theme,* edited by Michael Weinrich and John P. Burgess, 122–38. Grand Rapids, MI: Eerdmans, 2009.

Stam, F. P. van. *The Controversy over the Theology of Saumur, 1635–1650: Disrupting Debates among the Huguenots in Complicated Circumstances.* Amsterdam: APA-Holland University Press, 1988.

Stanglin, Keith, and Thomas H. McCall. *Jacob Arminius: Theologian of Grace.* New York: Oxford University Press, 2012.

Stewart, Kenneth J. "The Evangelical Doctrine of Scripture, 1650–1850: A Re-Examination of David Bebbington's Theory." In Haykin and Stewart, *Advent of Evangelicalism,* 398–413.

———. *Ten Myths about Calvinism: Recovering the Breadth of the Reformed Tradition.* Downers Grove, IL: IVP Academic, 2011.

Swinburne, Richard. *The Existence of God.* Rev. ed. Oxford: Oxford University Press, 1991.

———. *Faith and Reason.* Oxford: Oxford University Press, 1981.

Talbott, Thomas. "Christ Victorious." In Parry and Partridge, *Universalism.*

———. "The Doctrine of Everlasting Punishment." *Faith and Philosophy* 7 (1990): 19–42.

———. "A Pauline Interpretation of Divine Judgement." In Parry and Partridge, *Universalism.*

———. "Punishment, Forgiveness, and Divine Justice." *Religious Studies* 29 (1993): 151–68.

———. "Reply to My Critics." In Parry and Partridge, *Universalism.*

———. "Towards a Better Understanding of Universalism." In Parry and Partridge, *Universalism.*

Tanner, Kathryn. *Jesus, Humanity, and the Trinity: A Brief Systematic Theology.* Minneapolis: Fortress Press, 2001.

Thomas, G. Michael. *The Extent of the Atonement: A Dilemma for Reformed Theology from Calvin to the Consensus (1536–1675).* Studies in Christian History and Thought. Milton Keynes, UK: Paternoster, 1997.

Timpe, Kevin. *Free Will in Philosophical Theology.* London: Bloomsbury Academic, 2014.

———. *Free Will: Sourcehood and Its Alternatives.* 2nd ed. London: Bloomsbury, 2013.

Torrance, Thomas F. "Universalism or Election?" *Scottish Journal of Theology* 2 (1949): 310–18.

Turretin, Francis. *Institutes of Elenctic Theology.* Edited by James T. Dennison Jr. Translated by George Musgrave Giger. Vol. 1. Phillipsburg, NJ: Presbyterian & Reformed, 1992.

Tyack, Nicholas. *Anti-Calvinists: The Rise of English Arminianism, ca. 1590–1640.* Oxford: Oxford University Press, 1987.

Velde, Roelf T. te. *The Doctrine of God in Reformed Orthodoxy, Karl Barth, and the Utrecht School: A Study in Method and Content,* Leiden, Neth.: Brill, 2013.

Walls, Jerry L. *Hell: The Logic of Damnation.* Notre Dame, IN: University of Notre Dame Press, 1993.

———. *Purgatory: The Logic of Total Transformation.* New York: Oxford University Press, 2012.

———. "Why No Classical Theist, Let Alone Orthodox Christian, Should Ever Be a Compatibilist." *Philosophia Christi,* 13, no. 1 (2011): 75–104.

Warfield, Benjamin B. "Inspiration." In *International Standard Bible Encyclopedia,* edited by James Orr. Vol. 3, 1473–83. Chicago: Severance, 1915.

———. *The Plan of Salvation.* Rev. ed. Grand Rapids, MI: Eerdmans, 1975.

Webster, John. *Barth.* 2nd ed. London: T & T Clark, 2004.

———, ed. *The Cambridge Companion to Karl Barth.* Cambridge: Cambridge University Press, 2000.

———. *Confessing God: Essays in Christian Dogmatics II.* Edinburgh: T & T Clark, 2005.

Wesley, John. *John Wesley.* Edited by Albert Outler. Library of Protestant Thought. New York: Oxford University Press, 1964.

Williams, D. H. *Evangelicals and Tradition: The Formative Influences of the Early Church.* Grand Rapids, MI: Baker Academic, 2005.

Williams, Garry J. "Enlightenment Epistemology and Evangelical Doctrines of Assurance." in Haykin and Stewart, *Advent of Evangelicalism,* 345–74.

Wisse, Maartin, Marcel Sarot, and Willemien Otten, eds. *Scholasticism Reformed: Essays in Honour of Willem van Asselt.* Studies in Theology and Religion 14. Leiden, Neth.: Brill, 2010.

Wykstra, Stephen. "The Humean Obstacle to Evidential Arguments from Suffering: On Avoiding the Evils of Appearance." In Adams and Adams, *Problem of Evil.*

Index of Subjects and Names

Augustinianism, 7, 24n11, 97, 99,
102n8, 103, 105n11, 106–7,
111, 112, 114–16, 119, 121–24,
125, 135–37, 140–41, 148, 150,
206, 207, 211, 238; inclusivist-
universalist Augustinianism,
141–43; traditional
Augustinianism, 98, 99, 101–8,
110–16, 119, 123–24, 125,
135–37, 140, 148, 150

Balthasar, Hans Urs von, 133, 152,
242
Barth, Karl, 3, 7–9, 37n29, 42, 43,
55n9, 116–20, 127n2, 151–61,
163–74, 198
Bebbington, David, 24, 242;
Bebbington Quadrilateral,
24n10, 39, 40n31
Berkouwer, Gerrit C., 42, 56, 65,
66, 68, 242, 152n3
Boettner, Lorainne, 71–72, 76,
243
Brunner, Emil, 152n3, 243

calling, 66, 79, 93, 151, 182
Calvin, John, 2, 3, 55n9, 67, 74,
99, 100, 101, 117n24, 161,
221n8, 235
Calvinism, 1, 7, 26, 76, 80, 81, 83,
85, 87–89, 91–96, 99, 120–21,
137, 168n23, 170, 175, 216n4,
235–37, 239, 240
Christ, 5–11, 30, 35, 36, 41,
44–58, 61, 66, 83, 88, 93–94,

97, 111, 113–21, 124, 127, 134,
135, 138–45, 148, 151, 157,
158, 160–73, 175–83, 185,
187–97, 200–203, 206–10,
213–33, 235
Colquhoun, John, 50n6, 243
Cunningham, William, 27n18, 71,
95, 176n2, 188, 189n22, 244

Dabney, Robert, 10, 227–30, 233
Davenant, John, 8n8, 9–10,
82–83, 175, 180–81, 184,
189–97, 199–203, 206–7,
209–11, 230, 232–33
Davis, Stephen T., 123n31, 245
determinism, 4–6, 74, 75–78, 80,
88, 89, 91, 92, 94, 95, 96, 99,
168n21, 205, 208
Deviant Calvinism. *See*
Arminianism
divine justice, 105, 107, 131,
134–35, 147–48
double-payment objection,
213–15, 220–21, 224, 227–31,
233
double predestination, 2, 116,
117n24, 162, 175, 237
doxastic faith, 22, 23, 30, 79

ecumenism, 3, 42, 68, 69, 235;
ecumenical councils, 20, 21, 38
Edwards, Jonathan, 3, 5, 24–26,
27n19, 29, 30, 31, 40, 76, 104,
105, 112, 125

Hoeksema, Herman, 42, 49, 50n6,
248
Holy Spirit, 5, 20, 21, 25n13,
28–29, 32, 34, 38, 39, 41, 44,
45, 47, 49–54, 62, 80, 84n12,
87, 151, 180, 213, 225–27
Hunsinger, George, 8n7, 55n9,
152, 154, 156n7, 166, 248

infralapsarianism, 162, 165n16,
184

Jordan, Hal. *See* Oan Guardians
justification, 6, 41–69, 167, 172,
183n15, 191; anti-eternal
justification, 191

Kuyper, Abraham, 1, 42, 50, 65,
235, 236, 248

law, 17–18, 55–56, 61–64, 224
legislation, 18
Letham, Robert, 19n4, 176n2, 249
liberal theology, 36, 37, 40
libertarianism, 5, 6, 27n18, 75, 76,
79, 80, 81, 83, 86, 93, 126n1,
137, 167, 168
Little Blue Men. *See* Green
Lantern
Luther, Martin, 26, 30;
Lutheranism, 30, 31, 42, 236

MacDonald, Gregory, ix, 122n30,
123n31, 223n11. *See also* Parry,
Robin

Marx, Karl, 78; Marxism, 175
McCall, Thomas H., 188n20, 251
McCormack, Bruce L., 8n6, 9n8,
117n24, 152, 156n7, 249
McKim, Donald M., 235, 240, 249
Moore, Jonathan L., 16n3, 83n9,
176n2, 180–82, 185, 190n23,
195n26, 249
moral responsibility, 199, 202–9,
211
Muller, Richard A., 2n1, 27n17,
95n17, 96n18, 176n1, 178,
200n28, 236, 250. *See also*
Elleboogius, Cornelis

Nicole, Roger, 196–97, 250

Oan Guardians. *See* Little Blue
Men
Origen, 158–60
Owen, John, 9, 10, 138–40,
142–45, 229–30, 233

Parry, Robin, ix, 126n1, 223n11,
250–52. *See also*
MacDonald,Gregory
particularism, 7, 97, 121, 125, 126,
133, 136–38, 145
perseverance, 5n3, 28, 29, 195
Plantinga, Alvin, 129, 250
predestination, 43, 71, 75n5,
91n14, 100, 121, 122, 161–62,
187, 188n20, 190n23, 191–92,